DESIGN FOR THINKING

ALBERT UPTON

DESIGN FOR THINKING

A First Book in Semantics

STANFORD UNIVERSITY PRESS
STANFORD, CALIFORNIA
1961

STANFORD UNIVERSITY PRESS
STANFORD, CALIFORNIA

LIBRARY OF CONGRESS CATALOG CARD NUMBER: 61-14653

PRINTED IN THE UNITED STATES OF AMERICA

FOR ANNE

Icc hafe don swa summ þu badd annd forþedd te þin wille,

. . .

Affterr þatt little witt þatt me min Drihhtin hafeþþ lenedd.

. . .

Annd unnc birrþ baþe þannkenn Crist þatt itt iss brohht till ende.

ORM

FOREWORD

Did you ever notice—on waking one morning—that what your right eye saw of the pillow and sheet was not what your left eye could see? The near-up crumples and wrinkles—the white slopes, valleys, and ridges of that Alpine scene—looked strangely different, and yet were somehow the same. By wriggling about, trying to place the left eye where the right eye had been, you might almost manage to make the two views coincide. Squinting so, did you not feel you were on the track of some ultimate vision beyond vision itself, where what was seen (but with no physical eye) could make all views, and the viewings, combine, in their likenesses and their differences, to *make* sense?

Two eyes—two minds. It is hard to imagine a thinker, high or low, who hasn't, or isn't in, two minds, each forever hopefully or despairingly trying to see what the other sees. "An idea in the mind is to a Natural Law as the power of seeing is to light" said our Platonist Coleridge—and of Shakespeare's use of language. If so (and it is so) then there are Natural Laws that are in conflict—call it that—and thinking is their efforts to negotiate the peace which would be beyond understanding.

Two minds (at least) in one individual; in many individuals, more than as many. And, from our fearful recognition of this, endless absurd certitudes and convictions, pretentions and possessiveness. No doubt the word THE (the Type) is present in and, in a sense, belongs to, every *the* (the Token) on any page. In a sense! In a sense? What a divine escape phrase, letting us out into Reality, where THE along with the other words is trying, through us, to make up THE TRUTH.

I. A. RICHARDS

PREFACE

Even the titles of books are sometimes appropriately ambiguous. I have heard, for example, that Lancelot Hogben's *Mathematics for the Million* was not addressed to *hoi polloi* but to the one out of every sixty Englishmen who has what it takes to make sense of it. I have called this a "first book"; to a Basic English enthusiast "first book" seemed a better choice than "prolegomenon" or "propaedeutic." It is not a primer, however, if by primer we mean an easy first step for beginners. It is really *my* first book, the immediate result of twenty-five years of trial and error accompanied by no comforting sense of expertise and certainly not "written down" to the college freshmen for whom its successive revisions were primarily intended.

In conception it was designed to adapt the linguistic philosophy of *The Meaning of Meaning* to the American scholastic pattern; hence I have the honor of thanking Ivor Richards for many generous hours of counsel and criticism. It was due to his prompting that I finally tumbled to the profound importance of metaphor.

I have a similar obligation to Anne Upton, who first pointed out to me the obvious relation between the processes of semantic growth and the principles of analysis. Like Aristotle I have come to realize that in subjects like semantics, the obvious is always the hardest to discover.

There have been questions from time to time about the relation of this book to the General Semantics program. Was the failure to mention it intentional? The answer is No. If I were aware of so much as a word or a sentence derived from Lee, or Hayakawa, or Wendell Johnson, I should be proud indeed to acknowledge it, for I think that American education is distinctly in their debt. As for that "old white-bearded Satan" Korzybski, may God have mercy on his non-Aristotelian soul! What a pity that he could not have lived to read John Herman Randall's recent masterpiece!

Colleagues at Whittier College, Paul Smith, Charles Cooper, Roberta Foresberg, James Merrill, Gilbert McEwen, Frederick Harrison, and Mary Nash, complemented an attitude of encouragement with vigorous and indispensable cooperation. I am also embarrassingly beholden to Clara Dallas, who has the occult power to transcribe my most vermicular meanderings into something legible and relevant. I must also exercise the brief privilege and immunity of this preface to observe that there must be numerous choice spirits in the world who, if they should read it, would understand why I must express my gratitude to J. G. Bell and Gene Tanke of Stanford University Press for all that they have done for me and to me.

To those who find themselves taking this book seriously I dare to recommend three additional titles: *Teacher's Manual and Answer Book* and *Exercises in Semantics* by Anne Upton, Pacific Books, Publishers, Palo Alto, California, and *Creative Analysis* by Albert Upton and Richard Samson, Whittier College Press, Whittier, California.

ALBERT UPTON

Whittier, California
July 1961

CONTENTS

Call for some men of sound direction.
Let's want no discipline.

1 ORIENTATION

THIS IS A BOOK about the part language plays in human life. As such, it attempts to present a comprehensive and systematic account of the most important things we do, for language behavior is what makes us different from the higher animals. Man alone can tell the tale of yesterday; he alone can calendar the present or calculate the pattern of tomorrow. To use language, as language, is to be human; to use it with kindness, grace, and dignity is to be humane.

Today the study of language in our schools is somewhat confused. It is the most traditional of scholastic subjects being taught in a time when many of our traditions no longer fit our needs. You to whom these pages are addressed speak English and are therefore in a worse case than any other literate people.

People pondering the origin of language for the first time usually arrive at the conclusion that it developed gradually as a system of conventionalized grunts, hisses, and cries, and must have been a very simple affair in the beginning. But when we observe the language behavior of what we regard as primitive cultures, we find it strikingly elaborate and complicated. Stefansson, the explorer, said that "In order to get along reasonably well an Eskimo must have at the tip of his tongue a vocabulary of more than 10,000 words, much larger than the active vocabulary of an average businessman who speaks English. Moreover these Eskimo words are far more highly inflected than those of any of the well-known European languages, for a single noun can be spoken or written in several hundred different forms, each having a precise meaning different from that of any other. The forms of the verbs are even more numerous. The Eskimo language is, therefore, one of the most difficult in the world to learn, with the result that almost no traders or explorers have even tried to learn it. Consequently there has grown up, in intercourse between Eskimos and whites, a jargon similar to the pidgin English used in China, with a vocabulary of from 300 to 600 uninflected words, most of them derived from Eskimo but some derived from English, Danish, Spanish, Hawaiian and other languages. It is this jargon which is usually referred to by travellers as 'the Eskimo language.' "[1] And Professor Thalbitzer of Copenhagen, who did take the trouble to learn Eskimo, seems to endorse the explorer's view when he writes: "The language is polysynthetic. The grammar is extremely rich in flexional forms, the conjugation of a common verb being served by about 350 suffixes, equivalent to personal pronouns and verb endings. For the declension of a noun there are 150 suffixes (for dual and plural, local cases, and possessive flexion). The demonstrative pronouns have a separate flexion. The derivative endings effective in the vocabulary and the construction of sentences or sentence-like words amount to at least 250. Notwithstanding all these constructive peculiarities, the grammatical and synthetic system is remarkably concise and, in its own way, logical."[2]

Now as a first step toward understanding the present state of linguistic affairs in English, we must try to see why it is that Eskimo is easy for Eskimos but hard for explorers and scholars. Ordinarily we say that what is simple is but one thing, and that what is complex has two or more "parts"; the degree of complexity may then be measured by the number of parts. This would make a relatively small sand dune a very complex structure compared to a large electronic computer. But upon second thought we see that the sort of *com*plexity that causes *per*plexity depends not so much upon the multiplicity of parts as upon the number of connections among the parts. Upon third thought, we find reason to suspect that a still better measure of complexity would be the number of *sorts* of connections among the parts.

[1] *The Encyclopædia Britannica*, Fourteenth Edition, Vol. 8, p. 709.
[2] *Ibid.*, p. 707.

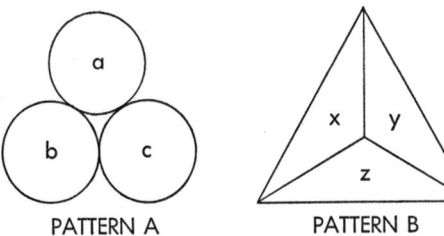

PATTERN A   PATTERN B

Thus patterns *a*, *b*, and *c* in the accompanying figure are simple continuous lines or circles. Pattern *A* is composed of *a*, *b*, and *c* and is therefore complex. Its principle of organization is mutual contact; *a*, *b*, and *c* are contiguous, each touching the others at two separate points. Patterns *x*, *y*, and *z* are complex, containing three parts each; they compose pattern *B*. Its principle of organization is mutual contact; *x*, *y*, and *z* are also mutually contiguous, but each touches the other two at one separate point and one common point. In addition, they are mutually collateral, each touching one whole side of the other two. Thus *B* is more complex than *A*, having not only more points of connection but also more sorts of connections among its parts.

If thoughts about parts, points, and sides could be heaped indiscriminately together like grains of sand, we might still measure complexity by counting the number of thoughts; but when our thoughts are of different sorts, we find that to understand them we may not put them together one after another, helter-skelter, but must manage somehow to fit them together according to some scheme. Until we discover a scheme that works, complexity makes for perplexity—unless we are content to wonder.

But before we return to the question "Why is Eskimo easy for Eskimos?" we must make a general remark about all language. We are able to have language because of our mental capacity to compare, or to see similarities; we need language because of our capacity to contrast, or to see differences. If we were not conscious of the resemblance between two seals we saw at different times, we would have no use for the word "seal." If we were not conscious of a difference between a seal and a walrus, we would have no need for the word "walrus." From this it would appear that two fundamental determinants of language are recall or *recognition* and the utility of recorded distinction; it is worth while to keep account in our minds of the different things that happen to us.

The more vital the differences are to survival, the harder it will be to see the similarities; hence from the civilized point of view the savage has many names for "the same thing." In our own tongue salmon are fry as babies, parr as children, smolt as adolescents, and grilse as adults. It is not difficult to see how salmon of different ages might acquire their several names long before some primitive ichthyologist discovered that they were all salmon. Names of acts and relations quite logically follow the same pattern; *we* play instruments, but as primitives we would blow horns, pluck lutes, and strum ukuleles; food is good *for* us, tastes good *to* us, but may not agree *with* us.

The first answer to our question "Why is Eskimo easy for Eskimos and hard for explorers and scholars?" should now be clear. Because he can't write and read, the Eskimo has developed his memory and has thus acquired a considerable vocabulary for things which seem important to him.

The second answer is a bit more difficult to present, but it moves us much closer to our main objective, which is to explain the present confusion in language studies. It has to do with what our commentators on Eskimo called inflection and synthesis. Here are four English sentences:

1. You sing her songs (entertain her).
2. He sang you songs (while you worked).
3. You might have sung *her* song (instead of your choice).
4. She sings her songs (which she composes).

Here they are in "broken" English:

1. You sing some song to she.
2. Yesterday him sing some song to you.
3. Yesterday you bad you no sing song she want.
4. She sing some song by she.

Here they are in classical Latin:

1. Cantiones puellae cantas.
2. Cantiones tibi cantabat.
3. Cantionem eius cantavisses.
4. Cantiones suas ea cantat.

In order to define our terms and provide a vocabulary for our present discussion, let us take the Latin word *cantavisses*. We call it a word and divide it into four syllables, each one of which has meaning. Nowadays a meaningful syllable or a one-syllable word is called a *morpheme*. Speaking roughly, we may say that *can* means "sing," *tav* means "have," *isse* means "might," and *s* means "you" (singular). We say that Latin is synthetic because, for example, the four morphemes are put together (or, better still, grow together) to form what we call a word. In Latin this one word can do the same job that in English requires the four-word sentence "You might have sung." We call English an analytic language because the speaker of English may be said to take apart complex ideas like the meaning of *cantavisses* and use a separate morpheme for each part.

You will see by comparing our two sets of English sentences that the standard English is not completely analytic, whereas the broken English is. The regular inflectional morpheme "s" for the plural is replaced by the word-morpheme "some"; the regular inflection of the masculine pronoun has been reduced to the single form "him" and the feminine to the single form "she." The standard English retains its ancient internal inflection (sing, sang, sung) but falls far short of the more primitively elaborate conjugation of the Latin.

At this point it may occur to you to think something like this: "After all, isn't it a mere convention whether we write 'He might have sung' or 'Hemighthavesung,' '*cantavisses*' or '*can tav isse s*'?" Two striking differences come to light with this question. The accent may fall upon any of the four English words, depending upon the sense; in the Latin the accent must always fall on the *iss*. And in Latin, if you say *tu* (you) you must express the same idea again with *s*; you can't say "*Tu cantavisse*."

Figuratively speaking we may say that analytic languages are informal whereas synthetic languages are formal. In English, words "come as they are"; in Latin, particularly "classical" Latin, they must wear the livery of their grammatical status. Thus in English we may say, "He yelled 'Down!' as he downed the ball down near the goal on the fourth down, but there was a mix-up in the down count." Continuing our figure we might say that "down" runs naked through our sentence except for the vestige of an old conjugation, the "-ed." In

Latin the first "down" might be *downavi,* the second *downabat,* the third *downe,* the fourth *downione,* and the fifth *downa.* The point is not simply that Latin is highly inflected, but that each grammatical type of word has a different set of inflections. You might therefore conclude that English is more like pidgin English than Latin and that Latin is more like Eskimo than English. But your conclusion would be a deceptive half-truth. The reason is a matter of history.

During the centuries in which English was rapidly losing its own elaborate set of inflections, the educational system of the English-speaking peoples was developing under an ever-increasing Latin influence. By the sixteenth century English had become the relatively "grammarless" tongue we speak today, but the education of an Englishman required the learning of more and more grammar because Latin was the principal vehicle of what we would call secondary and higher education. By the end of the eighteenth century, Greek, another synthetic language, was solidly established alongside Latin. The scholar and gentleman were brought up to regard the "humanities" as the most appropriate instruments of worldly wisdom, rhetorical beauty, and permanent discourse.

Two results of this emphasis on Latin and Greek bear directly upon our analysis of the present scholastic confusion. A dozen generations of schoolteachers have attempted to impose the manners of two great inflected polysyllabic languages upon the natural speech habits of an almost analytic tongue. With a pride born of their classical learning, they taught standards of grammatical "correctness" and rhetorical "elegance." A natural consequence of such instruction was the wholesale reintroduction of polysyllables into the vocabulary of a language that had learned to get along very well without them. By the middle of the eighteenth century the official vocabulary of English—as recorded, let us say, in Johnson's Dictionary—contained many more borrowed classicisms than native English words. Hence we find the following famous entry in that magnificent opus: "network: anything reticulated with interstices at equal distances between the decussations."

Now the acquisition of a polysyllabic classical vocabulary in addition to the "short and ugly" diction of his native tongue gave no trouble to an educated Englishman or American because the words were borrowed from languages he knew, and the individual syllables were meaningful. But in the late nineteenth and early twentieth centuries two irresistible forces radically changed the place of language in education. The obvious importance of scientific knowledge eclipsed the reverence for classical learning, and the rapid development of universal education in the English-speaking democracies placed the issue squarely upon an economic basis. Each generation saw fewer and fewer taxpayers willing to support the teaching of what they considered dead languages. In American schools, at least for practical purposes, Greek is now extinct and Latin is generally regarded as obsolete. The result is that even educated Americans speak a polysyllabic language the constituent syllables of which they do not understand. That the present state of communication among educated people is not worse is probably due to the fact that classical Greek and Latin were synthetic. When used in an analytic language some of the syllables are superfluous anyway; a language that can say "Don't go out in the *wet* without *rubbers,* you'll catch a cold," has learned to dispense with its own "-nesses," "-hoods," and "-ishes" and therefore carries the "-tures," "-tudes," "-tions," "-tives," "-ics," and "-icals" of its imports as mere excess baggage. To define "stealth" (as Johnson did) as "clandestine practice" instead of "hid work" is merely to spend breath or ink in the interest of gentility. The famous definition of "network" may be literally translated thus: "Anything made into a little net evenly X'd with holes between the X's." The great lexicographer simply used the Latin syllable *ret* for the English syllable "net" and followed it with a Latin description.

But Dr. Johnson's extraordinary capacity to grasp essentials was never stifled by his scholarship. The state of linguistic affairs which he viewed with such dignified alarm two centuries ago could not be more elegantly described today, even if we use the modern scientist's conception of "elegance" as a happy combination of rich detail and nice distinction. Here is that description:

Of the event of this work, for which, having laboured it with so much application, I cannot but have some degree of parental fondness, it is natural to form conjectures. Those who have been persuaded to think well of my design, require that it should fix our language, and put a stop to those alterations which time and chance have hitherto been suffered to make in it without opposition. With this consequence I will confess that I flattered myself for a while, but now begin to fear that I have indulged expectation which neither reason nor experience can justify. When we see men grow old and die at a certain time one after another, from century to century, we laugh at the elixir that promises to prolong life to a thousand years; and with equal justice may the lexicographer be derided, who being able to produce no example of a nation that has preserved their words and phrases from mutability, shall imagine that his dictionary can embalm his language, and secure it from corruption and decay, that it is in his power to change sublunary nature, or clear the world at once from folly, vanity, and affectation.

With this hope, however, academies have been instituted, to guard the avenues of their languages, to retain fugitives, and repulse intruders; but their vigilance and activity have hitherto been vain; sounds are too volatile and subtile for legal restraints; to enchain syllables, and to lash the wind, are equally the undertakings of pride, unwilling to measure its desires by its strength. The *French* language has visibly changed under the inspection of the academy; the stile of *Amelot's* translation of father *Paul* is observed by *Le Courayer* to be *un peu passé*; and no *Italian* will maintain, that the diction of any modern writer is not perceptibly different from that of *Boccace, Machiavel,* or *Caro.*

Total and sudden transformations of a language seldom happen; conquests and migrations are now very rare: but there are other causes of change, which, though slow in their operation and invisible in their progress, are perhaps as much superior to human resistance, as the revolutions of the sky, or intumescence of the tide. Commerce, however necessary, however lucrative, as it depraves the manners, corrupts the language; they that have frequent intercourse with strangers, to whom they endeavor to accommodate themselves, must in time learn a mingled dialect, like the jargon which serves the traffickers on the *Mediterranean* and *Indian* coasts. This will not always be confined to the exchange, the warehouse, or the port, but will be communicated by degrees to other ranks of the people, and be at last incorporated with the current speech.

There are likewise internal causes equally forcible. The language most likely to continue without alteration, would be that of a nation raised a little, and but a little, above barbarity, secluded from strangers, and totally employed in procuring the conveniences of life; either without books, or, like some of the *Mahometan* countries, with very few: men thus busied and unlearned having only such words as common use requires, would perhaps long continue to express the same notions by the same signs. But no such constancy can be expected in a people polished by arts, and classed by subordination, where one part of the community is sustained and accommodated by the labour of the other. Those who have much leisure to think, will always be enlarging the stock of ideas, and every increase of knowledge, whether real or fancied, will produce new words, or combinations of words. When the mind is unchained from necessity, it will range after convenience; when it is left at large in the fields of speculation, it will shift opinions; as any custom is disused, the words that expressed it must perish with it; as any opinion grows popular, it will innovate speech in the same proportion as it alters practice.

As by the cultivation of various sciences, a language is amplified, it will be more furnished with words deflected from their original sense; the geometrician will talk of a courtier's zenith, or the excentrick virtue of a wild hero, and the physician of sanguine expectations and phlegmatick delays. Copiousness of speech will give opportunities to capricious choice, by which some words will be preferred, and others degraded; vicissitudes of fashion will enforce the use of the new, or extend the signification of known terms. The tropes of poetry will make hourly encroachments, and the metaphorical will become the current sense: pronunciation will be varied by levity or ignorance, and the pen must at length comply with the tongue: illiterate writers will at one time or other, by publick infatuation, rise into renown, who not knowing the original import of words, will use them with colloquial licentiousness, confound distinction, and forget propriety. As politeness increases, some expressions will be considered as too gross and vulgar for the delicate, others as too formal and ceremonious for the gay and airy; new phrases are therefore adopted, which must, for the same reasons, be in time dismissed. *Swift*, in his petty treatise on the *English* language, allows that new words must sometimes be introduced, but proposes that none should be suffered to become obsolete. But what makes a word obsolete more than general agreement to forbear it? and how shall it be continued, when it conveys an offensive idea, or recalled again into the mouths of mankind, when it has once by disuse become unfamiliar, and by unfamiliarity unpleasing?

There is another cause of alteration more prevalent than any other, which yet in the present state of the world cannot be obviated. A mixture of two languages will produce a third distinct from both, and they will always be mixed, where the chief part of education, and the most conspicuous accomplishment, is skill in ancient or in foreign tongues. He that has long cultivated another language, will find its words and combinations crowd upon his memory; and haste and negligence, refinement and affectation, will obtrude borrowed terms and exotick expressions.

The great pest of speech is frequency of translation. No book was ever turned from one language into another, without imparting something of its native idiom; this is the most mischievous and comprehensive innovation; single words may enter by thousands, and the fabrick of the tongue continue the same, but new phraseology changes much at once;

it alters not the single stones of the building, but the order of the columns. If an academy should be established for the cultivation of our stile, which I, who can never wish to see dependance multiplied, hope the spirit of *English* liberty will hinder or destroy, let them, instead of compiling grammars and dictionaries, endeavour, with all their influence, to stop the licence of translatours, whose idleness and ignorance, if it be suffered to proceed, will reduce us to babble a dialect of *France*.

If the changes that we fear be thus irresistible, what remains but to acquiesce with silence, as in the other insurmountable distresses of humanity, it remains that we retard what we cannot repel, that we palliate what we cannot cure. Life may be lengthened by care, though death cannot be ultimately defeated; tongues, like governments, have a natural tendency to degeneration; we have long preserved our constitution, let us make some struggles for our language."[3]

It should be apparent that communication is in a far worse case today because even the "educated" reader must now deal with what we sometimes call "gobbledygook" without benefit of classical training. And there is no turning back. We cannot undo the results of five hundred years of Greco-Latin influence. We may avoid the use of "big" words in writing and speaking, but we would not deliberately cheat ourselves of the ability to understand them.

There would seem to be but one practicable answer to our problem. We must become expert with a good dictionary and make a vigorous effort to learn a minimum essential set of classical roots and affixes. We must get the habit of reading the etymologies as well as the definitions in our dictionaries.

And now a final word about attitude. English, with its insatiable and omnivorous appetite for imported food, has eaten until it has become linguistically unbuttoned. And the glutton has cloaked his paunch with the pride of the gourmet. We would not imply that a large vocabulary is bad, but rather that it is self-destructive if uncontrolled by a fine sense of distinction. Bodmer and Hogben, in their splendid *Loom of Language*, speak of grammatical usage as the "table manners" of language, Hogben at times with mischievous contempt; but we must not conclude that they think good table manners are bad. It is rather that a balanced diet and sound eating habits are more vital considerations in health education than using the

---

[3] Preface to Johnson's Dictionary.

proper hand or keeping the napkin folded across the lap, particularly in a society that, willingly or unwillingly, teaches "correctness" for its snob value. This book is written in the conviction that the knowledge of language behavior is the key to understanding and that the most important thing about language is meaning, not manners; that is why it is called "A First Book in Semantics."

Let it not be thought that we approach our subject from an anti-classical, or even an antischolastic, point of view. There is little indeed in these pages that is not at least implicit in the writings of Aristotle. He who would think clearly must think like a peripatetic even if he is unwilling to walk like one. Here is an example of Aristotelian thinking:

> If it is true (he said), that in the sphere of action there is some end which we wish for its own sake, and for the sake of which we wish everything else, and if we do not desire everything for the sake of something else, (for, if that is so, the process will go on *ad infinitum*, and our desire will be idle and futile), clearly this end will be good and the supreme good. Does it not follow then that the knowledge of this good is of great importance for the conduct of life? Like archers who have a mark at which to aim, shall we not have a better chance of attaining what we want? If this is so, we must endeavor to comprehend, at least in outline, what this good is, and what science or faculty makes it its object.[4]

Aristotle himself considered politics, in a very broad sense of the word, to be that science. For us it is also politics, but in an even broader sense; it is what Ivor Richards has called "psycho-politics."[5] Perhaps most of us would call it philosophy. Essentially it has to do with law and order, with the problem of finding out what makes good sense and what makes sense good. This is a book about the art of *making* sense. The focus of attention is upon language as the means, but the "end which we wish for its own sake" is freedom. By freedom we mean that state of mind you enjoy when you are aware of a choice and have the power to choose. We write in the belief that language is the chief tool by which we increase our awareness of choice and the discrimination with which we choose. We also believe that of all bad habits, bad language habits are the most likely to enslave us.

---

[4] *Nicomachean Ethics*, Book I, Chapter 1.
[5] *Fortune*, September 1942, p. 108.

The principles here put forth, then, are not new, but they are as timely as the theories of fission and fusion. And they have even greater promise for human happiness. We have worked hard to find words and ways that would make these principles simple and easy to understand. But although all but one are simple, few are easy to understand. "For as the eyes of bats," said Aristotle, "are to the brightness of daylight, so is the reason in our soul to the things that by nature are the clearest of all."[6]

But how are you to make sense of these very pages if we do not tell you what we mean by such historically ambiguous terms as "philosophy," "science," and "art"? And how can we do that without explaining the one thing about this book that might seem new and strange to the Philosopher? You see, Aristotle didn't know about neurones. He used history's most illustrious brain without knowing how it was put together. For him the notion of a central nervous system did not exist. For us a working idea of that marvelous tissue of gray must be introductory even to an introduction. But the briefest possible account of the central nervous system is material for a chapter. Our business now is simply to orient the reader.

In ancient Rome "orient" meant the direction toward the rising sun because "orient" means "rising" in Latin. For us it may mean as much as to tell what we are, where we are, whither we would go, and how we propose to get there. Here, then, is our orientation: we are English-speaking human beings; we live in a world full of conflict and distrust; we go in pursuit of the good life, which is liberty and happiness; and we set forth believing that the best way to do it is to use our heads, and to use them as a competent engineer might use a delicate instrument with appropriate care and skill. If you proposed to be a mechanical engineer, you would accept the challenge of the mathematical discipline as a matter of course; you would acknowledge the extreme utility of the slide rule and all it represents. The principles and procedures we invite you to consider stand in the same vital relationship to you if you would be civilized and free. They appear to us to offer the only solid ground upon which free men may ultimately stand between their loved homes and war's desolation—be the war within these homes or on distant shores or hilltops.

[6] *Metaphysics*, Book II, Chapter 1.

We have commented thus emphatically upon what seems to us the desperately important connection between freedom and language because we wish to make it clear at the start that this book presents a philosophy of life as well as a system for controlling the most characteristically human activity in it.

Now as language is the most characteristic sort of human behavior, so it is the most imitative, the most conventional, of all behavior. We might, therefore, study it as a social discipline. Of words we might ask many questions: "What do other people do with them?" "How do others arrange them—particularly the 'best people'?" "What is 'correct'?" "What are the 'rules'?" This is etiquette. It is critically important sometimes and has to do with such things as usage and grammar, "split" infinitives and the agreement of nouns and verbs; it frowns upon comma faults and misspellings. People call it "composition-rhetoric." You scorn it at your peril.

But in a democracy science is more vital than etiquette. Progress takes precedence over protocol. We shall leave important tasks undone or even unattempted if we dally overlong in getting democrats to say "pre-SEED-ence" instead of "PRESS-a-dence." We believe that the psychological approach to language study is more worthy than the conventional one, but we also know that if you become genuinely interested in the wonderful phenomena of linguistic behavior, much knowledge of the etiquette will come to you.

Be this as it may, our approach is the engineer's approach. We study not rhetoric or philology but linguistic engineering. We shall not be content with the mere description of language behavior or even the fascinating story of its historical development; we seek rather to make our language behave. Our study is really a branch of applied psychology; and like most other practical activities, it is an art which calls for a sound working knowledge of the anatomy and physiology of the subject. In our case, that subject is the conscious mind, which we here define as the highest function of the brain.

STUDY QUESTIONS

1. (A) Why is it that you who speak English "are in a worse case than any other literate people"? (B) Illustrate your answer to the above question by looking up the prefixes *com-* and *per-* in your dictionary and relating their meanings to *com*plexity and *per*plexity. (**c**) What does *re* mean in *re*cognition? In *re*cede?

2. On pages 2 and 3 three senses of "complex" are discussed. List these three senses in order of presentation. Using sense No. 1, which figure, *A* or *B*, is more complex? Using sense No. 2? Using sense No. 3?

3. Professor Thalbitzer says that Eskimo is polysynthetic. Look up "polysynthetic." If it isn't in your desk dictionary, does this mean there is no such word?

4. A child has seen a horse and has learned its name. Soon after, he sees another animal and calls it "horse." What fundamental mental capacity allows him to do this? If the second animal had been a cow, what would he have failed to do? When he named his second horse, how did the word *horse* change in meaning for him?

5. Dorothy Lee, in discussing the Trobrianders, a primitive culture, says: "The Trobrianders are concerned with being, and being alone. Change and becoming are foreign to their thinking. An object or event is grasped and evaluated in terms of itself alone; that is, irrespective of other beings. The Trobriander can describe being for the benefit of the ethnographer; otherwise, he usually refers to it by a word, one word only. All being, to be significant, must be Trobriand being, and therefore experienced at the appropriate time as a matter of course by the members of each Trobriand community; to describe it would be redundant. Being is never defined, in our sense of the word. Definition presents an object in terms of *what it is like* and *what it is unlike*; that is, in terms of its distinguishing characteristics. The Trobriander is interested only in *what it is*. And each event or being is grasped timelessly; in our terms, it contains its past, present, and future, but these distinctions are nonexistent for the Trobriander. There is, however, one sense in which being is not self-contained. To be, it must be part of an ordained pattern; this aspect will be elaborated below.

"Being is discrete and self-contained; it has no attributes outside of itself. Its qualities are identical with it, and without them it is not itself. It has no predicate; it is itself. To say a word representing an object or act is to imply the existence of this, and all the qualities it incorporates. If I were to go with a Trobriander to a garden where the taytu, a species of yam, had just been harvested, I would come back and tell you: 'There are good taytu there; just the right degree of ripeness, large and perfectly shaped; not a blight to be seen, not one rotten spot; nicely rounded at the tips, with no spiky points; all first-run harvesting, no second gleanings.' The Trobriander would come back and say 'Taytu'; and he would have said all that I did and more. Even the phrase 'There are taytu' would represent a tautology, since existence is implied in being; is, in fact, an ingredient of being to the Trobriander. And all the attributes, even if he could find words for them at hand in his own language, would have been tautological, since the concept of taytu contains them all. In fact, if one of these were absent, the object would not have been a taytu.

"Such a tuber, if it is not at the proper harvesting ripeness, is not a taytu. If it is unripe, it is a *bwanawa*; if overripe, spent, it is not a spent taytu but something else, a *yowana*. If it is blighted it is a *nukunokuna*. If it has a rotten patch, it is a *taboula*; if misshapen, it is a *usasu*; if perfect in shape but small, it is a *yagogu*. If the tuber, whatever its shape or condition, is a postharvest gleaning, it is an *ulumadala*. When the spent tuber, the *yowana*, sends its shoots underground, as we would put it, it is not a yowana with shoots, but a *silisata*. When new tubers have formed on these shoots, it is not a *silisata* but a *gadena*. An object cannot change an attribute and retain its identity. Some range of growth or modification within being is probably allowed, otherwise speech would be impossible; but I doubt whether they are conscious of it. As soon as such change, if we may introduce one of our concepts here, is officially recognized, the object ceases to be itself."

(A) Why is it hard for the Trobriander and other primitives to see abstract similarities?   (B) How does this relate to his having "so many names for the same thing"?   (C) Would it be likely that ambiguous terms (those having two or more senses) would exist in the Trobriander community? Why?

6. How do the answers to Question 5 relate to the question "Why is Eskimo easy for Eskimos and hard for explorers and scholars?"—i.e., why is Eskimo more *complicated* to the explorer and scholar?

7. What does *i.e.* mean as used in the above question? Where will you find it in your dictionary?

8. Look up *analytic* and *synthetic*. How do these definitions relate to the characteristics of analytic and synthetic languages?   (A) Why is the "broken" English "Yesterday him sing some song to she" more analytic than "He sang some songs to her"?   (B) Which would be more complex, an analytic or a synthetic language? Why?

9. What did the reintroduction of Latin and Greek do to analytic English?

10. Define "humanities" as it is used on page 6.

11. How would de-emphasis in teaching "dead languages" answer Question 1?

12. Dr. Johnson speaks in derision of a dictionary that can "embalm language." What does he mean by this? What reasons does he give as to why language *must* grow?

13. What does Johnson mean about language when he says on page 10, "it [new phraseology] alters not the single stones of the building, but the order of the columns"?

14. Johnson speaks of "words deflected from their original sense," as quoted on page 9. Look up *zenith* and *eccentric* in your dictionary and determine how they might be "deflected" when used in the contexts of "courtier's zenith" and "eccentric virtue of a wild hero."

15. What seems to be the answer to help clear up the misunderstanding arising through the Greco-Latin influence?

16. What concept of the teaching of language is the author demonstrating when he says, on page 10, ". . . but we must not conclude that they think good table manners are bad. It is rather that a balanced diet and sound eating habits are more vital considerations in health education than using the proper hand or keeping the napkin folded across the lap, particularly in a society that, willingly or unwillingly, teaches 'correctness' for its 'snob value'"? How does the definition of *semantics* relate to this statement?

17. By looking up "peripatetic," can you explain the statement, on page 11, "He who would think clearly must think like a peripatetic even if he is unwilling to walk like one"?

18. In the phrase "we must endeavor to comprehend . . . what this *good* is, and what *science or faculty* makes it its object," match the italicized words with the appropriate words in the sentence "the focus of attention is upon language as the means, but the 'end which we wish for its own sake' is freedom."

19. Define *civilized* as used on page 12. Note that in context with *free* you are considering a specialized sense of the term. The paragraphs on page 25 defining *civilization* and *citizen* may help you.

20. The author states, on page 13, that we seek to make our language "behave." How can we do this?

21. Look up *psychological* in the dictionary and upon the basis of your findings, defend the association of the "psychological approach to language study" and "the wonderful phenomena of linguistic behavior."

That hath a mint of phrases in his brain.

LOVE'S LABOUR'S LOST

2 BRAIN AND MIND

YOUR BRAIN is an organ. An organ is a whole part of an organism. You are an organism; so is an amoeba. An amoeba is a relatively simple organism; you are very complex because there are so many sorts of connections among your many sorts of parts. Organisms with brains have *purposes*; they can want things. An organ which helps an organism get what it wants has a *function*; it plays a part. An organism getting what it wants is a *system* "in being." Systems have purposes; organs have functions. Organs are also simple and complex. Thus a whole complex organ is made up of organic or interconnected parts. Your brain is the most complex organ in the universe. Indeed, Professor C. Judson Herrick once said that if the universe as we know it had but one human brain in it, that brain would be more complex than all the rest of the universe because of its almost infinite capacity for making interconnections among its millions of constituent parts.

It isn't as easy as you might think to define the term *part*. We shall make a more thorough attempt later; for the moment it must be enough to say that we measure the importance of a part by the number of connections it has with other parts. Thus, a "principal part" is a part with many connections. That is why the brain, like the heart, is called a principal part of the body.

The brain, being a complex part, has many functions. In this book we are concerned only with those that involve consciousness. For us the principal function of the brain is consciousness; and in dealing with the principal parts of the brain we deal only with the organs of consciousness. We want you to think of your mind as your private view of the working of three complex parts of your central nervous system; that is, of your brain with all the tributary branches of the nervous system that reach out into your body. We will call the complete set of sense organs one part; the organ or organs of emotion (which psychologists sometimes call "affection") a second part; and the organ of reason or logic that "sees" relations a third part. Now the logical or rational organ that sees relations or ratios is so called because its principal part is the language-using part of the brain; "logical" is made from the Greek word for "word." This language-using part will almost certainly be functioning whenever you are aware of a sensation or an emotion. Thus conscious states are never simple but always complexes of these primary brain functions: *sensation, affection,* and *reflection* (a somewhat more emphatic term for reason or logic). And any given moment of experience can, upon reflection, be more or less accurately resolved into these component parts.

"If you would carve an axe handle," says the Chinese proverb, "the model is in your hand." Now language is a tool of the brain, and it is the shape of that miraculous organ that will yield us the soundest principles of procedure. For our purposes we need not go into the intricate, technical description of the physical structure of the central nervous system, but in the language of Professor Herrick, "we wish to make it clear that we are not merely guessing when we say that it is possible to cite a wealth of facts about the location, structure, and physiological properties of the bodily organs employed in making mental symbols and in all those higher rational processes which employ them—in short, the semantic functions." Professor Herrick continues:

The transfer in higher mammals of the dominant control of conduct and of the course of conscious experience from brain-stem to cortex and from physiological to psychological technique has momentous consequences. The mental symbols elaborated in some unknown way by the integrative apparatus of the human cortex give to mankind new tools of adjustment which have extended the reach of his control from the present into the future. The human brain, as Sherrington aptly expresses it, is "fraught with a germ of futurity."

Mental symbols and their objective signs in language, mathematics, and so forth are the indispensable tools of the life of reason. With the help of these tools mankind can preserve and profit by the past experience of the race as recorded in tradition and literature and by imagination and invention enlarge his understanding and control of the inorganic, organic and human agencies of production and enjoyment. And of far more importance, he can predict the future and lay out his present course of action in the light of probable future consequences of the present act. The most intelligent brute lives mainly in the present. Men attentively bind the past and the future into their present and thereby become as gods, knowing good and evil.[1]

We may now return to our key words *art, philosophy,* and *science* and to a demonstration of the utility of our psychological defining technique. It is a fair assumption that each of these terms has a place in your vocabulary. It is a possibility that you have never taken stock of the numerous ways you use them. Let us assume for the moment that they have senses which could be used to sort out the characteristic behavior of the developed mind, or that we might sort intelligent men and women into three groups insofar as their activity is predominantly artistic, philosophical, or scientific. Now, if it is true that conscious mental behavior is made up of three components and only three, then it follows that these three components must be present in various degrees in the three different sorts of persons or activities, which we may define by component analysis.

If we further assume that one type of mental behavior is essential to each sort and that one type is either irrelevant or least relevant, do we not discover after a little thought that to the artist sensation is the essential? He works in the world of seeing, or the world of hearing, or the world of muscular rhythm, or the world of tasting, smelling, etc. The sensation is essential to the production of whatever affective state he may seek to "express." Although his work may withstand the most exacting logical analysis, he does not characteristically make that analysis himself either before or after the creative act. As Walt

[1] *Science Monthly,* August 1939.

Disney said of *Fantasia*, "We just make the picture and the professors tell us how we do it."

The philosopher, as such, is primarily concerned with value. To be a philosopher, he must "prize" something. He then makes use of whatever logical capacity he may possess to rationalize (that is, to make conformable to reason) his essential prizing. Prizing is basically affective. Desire is emotion; without feeling, there is no value.

The scientist is concerned primarily with law and order. He is nothing if not logical. His logic operates directly or indirectly upon the data of sensation, and emotion is as irrelevant to his activity as sensation is to the activity of the philosopher. A judge as such is a political scientist; his personal emotions are irrelevant to his judgment. As mercy seasons justice, judges become philosophers. Thus we have a neat, logical method of distinguishing among the three sorts of complex mental behavior, as shown below in tabular form.

Behavior:	*Artistic*	*Philosophical*	*Scientific*
Essential component:	Sensation	Affection	Logic
Relevant component:	Affection	Logic	Sensation
Irrelevant component:	Logic	Sensation	Affection

Now if you have been vigorously thinking of objections, particularly in the form of artists with elaborate color theories, philosophers who teach mathematics or logic, and scientists who prize freedom, you have simply switched your thought to the man as such, whereas we are thinking of the *characterizing* behavior. As an actual artist becomes less concerned with a particular world of sensation and more with the presentation of a particular emotion (like a Daumier or a Hogarth or a Blake) he is philosophizing. When a philosopher (like Whitehead or Russell) commits his intellect to the construction or exploration of a logical system, he is for the moment a pure scientist. And it would be the artist in Audubon that must have taken delight in the exquisite patterns of line and color that illustrate *The Birds of America.*

Thus the whole conscious behavior of whole men may be analyzed, and any given moment of thought may be distinguished as scientific, philosophic, or artistic according to the relationship among the three basic component functions.

But we have not said what we mean by "analyze." We will now take that necesary step by defining the three basic forms of analysis.

STUDY QUESTIONS

1. (**A**) Define *brain* by using the terms "organism," "organ," "whole part." (**B**) How would a "whole part" differ from a "part part"? (**C**) Using our definition of *complex* from Chapter 1, why is "your brain the most complex organ in the universe"? (**D**) How does *function* differ from *purpose*? (**E**) Can a part be a system? Explain your answer.

2. (**A**) Is *mind* as used at the top of page 18 a synonym for *brain*? For *consciousness*? (**B**) As the author uses the word "consciousness" on page 18, could a person be asleep and be conscious? Explain your answer.

3. (**A**) In Questions 1 and 2 we have attempted to lead you into making a distinction between an organ and its function. What are the three principal *parts* of your central nervous system? Where are these located? What are the functions of these parts? (**B**) Could we call these functions the three *modes* of consciousness? Why?

4. What reason can you discover in the dictionary for the fact that *reflection* is a "somewhat more emphatic term for reason or logic"?

5. (**A**) How can a symbol system "bind the past and the future into the present"? (**B**) Do you believe that man could think without the use of some symbol system?

6. Does the fact that you can think of a person who seems to you to act both as an artist and as a scientist make the art-science-philosophy classification of human behavior invalid? Why?

Let your reason serve to make the truth appear
where it seems hid.

MEASURE FOR MEASURE

3 ANALYSIS

THE LOGICAL OPERATIONS of analysis are extremely simple considering the indescribably complex organ that performs them and the astounding achievements that sometimes result from their application. For there are only three sorts of analytical questions that the rational intellect may propose and three sorts of rational answers it can get. It can ask (1) "What is this a sort of, or what are the sorts of this?" (2) "What is this a part of, or what are the parts of this?" (3) "What is this a stage of, or what are the stages of this?"

You may recall that we began Chapter 2 with an answer to the question "What is your brain a sort of?" By giving the answer "organ" to our question we took the brain into one of our most fundamental sortings—the sorting into things that are or have been alive and things that do not have the mysterious power to grow. We say that animals and plants grow. Clouds and dunes form.

Plants and animals are sorts of organisms; men and amoebas are sorts of animals. Now when we persistently and consistently ask and answer the question of sort, the results are what we call *classifications*, and we shall have more to say about them in this book. In biological science the study of classification is called *taxonomy*, which in Greek means the system or law of order. Here is a simple diagram showing how the system works:

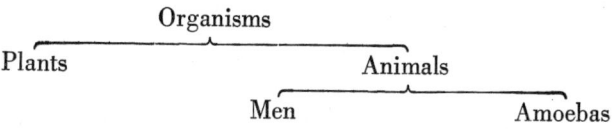

When you put the question "What is this a part of, or what are the parts of this?" you have in mind not what pigeonhole a thing belongs in, nor what sorts of things are in the same pigeonhole, but rather what the boundaries of things are and where and how they connect with the things that belong around them. You are thinking the kind of thoughts we think when we take things apart or when we put them together. We shall call this kind of analysis *structure analysis* because things that have parts connected to make wholes are called structures. An organism is a structure. A cloud is a structure, and so is a dune. In the science of biology, structure analysis goes by the name of anatomy, which comes from a Greek word meaning "to cut apart." A good anatomist, the Greeks would tell you, is like a good butcher—he knows how to cut where the joints are. When we talk about the connections or boundaries between the heart and the brain, or when we talk about the three parts of the brain that make up the organ of consciousness, we are anatomizing. Structure analysis really calls for pictures, but verbal statements of constituent parts and their arrangement may be conveniently presented thus:

$$
\text{Body}
\begin{cases}
\text{head} \begin{cases}
\text{skull} & \begin{cases}\text{crown}\\\text{jaw}\end{cases} & \begin{cases}\text{bone}\\\text{teeth}\end{cases}\\[2ex]
\text{organs} & \begin{cases}\text{brain}\\\text{sensory}\end{cases} & \begin{cases}\text{skin}\\\text{eyes}\\\text{etc.}\end{cases}\\[2ex]
\text{muscles}
\end{cases}\\[6ex]
\text{trunk}\\[1ex]
\text{limbs}
\end{cases}
$$

When the wholes that we take apart or put together in our minds are changing or moving wholes, the fourth dimension of time plays its part in our thinking; we then use the word *stage* or its synonyms for the constituent parts of the sort of wholes we call *operations*. Thus structures are three-dimensional and made up of parts. Events or operations are four-dimensional. Change takes time. Structures are wholes that have parts for parts. Operations are wholes that have stages for parts. The operation or process of taking events apart we shall call *operation analysis*. Because we never have events without things to evolve—that is, structures with changing relations among their parts—analysis of an event turns out to be the tracing of the functions of the parts, just as analysis of a structure is the tracing of the boundaries and the connections of the parts.

In biological science operation analysis is called physiology, which in Greek means, as you might expect, the science of natural change. We suggest the conventional outline form for representing operation analysis. For example:

I. Ingestion
    A. Mastication
    B. Swallowing
II. Digestion
    A. Stomachic
    B. Intestinal
III. Elimination

Here then are the three primary logical operations: classification, structure analysis, and operation analysis. Whenever you begin to see relationships in the world about you, one or more of these operations is going on in your head. Whenever you make a vigorous, systematic attempt to complete these operations you are being a scientist. Whenever these three operations are arbitrarily committed to some desired end and in Hamlet's phrase, "reason panders will," you are being a philosopher. When you revel in the richness of your observation of the world about you and display grace or skill in the manipulation of your environment, you are being an artist. And whenever you combine the three activities in harmony and balance you are being a statesman in the world of "psycho-politics," which is the Greek way of saying the city government of the soul. Franklin, Jefferson, and Madison were such statesmen, and two of the noblest documents of human history are partial records of their realistic solution to the problem of finding the good life.

At this stage in our discussion of language in mind and society, you are quite justified if you think that we are going to put great stress upon the importance of scientific behavior. Before taking our next step we must therefore explain clearly our theory of the status of science in the modern world. We think that there are two unfortunate, and ultimately unscientific, concepts concerning the nature of science and its relation to civilization. One is the idea of specialism, or as Professor Munro has said, "knowing more and more about less and less until you become intellectually unbuttoned"; the other is the idea that specialization is good because it makes for civilization which is, of course, good.

We suggest making a distinction between a highly developed or complex culture and a civilization. Culture may be defined in passing as the relatively rigid and unreasoned type of social behavior found in hives, lodges, and sometimes even in pentagons. It may be impressive and its achievements marvelous. We suggest, however, a meaning for "civilization" that would make it rather a special sort of complex culture in which the constituent parts have developed linguistic, that is to say, parliamentary, techniques for resolving the inevitable disputes that arise from conflicts of interest, real or apparent.

The basic unit of a civilization thus conceived is the citizen. The essential characteristics of a citizen are intelligence, health, and experience. He must be intelligent enough to recognize a conflict of interests and sufficiently healthy in mind and body to be personally responsible. But health and intelligence are not enough. If his experience has been too restricted, he will be enslaved by the specialization (division of labor) that develops in civilized communities; and he will be incapable of understanding the many persons whose experience has differed radically from his own. Thus, the ideal citizen is one who can behave as master or servant with equal dignity. Upon occasion, he must be able to make his own repairs and run his own errands. He will not be angry or fearful if, from time to time, he finds himself elbow to elbow or cheek by jowl with another citizen not strictly of his own caste. His social status at any particular moment will be determined less by his ancestry than by his immediate practical relations with those about him.

Now, it is an interesting and perhaps enlightening fact that the peoples of Europe and Asia that have clung tenaciously to a proud and warlike national spirit have preserved, in relative purity, what we might call authoritarian languages. Those nations, on the other hand, that have tended to put commerce and industry before national pride have evolved more democratic habits of speech.

The words in an authoritarian or so-called "synthetic" language have a more or less rigid system of strict rules to obey and are, as we have said, required to appear in the uniform proper to their status. The complicated grammars of German, Russian, and Japanese illustrate the point.

But in the so-called "analytic" tongues like English and Chinese a word is relatively free to do as it pleases, provided it takes a cooperative attitude toward its fellows. And in English, particularly, foreign immigrants are welcomed and naturalized with extreme hospitality. Thus the English-speaking peoples of the world have upon their tongues and before their eyes a constant reminder of the social and political principles that have made them what they are—people with a marked capacity for progressive adaptation. And the same might be said of the Chinese were it not for the fact that the liberalizing factors in Chinese thought have been counteracted by the worship of a primitive synthetic method of writing faithfully kept alive through the centuries by a scholarly priesthood. Command of the ten thousand characters necessary to the literate culture of a Chinese gentleman calls for the soul of a philosopher and the eye and hand of an artist which would be good, indeed, if it did not at the same time tend to repudiate the mental processes of the scientist. For it is the scientific method conceived as a way of life and an instrument of democracy that seems to offer the greatest promise of survival to those peoples who are unwilling to purchase security at the price of personal freedom.

If you would know the truths that are to make you free, you must learn to hew to truth's line and let the chips fall where they may. If you would build a world of social justice, you must model it after the world of science in which the individual is known by the fruits of his own achievement and by his capacity to get his own meaning out of his own environment.

The artist in us may be "pure and made apt for mounting to the stars" without knowing the how of his own mysterious "know-how."

The philosopher in us always "comes out by the same door as in he went." It is the rigorous process, however painful, of finding and facing the facts, however ugly, and the conscious ordering of facts into the inevitable patterns of promise or despair that must determine the procedure of a free mind. This is the analytic method.

That most miraculous organ behind your eyes and under your hat is, of course, a device for lowering those eyes and tipping the hat, but its most characteristic function is the function of asking questions and getting answers. The mind that cannot make meaning of the stream of experience, which comes pouring in through the channels of the senses setting up waves and eddies of emotion, cannot long remain a mind. If it stops making sense it is "lost."

Let us now ask ourselves just what happens when we do make sense. What is the meaning of *meaning*?

STUDY QUESTIONS

1. (**A**) What is the difference between saying "What is this a sort of?" and "What are the sorts of this?" (**B**) What is the difference between saying "What is this a part of?" and "What are the parts of this?"? (**C**) What is the difference between saying "What are the stages of this?" and "What is this a stage of?"? (**D**) All of these questions are employed in what primary brain function?

2. (**A**) We learned in Chapter 2 that the principal function of the brain is consciousness. What sort of analysis does *function* imply? (**B**) We also determined three complex parts of the central nervous system: sense organs, the organs of emotion, and the logical organ. What sort of analysis does this determination imply? (**C**) In placing intelligent men and women into three groups insofar as their activity was predominantly artistic, philosophical or scientific, what analysis was being applied?

3. What analysis is primarily involved in seeing similarities and differences? In seeing boundaries and connections? In seeing structures changing relations among their parts?

4. Define *pigeonhole* as used on page 23.

5. Define *part* as used to apply to structure analysis.

6. "Structures are wholes that have *parts* for parts. Operations are wholes that have stages for *parts*." How has the use of the italicized term *parts* changed?

7. What is meant by *four-dimensional,* and how is it different from *three-dimensional*?

8. (**A**) Must the analysis of an event necessarily proceed in chronological order? (**B**) What must an event have besides stages?

9. What is the effect of specialization on an individual?

10. (**A**) What can you say regarding a highly specialized individual in terms of his ability to run his own errands and make his own repairs? (**B**) We have seen in Chapter 1 that freedom is "the state of mind you enjoy when you are aware of a choice and have the power to choose." Why would specialization tend to restrict this freedom?

11. In his definition of the citizen, why do you think the author doesn't mention the characteristics of religion or patriotism?

12. (**A**) What can you say regarding an artist in terms of his ability to solve problems? (**B**) What happens to an individual when he cannot understand his own emotions?

13. Why would those who have put commerce and industry before national pride have developed more democratic habits of speech, i.e., why would English develop into an analytic tongue while Russian remained highly synthetic?

14. (**A**) "In the so-called 'analytic' tongues like English and Chinese a word is relatively free to do as it pleases, provided it takes a cooperative attitude toward its fellows. And in English, particularly, foreign immigrants are welcomed and naturalized with extreme hospitality." What characteristics of analytic languages are stated here? (**B**) What implication does this statement have concerning United States society?

15. (**A**) What part does the application of the analytic processes play in determining the free mind? (**B**) What arguments can you advance for the thesis that an analytic language would enable one to think more clearly, unhampered by the regimentation of a synthetic language?

My brain I'll prove the female to my soul;
My soul the father; and these two beget
A generation of still-breeding thoughts,
And these same thoughts people this little world.

RICHARD II

4 MEANING

SOMETHING OVER a generation ago two brilliant young Britons at Cambridge composed an essay that has played a large part in determining the form and direction of critical thinking in our time. They did not build better than they knew because they were keenly aware of the importance of their work; they were making a conscious effort to revive the profound and scientific understanding of the relation between language and thought possessed by Jeremy Bentham. And since both were competent students of contemporary psychology, they were able to make their enterprise a scientific rather than an academic operation. They called their essay (now in its eighth edition) *The Meaning of Meaning.*

This book contains few ideas indeed that do not have their origins or archetypes in *The Meaning of Meaning.* But we will not be frequently quoting from or referring to *The Meaning of Meaning,* or to the many other relevant essays of Charles Kay Ogden and I. A. Richards; for us, that would be like quoting Euclid on the principles of geometry or Aristotle on formal logic. This is because we are not dealing with matters of opinion but with relationships that anyone can see if he will only persevere in the attempt. Thus when we set out to answer the question "What is meaning a sort of, or what sorts of meaning are there?" we shall not riffle through the pages of *The Meaning of Meaning* to see whether we owe the authors a footnote. We shall keep to the direct course of giving the answers as we see them and as we think you must also see them if you look with care.

As you make your way step by step toward a clear understanding of anything, you must always try to get the most basic answers to your six fundamental questions first. A basic answer is one that is assumed in any other answer you get. For example, when we ask ourselves what sort of thing meaning is, a basic answer is that it is a sort of experience. Thus we must assume that whenever and wherever meaning is, somebody is—somebody with a central nervous system (which we will call c.n.s. for short) that has a cerebral cortex able to "see" relations.

Meaning is always a matter of relation. Nothing ever means itself alone; it can only be meaningful to somebody about something else. Meaning, then, is simply a function of the cortex in action; it is what goes on in a brain when it makes a thing or a connection between two or more things. We might say that meaning is the "stuff" of consciousness; it is what consciousness is made of.

Now if we begin to think of consciousness as if it were made of something, we may then ask our questions about structure. We then find that a meaning is a part of somebody's consciousness, which is a part of somebody's life. When we ask ourselves about the parts of a meaning, we find that we can get at least two basic answers. One we have already considered by pointing out that a meaning has sensory, affective, and logical components because of the sensory, affective, and logical parts of the c.n.s. This is the sort of structure analysis we make when we say that food is made up of fats, carbohydrates, and proteins, or that cars are made of metal, wood, rubber, and other materials. This is not really structure analysis, but classification using the language of structure analysis.

But what about the question "What are the parts of this?" when the answer is layers, filling, and frosting, or chassis, body, and motor? In this sense the question "What are the parts of a meaning?" is the profoundest of questions and its answer the most meaningful of answers. Indeed herein lies, it would seem, a psychological accounting for the trinitarian concept of God.

A unit of meaning—that is, a meaning that cannot at the moment be practically broken up into two or more lesser meanings—is made of a thing and the relation which connects it to another thing. (This reminds one that a neurone has two parts, an "axone" and a "dendrite," which connect it with other neurones in "synapses.") The implication is that in order to be conscious of a finite thing (a thing with known boundaries or a thing known to possess boundaries), we must have at least two other things: a boundary and another infinite or indefinite thing, whose boundaries may be either partially known or unknowable except where they bound the finite thing.

What do we mean when we say that boundaries and relations are things? Are not the water's edge and the land's end one and the same? Is the shoreline a part of the land or of the sea, or is it a line in its own right? It is easy to see that you cannot have a shoreline without a sea, a little harder to see that you cannot have a sea without a shore, and downright difficult for most of us to see that you can't have either without a shoreline. A person must draw that line somewhere. Wherever there is a sea, somebody must say to the water, so far you go and no farther; and to the land he must say, this is the end of you. And the relation between the one and the other is the act of delineation that went on in his head. The world is really a dynamic operation; only by means of symbols can the mind deal with it "as if" it were a static structure.

Relations, then, are spiritual (bodiless) or mental things that inhabit the world of consciousness. We may call them holy ghosts if they have to do with the relation between the finite and the infinite, the limited and the limitless, the conceivable and the inconceivable. Thus it is the very contrary of stupidity to say that you cannot be conscious of one thing and one only. In order to have one, you must have three: a thing, a relation, and another thing. The meaning of one of them is determined by your momentary awareness of the other two.

And so we move along to operation analysis; for a meaning is always a matter of moment. Meanings are not static, they are dynamic. Change takes place. Thoughts are events. Meanings have stages. They are four-dimensional operations; however swift they may be, they take time. If they start with sensory or affective activity, they become meanings when some appropriate relation is added; if they start with relations, they become meaningful with the addition of sensation, emotion, or another relation. But there must always be a relation.

Thought is the continuous flow of sensation and emotion punctuated into moments of consciousness by logical acts of relation. We might also call them moments of recognition because whenever we make a moment of experience meaningful by attaching a relation, the process is one of seeing some sort of resemblance to one or more of the past moments that have left their records in the delicate nervous structures of recall. Relations are simply patterns of resemblance, potential shorelines waiting to give definition to the land of sensation and the sea of emotion. The meaningful "things" that emerge from the moment of recognition are signs, and the "other things" they mean or signify fall into our patterns of analysis. That is, if we interpret an object as a car, it is a member of the car sort; if it means the plumber is here, it is a part of his equipment. If it is crushed up a bit, it may mean the entire event of a collision.

But for us, as students primarily concerned with the meanings we get from language, there is another and equally profitable way of sorting signs.

STUDY QUESTIONS

1. In Chapter 2 we discussed the question "Do you believe that man could think without the use of some symbol system?" In thus considering the relationship between *language* and *thought,* what can you say about the statement that "some feelings cannot be put in words" or that "sometimes people know things but they can't express them"?

2. What is the difference between *scientific* and *academic* as used on page 29?

3. Meaning is discussed through application of the "six fundamental questions." What are these?

4. Our first fundamental question, "What is meaning a sort of?" yields what answer?

5. The author states, on page 30, that "whenever and wherever meaning is, somebody is." Apply this statement to the classical question "If a tree falls in the forest and there is no one there to hear it, is there any sound?"

6. What is meant by "nothing ever means itself alone"?

7. Considering our definition of *consciousness* in Chapter 2, explain the relation between it and *meaning*.

8. Our second fundamental question, "What are the sorts of meaning?" yields what answer?

9. (**a**) Our third fundamental question, "What is meaning a part of?" yields what answer?   (**b**) When we talk of meaning being a *part* of consciousness, why is it "not really structure analysis but rather classification using the language of structure analysis"?

10. Our fourth fundamental question, "What are the parts of a meaning?" yields what answer?

11. (**a**) What is the trinitarian concept of God?   (**b**) Relate the Trinity to the psychological trinity in a unit of meaning.

12. (**a**) Explain the statement "Wherever there is a sea, somebody must say to the water, 'So far you go and no farther' " by relating it to the statement "a relation itself is a thing."   (**b**) What does *delineation* mean as used in the statement "and the relation between the one (thing) and the other (thing) is the act of *delineation* which went on in his head"?   (**c**) What significant morpheme is preserved within the spelling of *delineation*?   (**d**) Considering your answers to questions (**a**), (**b**), and (**c**), why is it "the very contrary of stupidity to say that you cannot be conscious of one thing and one only"?

13. Our fifth fundamental question, "What is meaning a stage of?" yields what answer?

14. What is meant by the statement "meaning is always a matter of *moment*"?

15. Applying our sixth fundamental question, "What are the stages of meaning?" what answer do we get?

16. How can a sensation become meaningful (become a sensation)?

17. How is recall involved in meaning?

5 SIGNS

THE COMPLEXITY of meaningful situations, which we may now call "sign situations," varies enormously. Suppose, for example, that a chain of three links is known to be situated so that energy may be applied only at link one; if link three moves, that is a sign that link two has been moved by link one, or that link two has moved link three, or that link one has moved. This is a very simple situation but the meaning that link two has moved link three is simpler than the meaning that link one has moved link two.

Now, if we are to sort meanings according to their complexity, how are we to measure the degree of that complexity? If one of these meanings is simpler than the others, how do we tell? Remember that we have said that complexity depends not so much upon the number of things but upon the sorts of connections among things. A person who can comprehend the interpretation of the movement of the third link of our chain would not experience increasing difficulty if we increase the number of links for there is but one type of connection between links, and no link has more than two connections. Now the number of connections that a given sign may have depends upon the situation in which we find it, and it might be well to add at this point that the term *situation*, as we have used it in the expression "sign situation," is synonymous with two other very important words, about which we shall have a good deal more to say: *context* and *matrix*. In interpreting the movement of our third link we had only to notice the simple structural characteristic of the chain and the fact that energy could be applied at one point only. These factors in our interpretation were significant elements in the situation, context, matrix, or (and here is one more widely used synonym) the "frame of reference."

It will be apparent that the factors which must be considered when we interpret A as meaning B may range from one to infinity; that is, we have a range of factors from A-means-B-when-C, to A-means-B-when-C_n (where n means any number of factors). For our present modest objective a threefold classification should be adequate. "A always means B" may stand as the pattern of the simplest possible sign situation, and B may stand as the simplest sort of meaning, which we shall call meaning from simple sign.

Now the most complex situations we are able to conceive are those we can find in the interpretation of great works of literary art —a play of Shakespeare's, a novel of Thomas Hardy's, the Book of Job, or Melville's *Moby-Dick*. In such complex sign situations, in order to get the sense of one word or one sentence we sometimes find it necessary to take into consideration not only words and sentences throughout the work itself, but numberless other considerations related to the life and time of the person who used the word or sentence. Thus we may take language signs as representing the maximum degree of complexity; to signalize this extreme difference from the simple sign, we shall give these most complex signs the special name "symbols."

For our immediate practical purpose the most important way-station on our scale of complexity between the simple sign and the complex symbol is occupied by the sort of meaning we get from shadows, photographs, maps, and the like. And when we say that A means B when and only when C is known, we suggest the possibility of various meanings for A. The conventional name for the sort of meaning we have in mind is "projection." Our answer to the question "What are the sorts of meaning according to the order of complexity?" is this: There are three sorts of meaning—meaning from simple sign, meaning from projection, and meaning from symbol. Meaning from simple sign may be defined as the sort of meaning we get from the fixed, natural, or necessary relation between things in the world, or from two events which happen together or in an inevitable sequence. Thus in an animal the head can mean the tail and vice-versa; and in the cause-effect relation the egg can mean the chicken or vice-versa.

Meaning from projection is the sort we get when we are able to imagine or construct one object by considering another because there is a point-for-point relation between them, provided that we know the connection or connections that make the point-for-point relation meaningful. We can get a very accurate notion of a room, for example, by interpreting the light and dark patterns on a photograph, provided that we know the nature of the lens used in the camera. Very serious mistakes may occur if we are ignorant of the variation in lenses. To cite a more extreme case, with a little training a skilled musician might learn to read or even to listen imaginatively to the music from a phonograph record by examining the groove under a microscope; for there is a point-for-point relation between the groove impressed on the disc and the music which produced it or the music which is produced by it—and any one of them may be said to mean the other two.

Meaning from symbol may be defined as the sort of meaning we get from a sign whose significant relation is not fixed in nature but established in accordance with the conscious interests of human beings. A sign or a projection has to mean what it means, or its interpreter is simply mistaken; we must say either that it has no utterer or that it is an utterance of nature. A projection may or may not be uttered. A shadow is not an utterance, but a map is; a photograph is an utterance when the lens is deliberately selected or the development of negative and print intentionally controlled; a recorded symphony is an utterance when the speed, volume, or tone is consciously adjusted. A symbol, on the contrary, is an arbitrary device, a mere matter of accord between two or more persons or a consistent adherence to one person's prearranged scheme. A bear track means something other than bear only on those very rare occasions when some crafty human attempts the imitation of a bear track. The map of a country, if it is a map and not a deliberate or careless misrepresentation, even though at first glance it bears no resemblance to the terrain, must be as it is, given the principles of construction or projection which produced it, and therefore must mean what it means. But a symbol is absolutely at the mercy of human intelligence insofar as you are willing to assume that that intelligence is free. Symbols, then, are arbitrary signs made by people who have free will. "Horse" (the word) means horse and "rabbit" (the word) means rabbit, but you are free to let "horse" mean workbench, and you might let "rabbit" mean hot cheese on toast; and if you had a silly streak you might let "horse" mean tincture of iodine and keep a diary wherein "rabbit" might stand for the end of the month. Sign, then, is a matter of necessity; projection, a matter of point-for-point relation; and symbol, a matter of convention.

Symbols are not only the most difficult of all signs to read because of the infinite number of ways they may be related to their verbal contexts (the words around them) and their matrices (their total environment), but they are the most valuable to us because it is by them and by them alone that we manage to differentiate ourselves from the other animals about us; by them and by them alone we can make appointments for the week after next; by them and by them alone we can tally the number of our flocks or discover that the square of the hypotenuse of a right triangle is equal to the sum of the squares of the opposite sides; by them and by them alone we can say "The Lord is my shepherd, I shall not want."

Symbols, as you might expect, perform a multiple function in our lives because of the multiple structure of the c.n.s. and the threefold aspect of our consciousness which that structure produces. By means of sensory operations—visual, auditory, and tactile—we produce comparable sensations in our fellows, and the result is the communication function of language.

Having discovered in this process that what is present can be made to stand for what is absent, we have learned how to make symbols serve as instruments for solving problems that could not otherwise be solved or even adequately conceived as problems. For the processes of sorting, and the special sort of sorting that we call counting, enable us to impose some modest degree of law and order on the innumerable phenomena of our experience and the vast complexity of their interrelations. Our symbol systems (among which our language is pre-eminent) are the instruments by which we modify our physical environment, rule the animal kingdom, and establish whatever norms of decency and order exist among us. The processes of definition and analysis constitute the problem-solving function of language.

It is doubtful that civilized man could survive the millions of artificial shocks his insatiable curiosity is heir to, or the tensions and frustrations that his contentions and confusions inevitably produce, if language did not offer him a means of relaxation or escape. Because the present word may stand not only for the absent thing but the thing of "airy nothingness," it becomes the instrument of the creative imagination and the means of psychological survival. With language in the form of poetry, as with the system we call music, we give a kind of necessary formulation to our feelings of weal and woe. This is the emotional adjustment function of language. We may call the functions of communication, problem-solving, and emotional adjustment the primary functions of language.

We are now ready to conclude our brief survey of the basic concepts for thinking about language and of the practices we encourage you to adopt. We have described words as sorts of symbols; symbols we have defined as the most complex signs of meaning, which require for their interpretation the constant reference to simple signs and, frequently, to projections. We have described meaning as a complex of the conscious processes of sensation, affection, and reason. Reason we have described as a threefold activity made up of classification, structure analysis, and operation analysis. Later we shall have occasion to point out the arbitrary and relative nature of classification. We shall, for example, set up a series of seven-fold sortings which will, to some extent, be arbitrary and designed merely to aid the memory and to illustrate the point; but we believe that the threefold classifications of ideas, language functions, and analyses are absolute and must be comprehended and utilized as the basic principles or laws of mental behavior.

There are several patterns that our presentation might follow from this point, which you would do well to consider. We are presenting a system of conscious behavior. Systems, as we have said, are complex dynamic wholes made up of related functional parts, and a complete account of any one of those parts must give its relationship to each of the other parts in the whole. That means that a complete account of each part cannot be given at any one time or in any one step. Take, for example, the system we call an automobile. A complete account of the carburetor would involve its relation to a spark plug, but any reference to a spark plug would have little meaning to a person who doesn't know what a spark plug is. If you will think about this matter for a few moments, you will see that it does not make much difference where you start when you are describing a complex system, for you will have to go from part to part, returning again and again to the more important parts because of their numerous connections with other parts.

For the simple reason that the communication function of language is its most obvious function and the one most grossly and unfortunately misunderstood, we shall begin with it. Because a survey of that function logically ends in the theory and practice of definition, which is a natural bridge to the problem-solving function, we shall discuss the problem-solving function next and conclude with the function of emotional adjustment.

But from a psychological point of view, the concept of ambiguity is fundamental to a consideration of all three functions. The definition and demonstration of ambiguity therefore seem desirable before beginning a systematic analysis of our subject.

STUDY QUESTIONS

1. Why is it simpler to see that the second link in a three-link chain has moved the third than to see that the first has moved the second?

2. What is our horizontal sorting factor when we sort meanings, i.e., what are we sorting according to?

3. The author gives us three synonyms for *situation* as used in the expression "sign situation": *context, matrix,* and *frame of reference.* Could we also substitute *environment* in the statement "Now the number of connections that a given sign may have depends upon the situation in which we find it"?

4. What factors determine the *complexity* of a sign situation?

5. In *A always means B,* is A the outside stimulus (thing) and B the interpretation by the mind of that stimulus?

6. As used on page 35, is *language sign* a synonym for *symbol*?

7. We consider a road map a projection because there is a point-for-point relation between the lines on the map and the actual road. What other factor would *have* to be considered to make the map meaningful?

8. Can you actually draw lines from the music to the groove that it produced on a record? What, then, does *music* mean in this sense? What is another sense of *music*?

9. (**A**) What does *utterance* mean as used on page 36. (**B**) Why is a map an *utterance*; why is a shadow *not* an *utterance*? (**C**) Discuss the words "projection" and "utterance" as used in relation to the shadow of an entertainer's hand cast upon a screen in the likeness of a goose.

10. (**A**) What does *arbitrary* mean? (**B**) Are the meanings of all words established arbitrarily?

11. What is the difference between *verbal contexts* and *matrices* as used on page 37?

12. The author states that "because of the multiple structure of the c.n.s. and the threefold aspect of our consciousness which that structure produces" symbols perform a multiple function in our lives. Which of the three aspects of consciousness would you choose as being the most closely related to the problem-solving function of language? To the emotional adjustment function? To the communication function?

13. What relation is there between words and the fact that what is present can be made to stand for what is absent?

14. Using a two-level classification diagram, analyze these concepts: (1) meaning is a complex of the conscious processes of sensation, affection, and reason; and (2) reason is a threefold activity made up of classification, structure analysis, and operation analysis.

Antiquity forgot, custom not known,
The ratifiers and props of every word . . .

HAMLET

They yawne at it, and botch the words up to fit theyr
owne thoughts.

HAMLET

6 AMBIGUITY

THERE SEEMS TO BE no way of accounting for the fundamental and widespread misunderstanding of the relation between language and thought unless the reason be the one quoted from Aristotle, that the mind is characteristically blind to things that are at once important and obvious. Be this as it may, the most important thing to know about language, regardless of any of its particular functions, is the principle of ambiguity. Signs and projections present from time to time examples of multiple meaning, but symbols, if they are to meet the innumerable demands of human thought with any degree of efficiency, must of necessity have many senses. It is our purpose now to show how simple, common words can give rise to profound misunderstandings merely because they *are* simple, common, and consequently ambiguous. By ambiguous we mean, of course, not vague, but capable of two or more interpretations.

Famous examples of ambiguity abound. Perhaps it is not too much to say that Hamlet's "To be, or not to be" soliloquy is the most famous passage in the most famous drama by the most famous dramatist of the western world. Since it has been scrutinized for three centuries by an endless succession of keen and interested eyes, one might reasonably suppose that its meaning would long since have been made abundantly clear. But as Alexander Bryan Johnson once said (*A Treatise on Language*), "the perverted estimation of language is so habitual" that generations of readers and playgoers seem to have misapprehended in one way or another the unhappy Hamlet's most obvious remarks.

Now the "perverted estimation of language" to which Mr. Johnson referred is the comfortable assumption that if one speaks simply and clearly in words common to him and his interpreter, his interpreter will understand him with little or no difficulty. The very opposite, however, is the fact, and the interpretations of Hamlet's too too familiar lines provide some striking examples of misapprehension.

We do not mean to suggest that here, at long last, we have plucked out the heart of Hamlet's mystery; we are not attempting a scholarly contribution to Shakespearean hermeneutics. We seek rather to impress upon the reader the essential fact of linguistic ambiguity and to make three points relevant to it: first, that the wide discrepancies of expert opinion relate to the meaning of familiar terms; second, that any defensible interpretation must of necessity proceed from a lively awareness of the law of matrix; and third, that rival interpretations should be evaluated according to the law of parsimony.

It would probably be a good thing if you would read the speech in question (Act III, Scene i) with some care. Here it is as it appeared during Shakespeare's lifetime in the second Quarto, which is now generally regarded as the exemplary text.

> HAMLET. To be, or not to be, that is the question,
> Whether tis nobler in the minde to suffer
> The slings and arrowes of outragious fortune,
> Or to take Armes against a sea of troubles,
> And by opposing, end them, to die to sleepe
> No more, and by a sleepe, to say we end
> The hart-ake, and the thousand naturall shocks
> That flesh is heire to; tis a consumation
> Devoutly to be wisht to die to sleepe,
> To sleepe, perchance to dreame, I there's the rub,
> For in that sleepe of death, what dreames may come
> When we have shuffled off this mortall coyle
> Must giue vs pause, there's the respect
> That makes calamitie of so long life:
> For who would beare the whips and scornes of time,
> Th'oppressors wrong, the proude mans contumely,

The pangs of despiz'd loue, the lawes delay,
The insolence of office, and the spurnes
That patient merrit of th'vnworthy takes,
When he himselfe might his quietas make
With a bare bodkin; who would fardels beare,
To grunt and sweat vnder a wearie life,
But that the dread of something after death,
The vndiscouer'd country, from whose borne
No trauiler returnes, puzzels the will,
And makes vs rather beare those ills we haue,
Then flie to others that we know not of.
Thus conscience dooes make cowards,
And thus the natiue hiew of resolution
Is sickled ore with the pale cast of thought,
And enterprises of great pitch and moment,
With this regard theyr currents turne awry,
And loose the name of action.

To give a complete account of the various interpretations of the disputed words in this passage would require a book rather than a chapter. There are two sorts of differences among the interpreters, different interpretations of the received text and differences of opinion regarding the accuracy of the text; for example, whether "to be" means to exist or to happen, and whether "slings" should read "stings," or "sea" should read "siege." The lines that have given the most trouble are the lines from "To be" through "end them"; "When we have shuffled off this mortal coil"; "When he himself might his quietus make"; "Thus conscious does make cowards"; "And enterprises of great *pitch* and moment" (the Folio and most editors read *pith*). There are over five thousand words in the footnotes to this speech in the Furness *Variorum* edition. Each succeeding editor sifts what he considers to be the wheat from the chaff of this voluminous commentary and adds a few kernels of his own.

The law of matrix, which we have already identified with the concepts of sign-situation, context, and frame of reference, means that a sign is without meaning except in a matrix, or that the meaning of a sign is relative to its matrix. Now there are two ways in which the kind of sign we have called a symbol can get into a matrix. When you use one, you put it into your own world of meaning. When another interprets the symbols uttered by you, he beholds them in *his* matrix—his world of meaning. We shall have much more to say about this later; now it may serve to point out that the interpreter must attempt to imagine what the speaker's matrix was like. We shall call the interpreter's conclusion the *theoretical matrix*. Our contemporary idea of how the words and things in Shakespeare's world must have appeared to him is our theoretical Shakespearean matrix. Most failures in communication between Shakespeare and posterity seem to be due to our reluctance to take the trouble to reconstruct Shakespeare's world. Indeed, some of us are outraged by that reconstruction if it tends to alter "our" Shakespeare or "our" Hamlet. Protestants, for example, are sometimes quick to resent the suggestion that Shakespeare thought Catholic thoughts with a mind nurtured by Catholic parents.

There are three indispensable instruments for setting up the theoretical matrix of a Shakespearean utterance: The Oxford English Dictionary, Bartlett's *Concordance* to Shakespeare, and a Biblical concordance of comparable scope. In the Oxford English Dictionary we may find an exhaustive and richly illustrated account of the way the English language was used up to and during the time of Shakespeare. In the Shakespearean concordance we may compare his every use of any given term throughout the plays and poems. In the Biblical concordance we may sometimes hit upon the very passages of scripture that apparently had some part in the formulation of his thought. Shakespeare's text abounds in Biblical allusions which have for some reason or other gone undetected by his professional interpreters. This is partly because the King James version has been used by the vast majority of English scholars, whereas it was not, of course, used by Shakespeare. We shall illustrate this point in suggesting an interpretation for the soliloquy.

The law of parsimony, sometimes called Occam's Razor, states that entities are not to be multiplied beyond necessity; this means that we are not to make unnecessary assumptions regarding the hypothetical matrix of a sign. Remember that the sign-situation must contain things other than the sign itself for the sign to have meaning. Now we have to guess what some of these other things are when we reconstruct a matrix. The law of parsimony urges a strict economy upon us; it requires that we never make a guess with two or three assumptions in it if we can make sense with one. One complex guess is better than three unrelated simple guesses. That is, if you arrive at the scene of a crime and find a shell, a pistol, and hole in the victim's head, *other things being equal*, it is better to guess that the pistol fired a bullet into the victim and ejected the shell, although you may have no proof that the pistol belonged to either the victim or the killer or that the shell had not been lying there long before the killing or that the hole had not been made with a spike.

It must be kept clearly in mind that we are talking about the interpretation of signs where there are two or more possible meanings and the "true" meaning cannot be determined. You can never know what Shakespeare "really" meant; but if you and a friend offer rival interpretations *each of which takes all the relevant signs and symbols into account*, by the law of parsimony your interpretation is the better if your hypothetical matrix contains fewer assumptions than his. We shall now illustrate this point with our reading of the soliloquy; and perhaps we should add that if you stay with us through the rather complex remarks we are about to make, nothing more we have to say in this book should seriously trouble your powers of comprehension.

Taking the first five lines we shall first attempt the somewhat complicated explanation of the ambiguity of "to be" and its effect upon the editorial history of the speech. Speaking generally, there are two main sorts of interpretation: those which regard "Whether 'tis nobler in the mind to suffer The slings and arrows of outrageous fortune, Or to take arms against a sea of troubles, And by opposing end them" as an expanded paraphrase of "to be or not to be"; and those which detect a change of subject. A great majority of commentators fall in the first class, which itself divides into two schools— those who see Hamlet as contemplating self-slaughter and those who understand him as debating the question of vengeance and its perilous consequences. The advocates of suicidal inclination constitute the main body of orthodox opinion, and they divide into two groups— those who read "to be or not to be" as meaning *to live or not to live* and those who read it as *Is this suicide of mine to be or not to be?* (See the accompanying chart.) Now the order of your paraphrase is determined by your reading at this point. If you say *to live*, you paraphrase it as "to suffer the slings and arrows of outrageous fortune," and *not to live* must then become "to take up arms against a sea of troubles." The scholarly effort to rationalize this position has been heroic, and we are asked to believe that Shakespeare had in mind

INTERPRETATIONS OF "TO BE OR NOT TO BE"

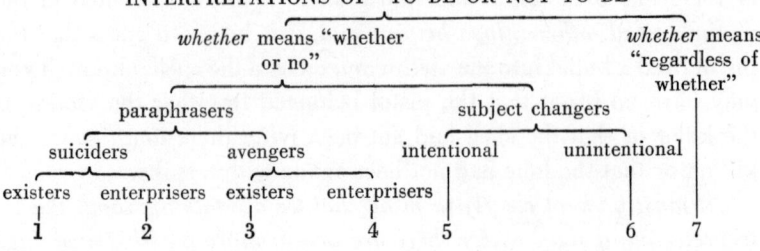

Interpretation by	Interpretation of "to be or not to be"	Interpretation of "whether 'tis nobler to suffer . . . or to take arms"
PARAPHRASERS		
Suiciders		
1. Existers	(1) To live (2) or not to live	(1) To suffer troubles (2) or to end troubles by suicide
2. Enterprisers	(1) Is this enterprise of suicide to take place (2) or not to take place	(2) To suffer troubles (1) or to end troubles by suicide
Avengers		
3. Existers	(1) To live (2) or not to live	(1) To suffer troubles (2) or to die fighting for vengeance
4. Enterprisers	(1) Is this enterprise of vengeance to take place (2) or not	(2) To suffer troubles (1) or to die fighting for vengeance
SUBJECT CHANGERS		
Intentional		
5. Johnson	(a) Life after death or not must be decided before consideration of	(b) To suffer or risk death
Unintentional		
6. Goldsmith	(1) To live (2) or not to live	(1) To suffer or to avenge
"REGARDLESS OF WHETHER"		
7. Upton	(a) To live or not to live is the question	(b) Regardless of whether it be nobler to suffer or avenge

Fleming's translation of Aelian's *History of the Celts* in which the Celts are said to "throw themselves into the fomey floudes with their swordes drawn in their handes, and shaking their javelines as though they were of force and violence to withstand the rough waves." This interpretation also acquits Shakespeare of the charge of muddling his metaphors and is, in this respect, superior to a certain professor's emendation of "arms" to "oars."

If, as an advocate of suicidal intent, you read "to be or not to be" as *Shall I or shall I not*, then you must reverse the paraphrase and *shall I* becomes "take up arms . . ." and *shall I not* is left to mean "suffer the slings and arrows . . ."

If you take the pro-vengeance gambit, you likewise enjoy the two "to be" alternatives. "To be" as *to live* becomes "to suffer . . ." and "not to be" becomes "to take up arms" *and lose your life in the scuffle*; and the alternative produces the reversal again. If "to be" is to avenge, it must mean *to take arms with fatal results* and "not to be" must mean "to suffer . . ."

If you refuse to follow the sheep over the cliff of paraphrase, you will find yourself among a curious but "clubable" group of companions. The first is Dr. Samuel Johnson, who attributes Hamlet's vocal incoherence to Shakespeare's craftsmanship in showing the distracted prince shifting his thought from his future to the dignity of his reason. Johnson reasons thus:

Of this celebrated soliloquy which bursting from a man distracted with contrariety of desires, and overwhelmed with the magnitude of his own purposes, is connected rather in the speaker's mind than on his tongue, I shall endeavor to discover the train, and to show how one sentiment produces another. Hamlet, knowing himself injured in the most enormous and atrocious degree, and seeing no means of redress but such as must expose him to the extremity of hazard, meditates on his situation in the manner: *Before I can form any rational scheme of action under this pressure of distress,* it is necessary *to decide whether, after our present state, we are* to be or not to be. That is the question, which, as it shall be answered, will determine *whether* 'tis nobler, and more suitable to the dignity of reason, *to suffer the outrages of fortune* patiently, or to take arms against *them,* and by opposing end them, *though perhaps with the loss of life.*[1]

---

[1] *Hamlet,* ed. Furness, Vol. I, p. 204.

The second member of the club is Oliver Goldsmith, the author of the *Essay on Metaphors* in James Prior's *Miscellaneous Works of Oliver Goldsmith*. Editors who revere both Shakespeare and Goldsmith repudiate the Oliverian authorship and in deference to them, we shall call him the pseudo-Goldsmith. Whoever he was, he had the critical audacity to say that "The soliloquy in Hamlet, which we have so often heard extolled in terms of admiration, is, in our opinion, a heap of absurdities, whether we consider the situation, the sentiment, the argumentation, or the poetry." Here is the passage relevant to our discussion:

The question is, "To be, or not to be"; to die by my own hand, or live and suffer the miseries of life. He proceeds to explain the alternative in these terms, "Whether 'tis nobler in the mind to suffer, or endure, the frowns of fortune, or to take arms, and by opposing, end them." Here he deviates from his first proposition, and death is no longer the question. The only doubt is, whether he will stoop to misfortune, or exert his faculties in order to surmount it. This surely is the obvious meaning, and indeed the only meaning that can be implied in these words, "Whether 'tis nobler in the mind, to suffer The slings and arrows of outrageous fortune, Or to take arms against a sea of troubles, And by opposing, end them."[2]

The third odd-ball who tumbles into the antiparaphrase pocket, if not the club, is also in appropriate disagreement with the other two members. He agrees with the orthodox position on the contemplation of suicide and the interpretation of "to be" as *to live*, but because he made an uninspired, but systematic, exploration of every potential ambiguity in the speech, the key to the enigma "lay in his way and he found it."

It is the present writer's considered opinion that the crucial ambiguity lies in the inconspicuous conjunctive adverb "whether." Let us attempt first of all to disrupt any predisposition on the part of the reader to use it as all previous commentators seem to have done. Here are some sample uses, all of which were in the language in Shakespeare's day: "Hand me that bodkin." "I can't decide *whether* that would be *right* or *no* (Shakespeare's habitual usage); I can't decide whether that would be *right* or *wrong*." "Well, *whether* it be right *or* wrong, hand it to me!"

---

[2] *Ibid.*, p. 206.

The tricky behavior of "whether" would seem to be due to the fact that looking to see whether a thing is so may be the same as looking to see whether it is so or not, but not necessarily so. It is a difficulty that arises in connection with the mental act of negation and is also exemplified by the "not" that tied us up in "to be or not to be." Now the reader is free to make up his own mind *whether* he agrees with Johnson or our pseudo-Goldsmith about Shakespeare's rhetoric, but *whether* he agrees with the one or the other on that score, we trust he will side with us on the ambiguity of *whether*.

But to return to Hamlet and his question. One of the several senses of "question" is "subject of philosophical debate" and specifically that sort of debate called dialectic that goes on in one's mind as one turns the question over to see its several sides. Ordinarily the question of revenge is an ethical one, and Shakespeare elsewhere approaches it as such. Here is the eloquent retort of the soldierly Alcibiades in *Timon of Athens* to the pious affirmations of the senators:

> FIRST SENATOR: You cannot make gross sins look clear:
> To revenge is no valour, but to bear.
> ALCIBIADES: My lords, then, under favour, pardon me,
> If I speak like a captain.
> Why do fond men expose themselves to battle,
> And not endure all threats? sleep upon't,
> And let the foes quietly cut their throats,
> Without repugnancy? If there be
> Such valour in the bearing, what make we
> Abroad? why then, women are more valiant
> That stay at home, if bearing carry it,
> And the ass more captain than the lion, the felon
> Loaden with irons wiser than the judge,
> If wisdom be in suffering.

Hamlet has apparently resolved this question for himself because he emphatically sides with Alcibiades in the lines:

> Rightly to be great
> Is not to stir without great argument,
> But greatly to find quarrel in a straw
> When honour's at the stake.

In our soliloquy, however, Hamlet is rather dismissing the ethical question, which has been transcended by the spiritual one. Let us take our cue from Dr. Johnson and rephrase Hamlet's thought: "Here I am, a reputable soldier, charged by my Father's ghost to avenge his most unnatural murder. But in my soul, ''tis bitter cold and I am sick at heart.' My Mother's outrageous behavior has so filled me with disgust that, as I said before, I would take my own life if 'the everlasting has not fixed his canon 'gainst self slaughter.' So you see, with me, regardless of whether it is nobler to suffer or nobler to fight, the immediate question is whether to live at all." If you are already familiar with the lines, it will be difficult to read "whether" and "to be" with appropriate emphasis and the succeeding words will have to go "trippingly on the tongue." But with a little practice you will be able to say:

> To *be* or not to *be*, that is the question,
> *Whether* 'tis nobler in the mind to suffer
> The slings and arrows of outrageous fortune,
> *Or* to take arms against a sea of troubles,
> And by opposing end them.

Once we free ourselves from the grammatical obligation of making "take arms" mean "suicide," we may easily dispose of the fanatical Celts in the editorial wastebasket and look for grounds more relative to Hamlet's thought.

In our methodical review of the multiple definition of "slings" we come upon a clue to the nature of Shakespeare's attendant images. The *O.E.D.* cites an occurrence of the word in *First Maccabees*, which turns out to be the most appropriate book in the Scriptures, as Shakespeare knew them, from which to derive Hamlet's solution of the ethical question. For Judas Maccabeus is the Hebraic exemplar of pious aggression, and in one of the most memorable battle passages of historical literature we come upon the magnificent picture of the sea of troubles breaking in outrageously upon the unfortunate sanctuary of Jerusalem.

And Judas departed from the castle, and removed the camp to Bethzacharam, over against the king's camp. ❡ And the king rose before it was light, and made his troops march on fiercely towards the way of Bethzacharam: and the armies made themselves ready for the battle, and they sounded the trumpets: ❡ And they shewed the elephants the blood of grapes, and mulberries to provoke them to fight.

And they distributed the beasts by the legions: and there stood by every elephant a thousand men in coats of mail, and with helmets of brass on their heads: and five hundred horsemen set in order were chosen for every beast. ❡ These before the time wheresoever the beast was, they were there: and whithersoever it went, they went, and they departed not from it. ❡ And upon the beasts, there were strong wooden towers, which covered every one of them: and engines upon them: and upon every one thirty-two valiant men, who fought from above; and an Indian to rule the beast.

And the rest of the horsemen he placed on this side and on that side at the two wings, with trumpets to stir up the army, and to hasten them forward that stood thick together in the legions thereof. ❡ Now when the sun shone upon the shields of gold, and of brass, the mountains glittered therewith, and they shone like lamps of fire.

And part of the king's army was distinguished by the high mountains, and the other part by the low places: and they marched on warily and orderly. ❡ And all the inhabitants of the land were moved at the noise of their multitude, and the marching of the company, and the rattling of the armour for the army was exceeding great and strong. ❡ And Judas and his army drew near for battle: and there fell of the king's army six hundred men.

And Eleazar the son of Saura saw one of the beasts harnessed with the king's harness: and it was higher than the other beasts: and it seemed to him that the king was on it: ❡ And he exposed himself to deliver his people and to get himself an everlasting name. ❡ And he ran up to it boldly in the midst of the legion, killing on the right hand, and on the left, and they fell by him on this side and that side. ❡ And he went between the feet of the elephant, and put himself under it: and slew it, and it fell to the ground upon him, and he died there. ❡ Then they seeing the strength of the king and the fierceness of his army, turned away from them.

But the king's army went up against them to Jerusalem: and the king's army pitched their tents against Judea and mount Sion. ❡ And he made peace with them that were in Bethsura: and they came forth out of the city, because they had no victuals, being shut up there, for it was the year of rest to the land. ❡ And the king took Bethsura: and he placed there a garrison to keep it. ❡ And he turned his army against the sanctuary for many days: and he set up there battering slings, and engines and instruments to cast fire, and engines to cast stones and javelins, and pieces to shoot arrows, and slings.

Here we have quoted the Douay version because it is easily accessible to you, although it was not available to Shakespeare when he wrote *Hamlet*. He might well have known the passage, however, as rendered in the Matthews Bible, which reads: "handbowes / fyrie dartes / rackettes to cast stones / scorpōs to shute arrowes / and slings."

And thus in the context of a great document in the history of human courage we acquit the author of *Hamlet* of the petty charges of bad grammar and faulty rhetoric. The four lines, "whether 'tis nobler in the mind to suffer The slings and arrows of outrageous fortune, Or to take arms against a sea of troubles, And by opposing end them" are not parallel but contrary to the line, "To be, or not to be, that is the question"; and "sea of troubles" is indeed a very appropriate metaphor *within* a most appropriate metaphor. Shakespeare would have us conceive of Hamlet, the soldier, when turning over the question of nonresistance versus pious aggression, as thinking in the terms and images of a soldier's scripture. When Hamlet thinks of "outrageous fortune," he thinks of it in terms, or rather images, of the outrageous fortune of besieged Jerusalem; and in his imagination he gazes out over her ramparts upon the approaching multitudes of the invading "Greeks" as they roll in, wave after wave, and beat upon the walls of the sanctuary. Hamlet thinks of the spiritual fortune of man in terms of the physical fortune of a city and the physical fortune of a city in terms of the behavior of the sea. "Sea" in this passage, then, does not mean the ocean, but an army; an army, however, which is not a real army, but a conceptual symbol for the outrageous circumstances that may trouble the soul of a man. Thus an appropriate metaphor within an appropriate metaphor has a reinforcing effect and is quite the opposite of a "mixed" metaphor, the influence of which may be psychologically disruptive, if not ludicrous.

Now if we are disposed to adopt the Maccabean derivation and the suggested reading of "whether," then further relevant conjecture is indicated. If Hamlet is dismissing the ethical question in the terms and images of its most classic formulation, why should he not turn to the same source for the words or images of the question he actually is presenting?

If a dramatist is creating a character who thinks in terms of Biblical recollections and is so overwhelmed by outrageous fortune that he would "shorten" his own life, what Biblical prototype would he be most likely to recall? Job, of course, and the seventh chapter of Job, at that. Now, if you read the seventh chapter of Job in the King James version, no compulsive sense of association may develop, but if you read it in the Catholic Vulgate as Shakespeare may have, or in the Matthews version, as he probably did, then you will be most emphatically reminded of Hamlet; for both soliloquies begin with military metaphors, both contain references to the one-way direction of hell-bent traffic, and both are uttered by soul-sick children of sinner Adam who conceive of themselves as overburdened soldiers "in for the duration" for whom this life is a prison and whose sleep is troubled by bad dreams. Compare Hamlet's "For me, Denmark's a prison, but I could be bounded by a nut-shell and count myself king of infinite space were it not that I have bad dreams." Here is the entire chapter from the closely parallel Douay version:

The life of man upon earth is a warfare [militia], and his days are like the days of a hireling [mercenarii]. ❡ As a servant longeth for the shade, as the hireling looketh for the end of his work; ❡ So I also have had empty months, and have numbered to myself wearisome nights. ❡ If I lie down to sleep, I shall say: When shall I arise? and again I shall look for the evening, and shall be filled with sorrows even till darkness. ❡ My flesh is clothed with rottenness and the filth of dust, my skin is withered and drawn together.

My days have passed more swiftly than the web is cut by the weaver, and are consumed without any hope. ❡ Remember that my life is but wind, and my eyes shall not return to see good things. ❡ Nor shall the sight of man behold me: thy eyes are upon me, and I shall be no more. ❡ As a cloud is consumed, and passeth away: so he that shall go down to hell [the King James has *grave*] shall not come up. ❡ Nor shall he return any more into his house, neither shall his place know him any more.

Wherefore I will not spare my mouth, I will speak in the affliction of my spirit: I will talk with the bitterness of my soul. ❡ Am I a sea, or a whale, that thou hast enclosed me in a prison? [the King James has *settest a watch over*]. ❡ If I say: My bed shall comfort me, and I shall be relieved speaking with myself on my couch: ❡ Thou wilt frighten me with dreams and terrify me with visions. ❡ So that my soul rather chooseth hanging, and my bones death. ❡ I have done with hope, I shall now live no longer: spare me, for my days are nothing.

What is a man that thou shouldst magnify him? or why dost thou set thy heart upon him? ❡ Thou visitest him early in the morning and thou provest him suddenly. ❡ How long wilt thou not spare me, nor suffer me to swallow down my spittle? ❡ I have sinned: what shall I do to thee,

O keeper of men? why hast thou set me opposite to thee, and I am become
burdensome to myself?   ❡ Why dost thou not remove my sin, and why
dost thou not take away my iniquity? Behold now I shall sleep in the
dust: and if thou seek me in the morning, I shall not be.

Let us check our course and position at this time. We are using
the soliloquy to demonstrate the bearing of the fact of ambiguity and
the laws of matrix and parsimony upon the process of interpretation.
In checking the multiple definition of "slings" we made contact with
the Scriptures, which in Shakespeare's time always included the
Apocrypha. This suggested a Biblical analogue for Hamlet's mood
as well as his imagery and uncovered the radical verbal differences
between the Matthews version and the King James *Job*. We find
ourselves, then, well advanced toward formulating a hypothetical
Shakespearean matrix. As one would expect, when a basic insight
is gained, incidental problems quickly resolve themselves and the
pieces of the puzzle fall into place. In this case the incidental problems have to do with the appropriate senses of "devoutly," "shuffled,"
and "coil."

One has the feeling that, except possibly by John Barrymore,
"devoutly" has usually been read with the sense of "sincerely" or
"wholeheartedly." Indeed, the Oxford Fathers cite the passage in
this generalized sense; but with Job in mind we must now prefer the
primitive sense of "piously" or "with appropriate reverence." It is
a legitimate question in casuistry whether the Everlasting's "canon
'gainst self-slaughter" implies a like proscription of the conscious
desire to die. It is apparent from the New Testament that the
conscience-clear Christian could "fall asleep in Christ" confident that
he would sleep soundly until the crack of doom. But it is also apparent from the Book of Job that however bitter the good man may
find his lot and however much he may yearn for death, he need not
necessarily fall from grace; for the "Lord blessed the latter end of
Job more than his beginning." Job, however, did not contemplate
the making of his own quietus. To wish to put an end to the thousand
natural shocks the flesh is heir to is not beyond the pale of "devout"
belief, for Job is a sacred precedent; but to seek release not in God's
due season but by one's personal act of will is to "shuffle off" this
mortal coil. It is a curious thing that editors have not noticed that

the appropriate sense of "shuffle" here is similar to that in the speech
of Claudius two scenes later (Act III, Scene iv):

> In the corrupted currents of this world,
> Offence's gilded hand may *shove by* justice,
> And oft 'tis seen, the wicked prize itself
> Buys out the law; but 'tis not so above,
> There is no *shuffling*.

We do not mean to say that "shuffle" in the verb phrase "shuffle off"
has the *same* sense as "shuffle" meaning "shove by." Denotatively
we may illustrate three early 17th century senses in such a sentence
as "The prisoner shuffled off his fetters, shuffled himself into a disguise, and shuffled by the guard." Connotatively they are all "bad"
or illegal. The word, of course, should be emphasized in reading
because it is the key word. It is when we willfully and deliberately
"shuffle" off this mortal coil that we break the divine law and therefore must expect to sleep the troubled sleep of the guilty until we face
the bar of judgment and receive our doom. The phrase has usually
been taken simply as a figurative synonym for "to die," thus creating
the redundancy "for in that sleep of death what dreams may come
when we have *died* must give us pause." Shakespeare has committed
worse, but if we regard him innocent until proved guilty, we do better
to read the line "for in that sleep of death what dreams may come
when we have made our *own* quietus must give us pause."

Now as to "coil": the *O.E.D.* says it here means "bustle or tur-
moil." It is true that it clearly has such a sense in the other contexts
used by Shakespeare—except for one. And as we might expect, that
one confirms our present train of thought. It is to be found in Act II,
Scene i, of *All's Well That Ends Well*. Count Bertram and his friend
Parolles are chatting with two young lords about to leave for the front:

FIRST LORD. O my sweet lord, that you will stay behind us!
PAR. 'Tis not his fault, the spark.
SEC. LORD. O! 'tis brave wars.
PAR. Most admirable: I have seen those wars.
BER. I am commanded here, and kept a coil with
    "Too young," and "the next year," and " 'Tis too early."
PAR. An thy mind stand to't, boy, steal away bravely.
BER. I shall stay here the forehorse to a smock,
    Creaking my shoes on the plain masonry,

> Till honour be bought up and no sword worn
> But one to dance with! By heaven! I'll steal away.
> FIRST LORD. There's honour in the theft.
> PAR. Commit it, count.

Here is the relevant semantic history from the *O.E.D.*: "1611, to coil cable; 1616, Coiled up in a cable like salt eels; 1661, These small coyled particles of the air . . . when the pressure is taken away . . . flie abroad into a Coyle or Zone ten times as big in Diameter as before; 1691, Coil, a hen-coil, a hen-pen." (All of which makes one wonder whether *in stir* [prison] is a development by way of folk etymology for an older *a* [in] *coil* based on the better-known "stir" sense of *coil*.)

This much, at least, is obvious: in the 17th century the noun "coil" derived from the verb "to coil" (as cable) was used to mean "area of confinement"; and that it makes better sense to interpret Bertram's remark "I'm kept a coil" as meaning "I'm kept in confinement," rather than, say, Kittredge's gloss of "fussed over."

So much for our consideration of the hypothetical matrix and the relevance of Holy Writ. Now for the principle of least effort—the law of parsimony, or the doctrine of Occam's Razor. There are two metaphors that give concrete expression to the central thought of the speech. The first is that of life as unhappy military service from which one is tempted to absent oneself without leave. The second is the act of bowling taken as a model or concrete expression of the concept of action. Another curious fact in the history of Shakespearean commentary is that commentators have not noted the persistence of the "bowls" metaphor. It first appears in the expression "Aye, there's the rub," the "rub" being any flaw or obstacle on the green or alley which deflects the course of the bowl.

The metaphor reappears in "puzzles," "pitch," "moment," and "current," although some commentators would have us believe that "pitch" refers to the zenith of a falcon's flight, that "moment" means "important," and that "current" refers to a stream. All commentators overlook the literal sense of "puzzles," which applies nicely to a rub as obstructing the bowler's intention and the fact that "pitch," "moment," and "current" are all common English words that literally express the qualities and behavior of a bowl. The whole discourse falls neatly into the pattern of scholastic philosophy slyly referred to in the *not* tautologous assertion of the sexton in Act V when Shakespeare has him say "an act hath three branches: it is to act, to do, and to perform."

Here we must bring in a relevant bit of Elizabethan legal history, best presented by John Dover Wilson in his superb Cambridge edition of *Hamlet* (p. 231):

10–20. *if I drown myself. . . . his own life.* An echo of the famous case of *Hales v. Petit,* heard 1554, of which reports were pub. in 1571, 1578, and which settled for the period the law regards suicide, recognising it as homicide and so distinct from some kind of felony for which there was a forfeiture. Sir James Hales, the suicide, was a Common Law Judge, and consequently the case would be noteworthy on that score; in any event it presents some striking parallels with the words of the sexton, e.g. (i) Hales committed suicide by walking into a river at Canterbury (cf. "if the man go to this water" etc.). (ii) The counsel for the defence argued that

> "the act of self destruction consists of three parts. The first is the imagination, which is a reflection or meditation of the man's mind whether or no it be convenient to destroy himself and in what way it may be done; the second is the resolution, which is the determination of the mind to destroy himself and to do it in this or that particular way; the third is the perfection, which is the execution of what the mind has resolved to do. And this perfection consists of two parts, viz. the beginning and the end. The beginning is the death, which is only a sequel of the act."

(iii) There was much discussion as to whether Hales was the "agent" or the "patient," in other words whether he went to the water or the water came to him; and the verdict was:

> "Sir James Hales was dead. And how came he by his death? It may be answered by drowning. And who drowned him? Sir James Hales. And when did he drown him? In his lifetime. So that Sir James Hales being alive caused Sir James Hales to die, the act of the living was the death of the dead man. And for this offence it is reasonable to punish the living man, who committed the offence, and not the dead man."

These parallels were first noted by Sir John Hawkins, the friend of Dr. Johnson (v. Furness). The same arguments are likely to have been repeated at any inquest upon a drowned person and so might come to Sh[akespeare]'s knowledge.

Now, the step between the "act" (which here means "intention")
and the doing is the willing. As Brutus says in Act II, Scene i, lines
61–69, of *Julius Caesar*:

> Since Cassius first did whet me against Caesar,
> I have not slept.
> Between the acting of a dreadful thing
> And the first motion, all the interim is
> Like a phantasma, or a hideous dream:
> The genius and the mortal instruments
> Are then in council; and the state of man,
> Like to a little kingdom, suffers then
> The nature of an insurrection.[3]

But fear of divine judgment after death "puzzles" the will, and like
the bowl, which has struck a rub, its current or course no longer
accords with the bowler's "enterprise" or intention. Thus that which
is *active*, meaning performed by an *agent* with a free will, becomes
passive, that which is acted upon. Our sense of the word "passion"—
a very active notion indeed—derives from the theory that when our
feelings get the better of our judgments we are no longer agents but
become "lapsed in passion"; we are "patients" acted upon by our
emotions, rather than acting in accordance with our wills.

By the law of parsimony the elaboration of the bowls metaphor
here set forth is a more probable interpretation of Shakespeare's symbols than those of the standard commentators because it provides one
structure (the game of bowls) as a frame of reference rather than
three: bowls, falconry, and water courses. You may not agree with
this interpretation, but if you do not, you will find it instructive to
examine the grounds of your own belief.

It is obvious that the chief cause of the wide variation in the meanings attributed to the soliloquy is the phenomenon of ambiguity (or
perhaps better, the phenomena of ambiguity), for there are several
distinct routes by which an old word may take on a new sense while
at the same time retaining its old ones. The principal difficulty in
accurate interpretation lies not in our inability to deal with the strange
new term, but rather in our strange unwillingness to deal systematically and understandingly with the old ones. The rules for playing

---

[3] In the third line quoted, "acting" means "performance"; in the fourth line,
"motion" means Cassius' "whetting."

the game of linguistic communication in English are at least as generous and flexible as the rules of jurisprudence in English-speaking
cultures. Any term, for example, may alter its grammatical status
almost at will, with the result that "down," which comes to us out of
the unrecorded past as a noun meaning "hill," is now set down in our
dictionaries as an adverb, an adjective, a preposition, and a verb.
But the phenomenon that causes the sort of difficulty experienced in
Hamlet's simple English periods is not grammatical innovation, but
the fact that established words naturally develop (according to what
we might call their birthright in the commonwealth of a free mind)
new but related senses in several determinable ways. It is the business
of our next chapter to show how this process comes to be.

STUDY QUESTIONS

1. (**A**) What is the definition of *ambiguous* as used in this chapter?
(**B**) What is the basis (cause) for ambiguity?   (**C**) Would you say that
our purpose should be to eliminate ambiguity so that communication
would be less of a problem?

2. What does Alexander Bryan Johnson mean by "the perverted estimation of language"?

3. (**A**) The chapter is organized around three points relevant to linguistic ambiguity. What are these?   (**B**) How does the first point relate
to the "perverted estimation of language"?   (**C**) There are two sorts of
differences among experts (interpreters) regarding the words in the "To
be or not to be" passage. With which sort are we primarily concerned
in this chapter?

4. (**A**) What is the law of matrix   (**B**) What does it have to do with
interpretation?   (**C**) How does the speaker's matrix differ from the interpreter's?   (**D**) What is a *theoretical matrix*?   (**E**) What is our theoretical Shakespearean matrix?   (**F**) What sorts of things would this
matrix include?   (**G**) How would "the three indispensable instruments"
aid us in setting up our theoretical Shakespearean matrix?   (**H**) Illustrate your familiarity with these tools by looking up the word *slings* in
the three sources.   (**I**) Would the use of these instruments by all experts
tend to decrease the differences among their interpretations? Why?

5. (**A**) What is the law of parsimony, or Occam's Razor?   (**B**) Why
would it be called "Occam's Razor"?   (**C**) What does it have to do with
interpretation?

6. (**A**) Consider carefully the chart on page 46. Define a "paraphraser." (**B**) How would he differ from a "subject changer"? (**C**) Could we have a paraphraser under the genus term "*whether* means 'regardless of whether'"? (**D**) How would an "exister-suicider" differ from an "exister-avenger"? (**E**) How would an "enterpriser-suicider" differ from an "enterpriser-avenger"? (**F**) How does Johnson's interpretation differ from Goldsmith's?

7. (**A**) Hamlet doesn't care whether he lives or dies. What does *whether* mean in the preceding sentence? (**B**) Whether he lives or dies, Hamlet's name will live. What does *whether* mean in the preceding sentence? (**C**) How can we be certain that the sense of *whether* as illustrated in sentence 7 (B) was in use in Shakespeare's day?

8. (**A**) What is the ethical question discussed in the quotation from *Timon of Athens*? (**B**) Hamlet apparently sides with Alcibiades in the lines:

> Rightly to be great,
> Is not to stir without great argument,
> But greatly to find quarrel in a straw
> When honour's at the stake.

But is this the important consideration of the "To be or not to be" soliloquy according to the author? If not, what is the important consideration? (**C**) How does the *Timon of Athens* quotation substantiate the assertion that "whether" means *whether or no*? (**D**) Which of the three facts relevant to linguistic ambiguity was primarily responsible for this decision?

9. (**A**) How is the quotation from *First Maccabees* relevant to the "To be or not to be" quotation? (**B**) Which of the "three facts" does its inclusion illustrate?

10. (**A**) How does a "mixed" metaphor differ from a metaphor within a metaphor? (**B**) How does consideration of the *First Maccabees* quotation "acquit the author of *Hamlet* of the petty charges of bad grammar and faulty rhetoric"?

11. The passage from the Douay version of the Bible relevant to the interpretation of *slings* is:

> And he turned his army against the
> sanctuary for many days: and he set
> up there battering slings, and engines
> and instruments to cast fire, and engines
> to cast stones and javelins, and pieces
> to shoot arrows and slings.

(**A**) In regard to the first use of *slings* in the passage quoted, which of the senses listed below fits best?

1. a siege engine
2. a flexible support
3. a type of ammunition
4. what David slew Goliath with

(**B**) What other word in the Douay passage justifies your choice?   (**C**) Fill in the blank in the passage below with a synonym that would indicate an understanding of the significance of the Douay passage:

> To be or not to be, that is the question,
> Whether tis nobler in the minde to suffer
> The .... and arrowes of outragious fortune,
> Or to take Armes against a sea of troubles.

12. (**A**) Why does the author include the Job quotation:

> Why dost thou not remove my sin,
> And why dost thou not take away my
> iniquity? Behold now I shall sleep in
> the dust: and if thou seek me in the
> morning, I shall not be.

(**B**) What sin does Job want removed?   (**C**) What does he mean when he says, "Behold . . . not be"?   (**D**) Is it being impious for Job to desire death? If not, why not?   (**E**) What would be impious for Job to do?

13. How does the Job quotation determine the sense of *devoutly* to mean "piously"?

14. (**A**) How would "shuffling off" this mortal coil break the divine law?   (**B**) How would the use of the Shakespeare concordance help us in determining the meaning of *shuffle*?   (**C**) Explain the change in meaning of *shuffle* in the sentence "The prisoner *shuffled* off his fetters, *shuffled* himself into a disguise, and *shuffled* by the guard."   (**D**) What do *denotatively* and *connotatively* mean as used on page 55?

15. (**A**) What is the most relevant sense of *coil* as it appears in the quotation from *All's Well That Ends Well*?   (**B**) What constitutes the *coil* for Bertram?   (**C**) What is Hamlet's *coil*?

16. (**A**) The author states that there are two metaphors "that give concrete expression to the central thought of the speech." What is a metaphor?   (**B**) In the passage "And enterprises of great pitch and moment With this regard their currents turn awry" *pitch* meaning "zenith of a

falcon's flight" refers to what frame of reference? (**c**) *Moment* in the sense of "important" refers to what frame of reference? (**d**) *Currents* meaning "a stream" refers to what frame of reference? (**e**) All these items may be included in what frame of reference? (**f**) What would each mean in this frame of reference? (**g**) Such a reduction of universes demonstrates what law?

17. Look up *puzzles* in the *O.E.D.* and determine the literal sense that would "apply nicely to a rub obstructing the bowler's intention."

18. (**a**) How is the speech by the sexton in Act V, "an act hath three branches: it is to act, to do, and to perform," relevant here? (**b**) What is the first stage of the Act? The second? The third? (**c**) How far does Hamlet go in completing his "act"? (**d**) What "rub" stops him? (**e**) How is the quotation from *Julius Caesar* relevant to Hamlet's "act"?

19. (**a**) How have the phenomena of ambiguity produced the wide variations of meaning of the "To be or not to be" speech? (**b**) How can these wide variations of meaning be resolved?

*Thou hast frighted the word out of his
right sense, so forcible is thy wit.*

MUCH ADO ABOUT NOTHING

*We commit no crime to use one language
in each several clime.*

PERICLES, PRINCE OF TYRE

7 SEMANTIC GROWTH

WE HAVE ALREADY suggested that language behavior is essentially
logical by observing that the Greek *logos* means "word"; we might
have added that it also means "reason." We might reasonably expect,
therefore, that the laws of reason would turn out, upon reflection, to
be the same laws that explain the growth of language. This is de-
monstrably the case, and our failure to realize the fact as basic to a
sound philosophy of education calls for an historical explanation.

In general we may say that artists, philosophers, and scientists,
as such, have not trusted one another. Plato, for example, banished
the poets from his ideal republic, and Aristotle, who was himself a
"triple threat" man, wouldn't let his left hand know what his right
hand was doing; he felt that figurative language had no proper place
in scientific discussion. There seem to be two confusions involved
here—the one between being imaginative and being unconventional,
the other between being "cut-and-dried" and being conventional. In
the first confusion we tend to associate imagination and "originality"
(being unconventional) as virtues of the artist because the one may
lead to the other, and we condemn, in the name of art, the sin of
producing the "cut-and-dried." But being imaginative and being unconventional are not necessarily the same, and convention may indeed

be a positive factor in great art. In the second confusion we tend to associate "standard practice" with the lack of imagination, require our scientist to stick to the actual, and forgive, in the name of scientific method, its cut-and-dried procedures. But being cut-and-dried and being conventional are not necessarily the same. Strictly speaking, when we are conventional we do as we do simply because that is the way others do, but this is not the reason that all scientists should behave in a similar manner. They have to behave alike because they *are* scientists. They must not harbor the artist's yen for being original; they must strive to cut and dry. But the insights necessary to see what to cut and how to dry it spring from the same "creative imagination" that we tend to think of as the property of the artist.

Now when a thinker gives an old word a new sense, he is violating a convention of his language, but the violations characteristic of poets, politicians, and all manner of special pleaders have been conventionally regarded with favor as rhetorical license. The flowers, if not the fruit, of rhetoric have nevertheless been forbidden to the scientist. In *The Tatler*, Steele complained of those who "affect the flowers of rhetoric before they understand the parts of speech," and Pope in his *Imitations of Horace* assured dear Murray that "plain truth needs no flowers of speech." The so-called "classical tropes" or "flowers of rhetoric" have been regarded for hundreds of years as the *ornaments* of style, and we children of modernity, with our ideal of functionalism, have banished them from our scientific republic, and incidentally have given them a sort of dishonorable discharge from our elementary and secondary curricula.

Meanwhile, our lexicographers, applying their own scientific principle of objective description as distinct from normative prescription, have recorded the license of innumerable poets, philosophers, and scientists in the pages of their dictionaries. For they know that old words take on new senses not only because of the human love of ornament or the urge to be different, but because of the intellectual need for linguistic economy.

Let us illustrate the distinction between what may be ornamentation and what is certainly linguistic economy by analyzing a bit of contemporary rhetoric. "John Foster Dulles stroked the shell of state with a masterly oar and the endurance of a champion." Now all the words in this statement are figurative with the exception of "John Foster Dulles" and "state." They make up a trope or flower called metaphor. Of course "trope," "flower," and "metaphor" are themselves figures, but we will focus upon the term "stroked." We consult the entry in a contemporary abridged dictionary. It contains 19 senses, the one clearly applying to our sentence being "to set the rate of rowing for a crew." Other related senses would be illustrated in such expressions as "the stroke of an oar," "the oar nearest the stern," "the oarsman nearest the stern," "the place of the oarsman nearest the stern," "the oarsman seated in his place with oar in hand," and "the rhythm of the stroke oar." Now, these are all derived or figurative senses, and they did not come about because oarsmen (or coxswains, for that matter) are licentious poets striving to be either imaginative or original. They came about because it is characteristic of the rational intellect to favor the law of least effort and adapt old tools rather than adopt new ones.

The basic laws of reason are simply statements setting forth the three analytical operations described in Chapter 2:

(1) A species (included sort) has the qualities of its genus (inclusive sort). This principle is called Aristotle's dictum; it is nothing more than a general way of saying that Fido must have the qualities of a dog in order to be one. The rules for operating with the *genus-species* relation are the rules for using the words *all, some, one,* and *none.*

(2) A structure is a system of related parts in space; or, a part has the relations of its whole; or, a part *belongs* to its whole.

(3) An event is a system of moments in time and space; or, a moment *belongs* to its event, a stage to its operation.

It should be noted that an event is more complex than a structure because an event is composed of a structure changing in time. Structures are static and three-dimensional, whereas events are dynamic and four-dimensional. The whole structure of an operation and the operation itself are said to have purpose; the constituent parts of the structure are said to have functions. Words are functional parts in the operations of communication, reason, and emotional adjustment. The changes, then, that make language grow are changes that take place on purpose. Somebody with intelligence sufficient to make conscious use of language consciously puts an old symbol to a new use. His operation is therefore a logical one; by performing it he commemorates a recognition that the present thing or moment has some definite connection with some thing or moment of the remembered past.

Now the basic logical operation is the simultaneous recognition of similarity and difference, which is the basis of what we have called the *genus-species relation*. One might say that this is the most important relation in our conscious life. It is by means of this relation more than any other that life makes sense. "Genus" is a Latin term that means "sort"; its plural is *genera*. "Species" means "particular sort" and its plural is *species*. A species is one of the *spec*ial sorts of a *gen*eral sort. In order to see that two species belong to a genus you must compare them; in order to tell them apart you must contrast them. Thus seeing differences and at the same time seeing similarities makes it possible to answer the questions "What is this a sort of?" and "What are the sorts of this?" And this is the process which, when systematically applied, we have called *classification*. In language growth we deal with it in its simplest and least conscious as well as its sophisticated form. Indeed, sometimes for no particular or cogent reason we use old words to give new names to things merely because we "imagine" resemblances.

When we see, or through any other sensory means observe, that one thing resembles another, we may give the one the name of the other. Innumerable objects, for example, have been named after their resemblance to parts of the body. Turn down the corner of this page and you have a "dog's-ear." Similarly, if two things produce similar emotions in the interpreter the one may be named after the other. Perhaps the term "dogfight" as applied to an unsystematized combat of fighter planes in World War II developed from the emotional excitement which dogfights occasion in some beholders; or again, "bombshell" in the sense of extreme surprise may refer to the same emotional component that is symbolized in the word "surprise" itself. We also may proceed in the same manner with logical resemblances. The sense of "father" used in the Catholic church is such a growth. Let us call the three types of growth we have now illustrated sensory, affective, and logical similitudes, and define "similitude" as a name that has been transferred to a thing or quality because it refers to a similar thing or quality.

There is a popular American song, still to be heard occasionally, in which a woman is called "a great big beautiful doll." Now if an admirer uses the term because the woman looks like a doll, we have a sensory similitude; if he uses it because he's "*afraid* she'll break," we have an affective similitude; if he uses it because he thinks of dandling her upon his knee, we have a logical similitude which may be expressed as the proportion *a* is to *b* as *c* is to *b*. The name of *a* (doll) may be applied to *c* (woman) because of the similar relation to *b* (man). Sensory similitudes are very common in language; logical similitudes are comparatively rare.

When the mind has reached the stage of being aware that it makes similitudes, it is ready to take the next step in linguistic sophistication and become aware of the specific and limited number of qualities that constitute the resemblance in any given instance. When we call the folded corner of a page a "dog's-ear" it is because it reminds us of a dog's ear. But that resemblance, after all, is quite limited and can be defined. But in saying what it is that the page corner and the dog's ear have in common, we require a different kind of language from the sort to which "page corner" and "dog's-ear" belong. Abstract language, we call it, because we have used words to draw the quality away from the things that possess it, in this case the appearance of a triangular flap lapping down over the object to which it is attached along one of its sides.

Thus we become aware of qualities as "things" distinct from the "things" that "possess" them. We shall have much more to say about the psychology of this process in the chapter on qualification. It is to our present purpose to note that when we distinguish a quality as such from a thing as such, we have created a situation in which it becomes convenient to name the quality after the thing or the thing after the quality. For example, we have the color "orange" named after a specific quality, the color of the fruit we call an orange; and we name the carnation after the specific quality, flesh-color, of the flower that possesses it. Let us call the relations here described *abstract-concrete relations* and call the orange type an *abstraction* and the carnation type a *concretion*, because in the one we go from the

concrete fruit to the abstract color and in the other from the abstract
color to the concrete flower.

With the elementary similitude and abstract-concrete relations
established, the mind is ready for the more deliberate processes which
we have already identified as analysis. The genus-species relation
which, when systematically applied, produces the type of analysis we
have called classification also produces the growth of two types of
sense. The two processes, *generalization* and *specialization*, are exceedingly common in language and it is highly important that we
understand and control them.

Take the word "dog," for example, and assume that its initial
sense is that expressed in the sentence "Fido is a good dog." Now,
seeing about us in the animal world such animals as coyotes, jackals,
wild dogs, wolves, foxes, and various others that bark and circle
before lying down, and needing a name for them all, we select the
name of the one most familiar to use. Hence we get the sense of "dog"
in "A dhole is a wild dog; a shepherd is a domestic dog." When the
sense of a term is expanded in this way to include more species (in
the logical sense of *species*), we call the new sense a "generalization."
Generalizations are exceedingly frequent in dictionaries where lexicographers lack the space to cover numerous similar senses in detail.
There are, for example, several fields in which mechanical devices are
employed which are called dogs—usually through one of the similitude relations. But when the dictionary-maker defines "dog" as "any
of various devices usually of simple design for holding, gripping, or
fastening something" he has then and there developed a generalization.

A "specialization" is the result of the same process in reverse.
Take the word "dog" again in either the sense of "a member of the
dog family" or "domestic dog" and compare the sense "male dog" as
expressed in the sentence "He preferred to train bitches rather than
dogs." Here you have a specialization. In this very chapter "abstraction," "generalization," and "specialization" are themselves specializations. First we start with the general sense of the term "similitude"
in which it is synonymous with "comparison." The comparison of a
hog's back and a mountain implied by using "hogback" to refer to
a mountain is a species of a genus similitude, and the term as used

in this chapter refers to that species and only that species; hence we call it a specialization, and in so doing we mean only that type of specialization in which an old word gets a new sense.

Whenever a thing is or may be conceived of as a structure, a group of constituent parts in their respective positions, the logical intellect seeks naturally or by training to identify the parts and note their relationship to one another; it tries to discover the joints or articulations. Consequently a condition comes about in which it is convenient to name a particular part in which we, for the moment, may have a special interest after the whole structure or to name the whole structure after a particularly significant part, or to name one part after another. By abstraction (to use our newly coined sense) let us call the resulting senses *structurals*. The term "duckbill" as the name of the mouth of a platypus is a similitude, but as the name of the whole animal it is a structural as is also the synonym "platypus," which is simply Greek for flat-foot. From almond, the tree, we get as structurals both almond, the fruit, and almond, the kernel of the fruit.

The third type of analysis, operation analysis, is manifested in the field of semantic growth when we deal with structures in the process of change. We are confronted here with the subtle variations of meaning of the word *part*. A nut is a part of a tree. To say that a nut is a part of a tree is not to say the same thing as to say that an act is part of a play or that an actor is part of an act. Complex operations may be complex because they have several stages, or because the structures that perform them have several parts, or both. Thus we have not only the reciprocal relation of the stage and the whole event or operation, but also the reciprocal relations of stage and stage, structure and operation, stage and operation, part and stage, part and operation, part and structure, and part and part. All of these relations may give rise to semantic growths. Let us call them, again by abstraction, *operationals*. The last two relations, it should be noted, are not the static structure relations for which we used the terms "articulation" and "joint," but dynamic relations involving time. Let us call the relations among the moving or static physical objects that constitute the structure of an operation *connections*. The connection between the original and derived senses may be so tenuous as to become a matter of history, and several sense growths may have intervened. Thus we may call Gladstone meaning "bag" or Gladstone meaning "carriage" an operational because of the connection between the part William Ewart Gladstone and the part "this bag here" or "that carriage there," but there must have been intervening similitudes and generalizations.

The operational category is a convenient means of keeping our classification of semantic growths to our seven rules of semantic economy. If you think of such an inclusion as Gladstone somewhat far fetched, reconsider it in these terms: "I have here a Gladstone. It is a concrete manifestation of the influence of a great Englishman upon my life and is therefore a part of the total operation influence-of-Gladstone. In order to see why I call it Gladstone, I have to see the connection between the bag and the Prime Minister and that connection is a complex series of historical events (stages). His 'function' in this case was to provide a name for my bag."

We may name a surgical operation after the organ that is removed, the instrument used to remove it, or some critical stage in the operation itself. Operational growth often produces a change not only in the sense of a word, but in the grammatical function of the word. Thus, an operation performed upon a skull with a special sort of saw called a trephine is trephining. We may say that the operation is named after the tool. But the tool's name has been turned from noun to verb in such a sentence as, "They had to trephine." (It should be noted here that if the grammatical change merely added the idea "to make use of" there would be no semantic growth.)

The attempt to classify a given growth according to the system here being developed by examining the "old" and "new" senses is a rigorous logical discipline demanding patience and practice. Here is a paradigm illustrating the fourteen types of operationals. It must be kept in mind that the "universe" of an operation is arbitrary and relative. In operation automobile the driver and highway might be excluded; in operation automotive transportation they would be functional parts.

1. Operation-stage
   A. Old Sense: *trephining*, using the trephine
      New Sense: *trephining*, the complete operation
   B. Old Sense: *tragedy*, related series of dire events
      New Sense: Fortinbras missed the *tragedy* (i.e., the bloody end)

2. Operation-structure
   A. Old Sense: *escapement,* act of escaping
   New Sense: *escapement,* pallet and toothed wheel of a timepiece
   B. Old Sense: *moon,* celestial body
   New Sense: *moon,* the moon moving through one orbit

3. Operation-part
   A. Old Sense: *birth,* to give birth to
   New Sense: *birth,* the organism born
   B. Old Sense: *kitten,* newborn cat
   New Sense: *kitten,* to bear kittens

4. Stage-stage
   Old Sense: *childhood,* between infancy and youth
   New Sense: second *childhood,* dotage

5. Stage-structure
   A. Old Sense: *finish,* the final stage
   New Sense: *finish,* photo-finish (i.e., structure at finish)
   B. Old Sense: *bloom,* a flower
   New Sense: *bloom,* in flower

6. Stage-part
   A. Old Sense: *exhaust,* escape of gas
   New Sense: *exhaust,* the pipe
   B. Old Sense: *stomach,* organ of digestion
   New Sense: *stomach,* as in "He could swallow it, but he couldn't *stomach* it"

7. Structure-part
   A. Old Sense: *house,* theater with audience
   New Sense: *house,* audience as in "The whole *house* applauded"
   B. Old Sense: *fly,* a fishhook
   New Sense: *fly,* as in "You take trout with a fly (i.e., fly-rod, reel, line, leader, and hook)"[1]

8. Part-part
   Old Sense: *cannon,* the instrument in operation cannonade
   New Sense: *cannon,* as in "I hear *cannon* (i.e., the air waves that excite the air)"

There is one more relation which we must add to the list of simple semantic growths before proceeding to the complexities of proportional metaphor. The Greeks, likewise, had a word for it; the word

---

[1] But you wouldn't use the term except in the operation; in a pure structure-analysis situation the term would apply no further than the gut by which the hook is bent to the leader.

was "irony." When we call a thing by the name of its opposite, we develop a new sense by the *ironic relation*. Now this type of growth is exceedingly infrequent, but it may be psychologically impressive and may occasionally cause complete misunderstanding. Of course, when we say "infrequent" we mean with respect to the semantic growth of individual words that lasts long enough to become established in one's vocabulary, if not in the dictionary. The ironic use of groups of words such as sentences or, for that matter, whole ironic compositions, is characteristic of a certain type of personality and by no means rare. "Welsh rabbit," "mare's nest," "Robin Hood's barn," "Hobson's choice," "busman's holiday" are instances of irony which enjoy tenure in our language.

We have now defined and illustrated six relations which prompt the mind to give new senses to old words; by means of the similitude, abstract-concrete, genus-species, structure, operation, and ironic relations we manage to increase the utility of our vocabulary while at the same time making meaningful connections between the present and the recollected past. For the most part, and for most of us, the process is not a systematic one but goes on in a most haphazard and capricious manner. But the result is the astonishingly elaborate and efficient device that enables us to express the infinite difference in the behavior of men and apes. It is difficult for us to realize that this marvelous tool, which each of us has been developing as far back as he can remember, plays the elaborate and definitive role it does. But it is literally by means of the six operations we have just reviewed, by the way in which they keep our thoughts in more or less organized arrangements, that we manage to create whatever order and integrity our conscious selves may have. Vocabulary and grammar provide the fixed warp upon which we weave the fabric of meaningful experience according to these variable patterns of essential relatedness.

A seventh type of language growth, which becomes available to us with the semantic sophistication gained in the exercise of the other six, is the very hallmark of linguistic maturity and justly deserves the attention of a separate chapter. Let us now consider with care and in detail just what goes on when, for example, we speak of language as if it were a weaver's thread and meaning the pattern growing upon his loom.

STUDY QUESTIONS

1. (**A**) The author states that the essentially logical "laws of reason" turn out "to be the same laws that explain the growth of language." What are the laws of reason? (**B**) How do they apply to each of the six semantic growths illustrated in this chapter?

2. (**A**) Aristotle felt that "*figurative* language had no proper place in scientific discussion." What does *figurative* mean here? (**B**) The author goes on to show that through the centuries giving a word a new sense has been praised when utilized by the artist to produce a stylistic effect, but forbidden to the scientist because his language is to be "cut-and-dried" and "conventional." In Chapter 1 Dr. Johnson is quoted as speaking of "words deflected from their original sense"; he gives examples of a "courtier's *zenith*," the "excentrick virtue of a wild hero," and the "physician of *sanguine* expectations and *phlegmatick* delays." How have the words in italics been "deflected" from their original senses? (**C**) How do your findings in question 2 (**A**) relate to the statement "but the insights necessary to see when to cut and how to dry it spring from the same 'creative imagination' that we tend to think of as the property of the artist"? (**D**) How would the "basic laws of reason" relate to "creative imagination" in the above quotation? (**E**) How have the lexicographers "applying their own scientific principle of objective *description* as distinct from normative *prescription*" demonstrated that "creative imagination" is characteristic of both artist and scientist? (**F**) How is *description* distinct from *prescription* in the previous quotation? (**G**) What would happen to our language if the rational intellect didn't "favor the law of least effort and adapt old tools rather than adopt new ones"?

3. (**A**) The author states, on page 65, that "of course *trope, flower* (of rhetoric), and *metaphor* are themselves figures (of speech)." Look up these words in your dictionary. How are they themselves figures? (**B**) Consider the meaning of tropism in the words *phototropism* and *thermotropism*. Is tropism "deflected" in these words? (**C**) Two of the classical tropes were *synecdoche* and *metonymy*. Look these up in your dictionary and determine which of our six semantic growths could be included under these classifications.

4. Using our definitions of *complex* established in Chapter 1, how is an event more *complex* than a structure?

5. What intelligent act is required to put an old word to a new use?

6. In the discussion of sensory similitudes, we are told that "innumerable objects have been named after their resemblance to parts of the body." Verify this statement by looking up *hand, head, foot, leg,* and *arm* in your dictionary.

7. In the formula $a/b = c/b$, would the common factor, b, necessarily have to stand for a thing? Why?

8. In the abstract-concrete relation we name the quality after the thing or the thing after the quality. Would the *shape* of a thing be part of the thing or a quality of the thing?

9. On page 68 the author states that "in this very chapter 'abstraction,' 'generalization,' and 'specialization' are themselves specializations." Explain this statement.

10. (A) It is stated that operational growth often produces a change in the grammatical function of a word. If a word is changed merely from noun to verb by adding the idea "to do what you do with," there would be *word* growth but no *semantic* growth. Why? (B) Is there a *semantic* growth in the following?

Old Sense: The carpenter used his *saw* to cut the wood.

New Sense: The carpenter *sawed* the wood.

Old Sense: Dinner is on the *table*.

New Sense: They voted to *table* the matter until next meeting.

11. What is a village *square*? Why do we call it a square?

12. (A) What sorts of things are a covering of paint, a jacket, and the hair of a dog? (B) If we call the *hair* of a dog a coat, are we making the word *coat* express a specific or a general thing? (C) If we say a coat is a *covering*, are we using "coat" to mean a specific or a general thing? (D) Which can you draw, touch, see, etc.—a jacket or a covering?

13. If the word "drink" has always had a general meaning for you and included any sort of drink, but in certain groups is used to mean only alcoholic beverages, would you call the growth of the use of the word a generalization? Why?

14. Have you ever heard a bicycle called a *wheel*? Which semantic growth does this illustrate? Why?

15. (A) What does *carbon* mean in the sentence "I made three *carbons* and with the original I have four copies"? (B) Why are carbon copies called *carbons*? What analytic process is used to make the word do its new job?

16. What is a *hand* in the sentence "He has a legible *hand*"? Through what process has this word acquired its new meaning?

17. Why is "Welsh rabbit" ironical? "Hobson's choice"?

8 METAPHOR

METAPHOR IS ANOTHER loan word from the inexhaustible treasury of Greek and is nicely translated for us in the more common Latin word "transfer." In discovering how metaphors work we will be helped by the concept of a *universe of discourse.* A universe is a whole system that is not at the moment regarded as part of another system. "Discourse" means regular or rational thinking and, of course, includes the necessary symbol system or systems. We may say, therefore, that a universe of discourse is a world of thought with its vocabulary, grammar, and syntax—that is, its stock of words, the rules for changing their forms, and for arranging them in relation to one another.

Whenever we make metaphors we transfer the language of one universe to another. Thus our analysis of the metaphorical operation will require us to think in three different universes: the universe from which the language is borrowed, or the metaphorical universe; the universe in which the borrowed symbol is put to use, or the contextual universe, the universe of the other nonmetaphorical words around the metaphor; and finally, the universe in which we are now thinking, the comprehensive one which includes both the metaphorical and contextual. Semanticists call this last universe the metauniverse and the language we use to discuss the metaphorical *and* contextual universes a metalanguage. (This sense of "meta-" meaning "over" or "beyond" or "after," is, of course, different from the sense of meta- in metaphor, which, like the *trans-* in transfer, means "across.")

Aristotle used the term "metaphor" to include what we have called similitudes, and some rhetoricians have even stretched it to include explicit comparisons like the simile. We here limit the term to what Aristotle called "proportional metaphor." We shall have more to say about proportional metaphor because it is the most important linguistic consideration in the study of our conscious life. Here we introduce it simply as the most complex form of semantic growth, the most impressive way in which an old symbol can take on a new sense.

Aristotle, by the way, was keenly aware of the subtle magic of metaphor. In the *Topica*, a treatise on clear thinking, he warns that "metaphorical expression is always obscure," but in the more poetical *Rhetoric* he says, "Now strange words simply puzzle us; ordinary words convey only what we know already; it is from metaphor that we can best get hold of something fresh."

Now this refreshing function of metaphor in which an old word gets a new sense at the same time that an old situation is seen in a "fresh" new light is brought about by the imaginative substitution of things for words. Universes of discourse are inhabited by things as well as words, and the secret of metaphorical utterance or interpretation is the trick of arranging the right things in the right way in the peep show of the imagination. When we successfully interpret a metaphor it is not simply because we can substitute the language of one universe for that of another, as in the translation of a foreign tongue, but because we are able to see that things in the one universe stand in the same relation to one another as do things in another universe. In the proportional metaphor some thing a is seen to be in some meaningful relation to some thing b that has a meaningful resemblance to the relationship between some thing c and some thing d. For the sake of clearness and convenience let us consistently use the ratio a/b to represent the things and their relationship in the metaphorical universe and the ratio c/d to represent the things and their relationship in the contextual universe.

Now let us make the concept of metaphor amenable to the process of analysis by representing it in diagrammatic form. And let us analyze a simple metaphor in our diagram, using boxes in place of ratio signs so as to explicitly symbolize the relations implied in the metaphor. Here is a classic example:

"The Lord is my shepherd"

Animal husbandry:	Religion:
Metaphorical universe	Contextual universe

A. The shepherd   C. The Lord

tends	$=$	encourages

B. the sheep   D. the psalmist

Relevant relation:
promotes welfare of

You will note that the base line of our diagram contains what we have called the relevant relation. It is a genus term that includes the metaphorical and contextual relations as species. Thus it is in fact an explicit formulation of the resemblance represented by the equals sign in the diagram. And the language of the relevant relation is a metalanguage. "Tends" and "encourages" are species of the genus "promotes welfare of."

In the rigorously defined nomenclatures of technology, that is, in universes where you "split hairs" or "get technical," there will tend to be more or less exact terms for expressing either of the ratios in the proportion or for naming the things that are related in each universe. But in the haphazard vocabularies of general discourse, where unconscious custom has not been replaced by deliberate regulation, the selection of the "proper" term will be a matter of experiment or taste. In diagramming metaphors you will frequently find that the language of the contextual universe will do just as well for the metauniverse. And for the same reason you will often find that the language of the metaphorical universe is more precise; indeed, this is probably one of the reasons for its use.

Be this as it may, the intellectual exercise of metaphor analysis as represented in our diagram is an extremely efficient method of cultivating an awareness of the nature of language behavior. The act of selecting a suitable name for the metaphorical universe, the act of matching this name with a term from a comparable level of abstraction and appropriate "style" to name the contextual universe, the explicit formulation of the two relationships, and finally the wording of the relevant relation are all fundamental operations in the exercise of verbal selection and control.

And what is perhaps still more important, the recognition of the things symbolized by *A*, *B*, *C*, and *D* is the fundamental analogical act that characterizes the procedure of creative intelligence. To be able to see analogies, which we have called "proportions," is to be able to make sense of the constantly changing panorama of life. We have witnessed hundreds of instances in which systematic training in the interpretation and formulation of metaphors has been the only factor that could account for a marked increase in the intelligence quotient. Just as certain types of exercise may increase the capacity and coordination of muscular tissue, so appropriate and repeated experience in analogical thinking develops the power to get meaning, and particularly that most difficult of all types of meaning involved in the adept solution of problems that are new and strange.

Metaphors aid us in two ways with the process of abstract thinking. They make complex abstract ideas easier to "see" and easier to remember. Let us analyze another one to "clinch" the point; consider once more the sentence "Vocabulary and grammar provide the *fixed warp* upon which we *weave the fabric* of meaningful experience according to these variable *patterns* of essential relatedness." The italicized words are borrowed of course, from the universe of websters to whom, by the bye, we ultimately owe our synonym for "dictionary." Here is the metaphor analyzed:

Weaving: Language:
A. The fixed warp   C. Vocabulary and grammar

provides framework upon which the woof or filling is woven into a fabric in accordance with	=	provide fixed forms to which sense or content is given to produce meaning according to

B. a pattern   D. laws of semantic growth

Relevant relation:
provides basis upon which
something may be developed

By means of the terms "warp" and "woof" we are able for the moment to visualize the meaningless "form" of a word as something separate and different from its sense or "content" when put to use. The term "pattern" then suggests how the known modes of relationship determine the senses that a given word-form may take in the act of progressive symbolization which we know as thinking or consciousness. What perhaps is most noteworthy about many metaphors is that they have a sort of fertilizing effect upon our thinking. In this instance for example, we are reminded that fabrics are artificial or man-made; then we consider whether conscious thought is likewise an artifact. Thus we increase our realization that language is an instrument subject to control and thought the product of its operation.

Here is another application of the weaving metaphor in which the woof is used to represent this very concept of human purpose. It is from *Moby-Dick*:

Queequeg and I were mildly employed weaving what is called a sword-mat, for an additional lashing to our boat. . . . As I kept passing and repassing the filling or woof of marline between the long yarns of the warp, using my own hand for the shuttle, and as Queequeg, standing sideways, ever and anon slid his heavy oaken sword between the threads, and idly looking off upon the water, carelessly and unthinkingly drove home every yarn: I say so strange a dreaminess did there then reign all over the ship and all over the sea, only broken by the intermitting dull sound of the sword, that it seemed as if this were the Loom of Time, and I myself were a shuttle mechanically weaving and weaving away at the Fates. There lay the fixed threads of the warp subject to but one single, ever returning, unchanging vibration, and that vibration merely enough to admit of the crosswise interblending of other threads with its own. This warp seemed necessity; and here, thought I, with my own hand I ply my own shuttle and weave my own destiny into these unalterable threads. Meantime, Queequeg's impulsive, indifferent sword, sometimes hitting the woof slantingly, or crookedly, or strongly, or weakly, as the case might be; and by this difference in the concluding blow producing a corresponding contrast in the final aspect of the completed fabric; this savage's sword, thought I, which thus finally shapes and fashions both warp and woof; this easy, indifferent sword must be chance—aye, chance, free will, and necessity—no wise incompatible—all interweavingly working together. The straight warp of necessity, not to be swerved from its ultimate course—its every alternating vibration, indeed, only tending to that; free will still free to ply her shuttle between given threads; and chance, though restrained in its play within the right lines of necessity, and sideways in its motions directed by free will, though thus prescribed to by both, chance by turns rules either, and has the last featuring blow at events.[1]

Perhaps a page from a seaman's manual will suggest to you the sort of mental picture necessary for the adequate interpretation of Melville's paragraph. And even though you are not moved by this rather complex metaphor to attempt your own diagrammatic analysis, it may well serve to promote the realization that metaphor may be infinitely more than mere literary ornamentation or journalistic cleverness. Here is the description of a sword mat loom from a seaman's manual:

Two bars or tightly stretched ropes are fixed at a distance apart the length of the required mat. On them is wound the rope which is to form the warp.

Two pieces of wood, *A* and *B*, are laid across the warp. *A* is connected to every alternate line of warp by means of loose loops of yarn, and *B* is similarly connected to the other lines of warp as shown in the figure. By lifting *A*, every alternate line of warp is lifted and the weft *C*, is passed. It is then pressed home by the sword *D*. This is a flat piece of wood usually slightly bevelled on one edge.

The sword is withdrawn, *A* is lowered and *B* is raised, bringing with it the other series of warp lines. The weft is passed back and pushed home by the sword as before. This process is continued until the mat is finished. At the end there will be no room for the sword so the weft must be got in by using a marline-spike.[2]

It is an irresistible temptation to note that for Ishmael chance enjoys "the last featuring blow," while for the author of the seaman's manual the doughty marline-spike stubbornly insinuates the woof of free will to the bitter end. In the same vein we might mention Sir Charles Sherrington's reference to the human brain as an "enchanted loom where millions of flashing shuttles weave a dissolving pattern, always a meaningful pattern, though never an abiding one; a shifting harmony of sub-patterns."[3]

Metaphor has been introduced here simply as the last and most complex of several ways in which old words take on new duties, but

[1] *Moby-Dick*, Chapter 47.
[2] Charles Spencer, *Knots, Splices, and Fancy Work*, p. 160.
[3] *Man on His Nature*, Chapter 7.

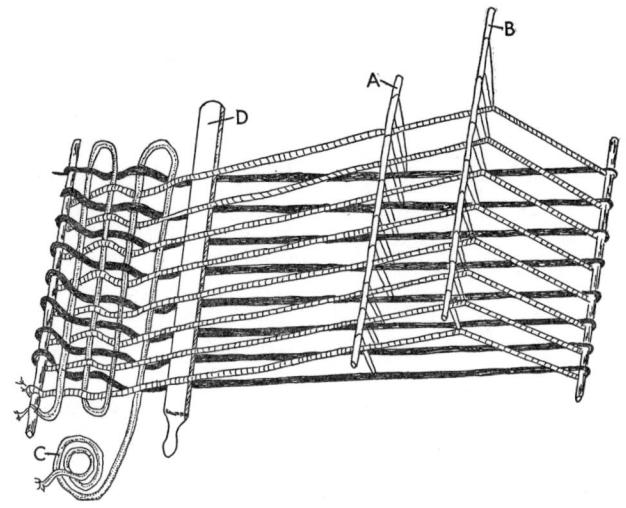

SWORD MAT LOOM

Charles Spencer, *Knots, Splices, and Fancy Work* (Glasgow, 1946).

in due season it will be our task to demonstrate that the new duties of metaphorical growth concern the very life of science, art, and religion. And before leaving the subject of semantic growth, we would re-emphasize the point that we are not here concerned with the history of language; we do not suggest that it is important for you to know that "queen" meant "woman" in 756 A.D. or that it once took on the meaning of "wench." We are instead "concerned" (and here we use the term in the Quaker sense) that you acquire a set of rules for understanding not only the evidence of ambiguity on every page of your dictionary but a set of rules for interpreting every page you read and every utterance you hear. This is the sort of knowledge that, in Coleridge's phrase, returns again as power.

It is essential to realize that the view of semantic growth here put forth differs in one fundamental respect from the formidable theory of the learned Dr. Johnson, which we presented in Chapter One. He assumed the existence of an "original" or "proper" meaning for each morpheme. Actually these original senses are merely the earliest recorded senses and have no other claim to originality. In our view any term, however new and definite, must, to be generally useful, develop a set of related senses by our seven rules of semantic economy. It is not only because of ignorance, caprice, or poetic imagination that old words take on new senses; it is also because the modern mind must contrive to do its business with an efficient minimum of linguistic machinery in an environment of ever-increasing complexity. This is the doctrine of essential ambiguity.

STUDY QUESTIONS

1. By looking up *sophisticated* in your dictionary, explain the author's statement that metaphor is the very height of semantic *sophistication.*

2. Considering the definitions of *complex* as established in Chapter 1, why is metaphor "the most complex form of semantic growth"?

3. How do the basic laws of reason apply to the semantic growth of metaphor?

4. How does metaphor help us to "get hold of something fresh"?

5. (A) Metaphorical growth is achieved "by the imaginative substitution of *things* for words." Explain this statement.   (B) What does *things* mean in the above quotation?

6. In what way or ways is a logical similitude different from a metaphor?

7. Why is it logical to assume that the repeated analysis and formulation of metaphors will account for a marked increase in the I.Q.?

8. The author illustrates the two ways in which metaphors aid us with the process of abstract thinking. What are these two ways?

9. How does the view of semantic growth presented in this text differ radically from Dr. Johnson's assumption (Chapter 1) concerning "original" and "proper" meanings for each morpheme?

10. *Universe of discourse* has been defined as "a world of thought with its vocabulary, grammar, and syntax." In what universe of discourse are we speaking when we use each of the following sets of terms: (A) Keel, compass, mast, course, secure.   (B) Apples, flour, shortening, cinnamon, 425°.   (C) Value, ethics, principle, right, wrong.   (D) Revenge, Hebrew, eye, tooth, God.   (E) Fear, associations, subconscious, analysis, ink blot.   (F) Level, chain, contour, measure, tract.

11. (A) In the metaphor from Chapter 7, "John Foster Dulles stroked the shell of state with a masterly oar and the endurance of a champion," we have transferred the language of one universe of discourse to another.

Which terms are we transferring? (**B**) Name the metaphorical universe from which we are borrowing. (**C**) Name the contextual universe in which we are putting the symbols to use. (**D**) Which universe tells what is *said* and which tells what is *meant*? (**E**) In order to analyze the metaphor, we must consider not only the metaphorical and contextual universes, but the metauniverse as well. What is a *metauniverse*? How is it a genus term?

(**F**) Analyzing metaphor has been made possible by an arbitrary diagram. On which side of the diagram do we place the metaphorical terms? The contextual? (**G**) In determining the $a/b = c/d$ relation, we say that *things* stand in relation to each other. What part of speech do we use to symbolize them? What "things" are involved in our "John Foster Dulles" metaphor? Determine the $a/b = c/d$ relation. (**H**) The boxes contain the relations implied in the metaphor. What part of speech are these relations likely to use? What relation word is already given in the metaphor above? Does it belong in the metaphorical or contextual universe? By analyzing this relation, determine the other box. (**I**) The language of the relevant relation is a metalanguage. Why is it true that the language of the contextual universe will often do just as well for the metauniverse? Do you find that you can use the contextual relation of the metaphor above as the relevant relation? Reproduce your analysis of the metaphor on a diagram like the one shown on page 78.

No man is the lord of anything, though in and of him there be much consisting, till he communicate his parts to others.

TROILUS AND CRESSIDA

9 COMMUNICATION

IF WE HAVE NOW MOVED you to a lively awareness of the fact that our most important and most useful words are ambiguous, or as Dr. Richards prefers to say, "resourceful"; if you are ready to agree, after a survey of the seven ways in which an already familiar symbol can take on a new sense, that most ambiguity derives from desirable, not to say necessary, psychological convenience; and finally, if you have considered, however briefly, the profound implications of the fact of ambiguity for any practical theory of language behavior, then you are ready and willing to think with us about that first and most obvious function of language, communication.

Let us describe with care and in some detail just what goes on when one human being communicates with another. We must begin by defining two fundamental concepts which we may call "complementary structure" and "complementary experience." "Complementary structure" is for us a purely physical term. It is exemplified by the audible response, say, of a tuning fork to a whistle, or of any other physical object to another physical object which is producing a sound of the same pitch. The vocal apparatus of an utterer and the auditory apparatus of an interpreter must first of all be complementary in structure if one is to communicate with the other through the medium of sound. Similarly, an interpreter of visual symbols must be visually complementary to the writer or printer of the symbols, and an interpreter of Braille must have a tactile structure complementary to an utterer in Braille.

Most of us do not realize the extent of our deficiencies, particularly in speaking and listening, and it is surely the proper business of any thoroughgoing approach to the problems of communication to recommend the measurement of one's capacity to hear as well as his capacity to see. In this study, however, focused as it is upon the psychology of meaning, adequate complementary structure between utterer and interpreter is assumed.

What is more important for us here is the second fundamental concept—the concept of complementary experience. It is based upon the kind of psychological behavior called conditioned response. If you make a marked increase in the amount of light falling upon the normal eye, you observe an immediate adjustment of the iris to reduce the size of the pupil. This is called an unconditioned response, and the increased light is called an unconditioned stimulus. Now, if you make numerous trials taking care to sound a buzzer whenever the light is increased, the iris can be "taught," that is to say, conditioned, to reduce the pupil at the sound of the buzzer alone. This learned response is called a conditioned response and the sound of the buzzer, a conditioned stimulus.

Now symbols are our most important conditioned stimuli, and successful communication depends upon complementary conditioning, or, as we have already called it, complementary experience. It is one of the curious facts of life that we pay so little heed to this most fundamental of all psychological phenomena. Just as we find ourselves shouting at listeners who do not speak our language, so by a similar irrational impulse we assume that those with whom we attempt to communicate are equipped with complementary sets of conditioned responses to our own common stock of symbols.

It is easy to see the stupidity of expecting one who does not speak English to converse with you in English. It is not so easy to realize that one who does speak English may not have been conditioned to operate with the same set of senses for the familiar terms common to your vocabulary and his.

Let us first make a somewhat oversimplified structure analysis of a complementary pair of communicants. In addition to the similar bodily structure which we have already suggested, such as comparable eyes and ears, we must remember that the necessary similarity includes all those complex mechanisms of the brain that produce the conscious states we have called sensations, affects, and relations.

Let us consider a hypothetical pair of communicants, utterer and interpreter, from the operation point of view. We shall assume that our utterer has six hats: red, blue, yellow, black, gray, and white. If the rods and cones (the tiny end organs packed together on what corresponds to the sensitive films in a stereoscopic or double-lens camera) of the retinae of his eyes are not defective, he will be able to see that the six hats differ even though they are of the same shape and material. If we reduce the light so that he can barely see, the white and the yellow will seem to be the same. But as the light grows stronger he will be able to see that the red, blue, and yellow affect him differently from the black, gray, and white. He now has sufficient experience (remember, this is all grossly oversimplified) to conceive of color and shade. But he can also distinguish the red hat from the blue and yellow hats, the yellow from the blue and red, and so forth. He is thus ready for the concepts red, blue, and yellow if, for example, we provide him with a red feather, a blue feather, and a yellow feather. Indeed, he may have the human impulse to decorate the hat with the corresponding feather. And if the feathers seem to have more in common with the white hat than the other hats have in common with the white hat, he can see that his concept of shade will determine the difference between the two reds, the two blues, or the two yellows, and he will have need of the concepts of light and dark. And as we increase the number of shades he will require relation concepts like those expressed in the suffixes -er and -est. By repeating the conventional symbols hat and red with the red hat, he conditions the sound of the words to the sight of the hat. If he sees that the relation of each feather to its hat is similar to the other two, he has need of a relation concept like the one expressed by the preposition in, and he is thus prepared to say to himself "light red feather in dark red hat." Now in the dark he is not able to tell one hat or one feather from another; but in the middle of a moonless night he is able to think "red feather in red hat" simply by uttering the appropriate symbols to himself. And with his human impulse to try new combinations, he can even think "yellow feather in blue hat" without ever having seen them thus combined.

Now it is easy to see that an interpreter who has been similarly conditioned to the same set of words and things is capable of similar concepts, and that with a little practice the two can communicate in the universe of feathered hats.

When Yankee Doodle stuck a feather in *his* hat he called it "macaroni" because he was very pleased with its appearance. But the result was a failure to communicate the affective component of his experience to untold millions of his American interpreters who do not speak Italian. Then there is the incalculable confusion of the millions of others who have tried to make some sort of sense out of a hat, a feather, and a staple article of diet. Italian symbols are ambiguous too, and *macaroni* is internationally ambiguous and has a history sufficiently complicated to require the services of a good dictionary.

The simplest conceivable situation, then, in which one human being may communicate with another is one in which structurally complementary communicants have been conditioned to associate the same words with the same things.

But most communication is not of this type. When we talk about hats most of our conditioning has been in connection with different hats, and successful (that is to say, accurate) communication depends upon the chance that our hat experiences have been sufficiently similar. And if we include our emotional attitudes in any attempted "exchange" of ideas, the variation in our experience may be great. Communication about very similar hats (Stetsons, for instance) may be corrupted by the fact that whereas one learned to admire them on Canadian Mounties, another learned to detest them on cattle thieves.

The third situation—one in which we find ourselves attempting to communicate nearly every day of our complicated modern lives— is the one in which we try to converse about hats with some one who has grown up where everybody goes bareheaded. In such a situation an abstract term like "headdress" may call for very careful definition if adequate communication is to take place, even though the objects under consideration are physical and external to us. When we take up the discussion of our private "states of mind" with regard to such abstract considerations as to whether appropriate dress is essential to good manners, accurate communication is likely to require patient and careful experiment.

We may repeat, then, that there are three general types of simple communication situations: those in which we communicate our responses to the same external physical objects; those in which we communicate with reference to similar objects; and those in which we communicate our sensations, emotions, and logical conceptions without reference to external and verifiable "check points."

Successful communication with reference to external stimuli would seem to depend on a careful consideration of the sensory mechanisms involved and the relative times and places of the communicants. But when we attempt to communicate about the innumerable goings-on within our own skins and skulls, things may become complicated indeed. When we deal with such utterances as Keats' "What is there in thee, Moon, that thou shouldst move my heart so potently?" or Shelley's "fair coquette of heaven," or Shakespeare's "moist star upon whose wat'ry influence Neptune's empire stands," our symbols seem to refer not only to the moon, but also to emotional states (affects) and logical deductions (concepts) that accompany our sensory perceptions of the physical patterns of moonlight. Such goings-on seem to be determined not so much by the general structure of our organs as by the conditioning experiences those organs have suffered or enjoyed. Hence emotions and conclusions are relatively private and thus present far greater problems of communication. Communication takes place insofar as the meaning of utterance corresponds to the meaning of interpretation. Since both are in large part conditioned responses, the success of the communication depends upon the extent to which the past experiences of the communicants have been similar; similar, that is, so far as the conditioned stimuli (the symbols in the utterance) are concerned.

In complex symbols containing a high proportion of subjective referents, communication is a matter of chance unless the communicants are alert. For the semanticist, alertness is a matter of being constantly and consciously aware of the fundamental principle of symbolic meaning. This principle is usually called the *law of context*, and is so called by Ogden and Richards; but we shall use Professor Dewey's term *matrix* because "context" for most interpreters refers merely to the immediate textual environment of a symbol. The law is: *A symbol has a meaning only in a matrix,* or *the meaning of a symbol is relative to its matrix.*

And what is a matrix? It is everything except the symbol itself— everything under the sun, the sun itself and all the stars, and the curved spaces beyond the stars. The other words of Marcellus, the *Tragedy of Hamlet,* the Age of Shakespeare, English Society, British Civilization, Western Culture, Human History, Cosmic Evolution, the Everlasting All, are but expansions of the field of vision as we consider the symbol "Something is rotten in the State of Denmark!"

But matrices are limited, nevertheless; for a symbol can get into a matrix only by being used in an utterance or interpretation. Now an utterance or interpretation, as we have already taken pains to point out, is simply a complex event in somebody's central nervous system. The first matrix of Marcellus's speech, therefore, was the rest of Shakespeare's central nervous system (or Bacon's, if you prefer), the rest of Shakespeare's universe. When you make use of the same symbol in your interpretation, the matrix is the rest of *your* central nervous system, the rest of *your* universe. And if you conjure the wandering stars to make it a wide matrix, they are but your stars wheeling in the orbits of your own central nervous system.

So it is that the act of interpretation, when performed with conscious care, is largely a process of building up a theory of the matrix of the utterance. Such a process must always come to a stop short of the actual reference of the utterer. You can't crawl through the tortuous convolutions of his cerebral cortex to have a look around. Because reconstruction of the complete matrix of a symbol would be possible only to an interpreter of infinite knowledge, it is something more than a foolish wisecrack to say that only God knows what Shakespeare meant when he had Marcellus say "Something is rotten in the State of Denmark!"

The reader may object at this point that he sees no practical connection between our rhapsody upon the cosmic dimensions of a matrix and the interpretation of a symbol like "Please pass the butter." The objection suggests the need for two terms: *complete theo-*

retical matrix and *practical matrix*. For it is, of course, true that
we are not as a rule concerned with those parts of the matrix of a
symbol that seem to have no meaningful (significant) relation to it.
We limit ourselves to what is commonly called the "frame of reference."

But imagine for a moment that you have been entertaining at
luncheon two learned physicists who have entered into a lengthy
argument over the distance between the earth and Betelgeuse. After
fifteen minutes of respectful exasperation, imagine yourself as having
said in a cautiously remonstrative tone, "Dr. Drystein, do you mind
passing the butter to Professor Heddington?" Now if the name of
that most magnificent luminary meant no more to you than "beetle-
juice," your request would be entirely innocent of the subtle meaning
it might possess if you were even amateurishly aware of the mathematical incongruity between the distance the butter had to travel
from Drystein to Heddington and the number of light years that it
is supposed to take a photon to make the trip from Betelgeuse. You
might be mischievously suggesting that your learned guests tempo-
rarily change the subject from astronomy to gastronomy. And if it
still seems to you that we "consider too curiously, to consider so,"
you might consider the etymology of *consider*.

If we would have a clear understanding of complicated things
like matrices, it is well to dissect them into their distinguishable
aspects. A matrix has two principal aspects. Whenever a symbol is
"born" in an utterance, it immediately presents, to a critical interpreter, two considerations which may appropriately be called the
aspect of environment and the aspect of heredity.

The environment of a symbol is all that lies around it at the
moment of birth. Unfortunately for the interpreter, he is not always
able to be present at the blessed event. In the case of the printed
or written symbol, the interpreter resembles the tardy visitor who
arrives at the hospital with his arms full of flowers and his head full
of curiosity, only to learn that mother and babe have gone home.
He must reconstruct the environment of the utterance as best he can.

Whether you approach an utterance from the standpoint of the
utterer or of the interpreter, it may exhibit seven phases if your
knowledge of it is not in some way obstructed. There is the "plain"

sense of the words; a *secondary sense* if the symbol is a metaphor, a pun, or irony; the *tone* of the utterer; the *feeling* that accompanies the utterance; the utterer's apparent *intention*; the utterer's *motive*; and occasionally a seventh phase, which we shall call *referential effort*, for the apparent ease or difficulty with which the utterer "finds" words for his thoughts sometimes throw light upon his meaning. A halting utterance may express a faulty meaning or it may imply that the utterer is groping for words to express a difficult thought and that the interpreter should take similar pains with his interpretation.

An instance of one form of irony will serve to bring out the interdependence of the phases and the fact that the plain sense is but one phase of the complete meaning. In the Old Testament story of Job, we find Job sitting in misery upon a dunghill, suffering through a visitation of some of his talkative and self-righteous neighbors. Finally Job reaches the end of his patience and exclaims, "No doubt but ye are the people, and wisdom shall die with you!" Now the sense of these words in most environments would probably be that the persons addressed are the elite; they "know all the answers"; indeed, they enjoy a monopoly in brain power; they are the brain trust and when they die there won't be any judgment left in the world. But Job's tone is itself symbolic; there is a certain tone of voice which we call *ironic* that signals the interpreter to take the symbol in a sense opposite to the one it usually bears. This ironic tone is sometimes mischievously humorous, but here the environmental signs imply that it is sarcastic. Job speaks with a *feeling* of indignation. His apparent *intention* is to compliment but his *motive* is to rebuke.

Or take the case of another famous utterance. In 1381 John Ball, the leading labor agitator of his day, travelled about England inciting the striking peasants to riot. With fanatic zeal he would shout, "When Adam delved and Eve span, who was then the gentleman?" The mere words might have the unemotional sense of the question, "In the time of Adam and Eve, who held the social status of a gentleman?" But surely not so with Ball! No doubt his audience was expected to roar back an enthusiastic "Nobody!" or an equally emphatic "Adam!" In terms of its medieval environment his utterance would expand into something like this:

"You have been told that the *status quo* is ordained by God; that gentlemen are gentlemen by divine right of inheritance; that the plowman is bound to his plow by the eternal nature of creation. Fellow sinners, do not be deceived. Are we not all descendants of Adam? Was he a gentleman as he tilled the earth in the sweat of his brow? If so, you are his heirs; if not, what then is divine and eternal about gentility?"

Ball's *tone* was bitter, for hot was the *feeling* within him. His *intention* was action, and he got it. "When Adam delved and Eve span, who was then the gentleman?" was a slogan; it "meant" trouble for London.

To grasp the total meaning of a symbol, knowledge of all its phases is required. But this is scarcely to be had without considerable information about the environment of the symbol. We frequently need to know where and when it was uttered, facts which we may refer to as its environmental *dimensions*. The dimensions of place and time provide us vital clues to what is usually called the "universe of discourse." A universe of discourse, remember, is a community of minds in which a common set of symbols (vocabulary) operates according to a common set of rules (grammar and syntax). The great universe (macrocosm) of English is made up of many little worlds (microcosms), which possess their own special vocabularies and even their own grammars. Our word "matrix," for instance, has a half-dozen different senses in a half-dozen different universes of discourse. "We ain't got no grub in the joint" is the "proper" way to say in one universe what is properly symbolized by "There isn't a thing in the house to eat" in another more "proper" universe of discourse.

By noting the time and place of an utterance we may achieve a far more accurate idea of the precise sense in which an ambiguous symbol is used. Many a modern reader has missed many a point in the reading of Shakespeare by neglecting to allow for the fact that his plays were written three and a half centuries ago in England. Take, for example, the audacious speech of Hamlet (in Act IV, Scene iii) to his uncle, King Claudius, whom he justly believes to be the murderer of his father. Hamlet says "A man may fish with the worm that hath eat of a king, and eat of the fish that hath fed of that worm." "What doth thou mean by this?" asks Claudius. "Nothing," says

Hamlet, "but to show you how a king may go a progress through the guts of a beggar." The modern reader has no difficulty in making satisfactory sense of this, but he misses a bit of superb irony if he does not know that in Shakespeare's England the word *progress* meant a royal journey of state from castle to castle made with all the pomp and circumstance of a Shriners' parade—the gaudy heralds sounding their bannered trumpets in the van, the "black guard" of ruffian scullery boys with their sooty pots and kettles rattling and clanking in the rear.

It is relevant here to note the traditional practice of rhetoricians and pedagogues of training their victims in the one "proper" way. And an occasion comes to mind in which a group of English instructors were exchanging ideas on the subject of method. A set of exercises based upon groups of related words was submitted. The student was to be given such words as "hand," "fist," and "paw" with which to complete the sentence, "The bride approached the altar with a lily in her ———." If he filled in the blank with "hand," he was good; if he used "fist," he was bad; if he used "paw," he was terrible.

But we recalled a certain buxom bride as she moved irresistably down the aisle with her jaw set and a grim look of unconquerable determination upon her none too winsome phiz. We couldn't quite remember whether she was toting a lily, but we were certain that, if she was, it must have been strangled mercilessly in her fist. And if her mother had had a church wedding, we'll swear that she must have clutched her lily in her paw. This merely goes to show that there are times and places in which words may appropriately be transferred from one universe of discourse to another.

There is another aspect of symbolic environment which has enjoyed perhaps too much emphasis in English instruction. Some teachers even go so far as to discourage the use of the dictionary as if it were a sort of "pony." "Learn to get the meaning from the context," is their maxim. "Context" here has the sense of *surrounding symbols*, and the implication is that you can guess the sense of a word or group of words by scrutinizing the adjacent words with which you are already familiar. We shall substitute for "context" the term "textual environment" and conclude with the warning that the context maxim is a fair invitation to an excellent guessing game, but dangerous advice for beginners. And few of us, indeed, get very far beyond the beginner's stage in mastering the vast vocabulary of the English tongue.

So much for the immediate environment of a symbol as embodied in the nonsymbolic aspects of its meaning, the circumstances (dimensions) of its utterance, and its textual relations. We still have its heredity to consider.

By the hereditary aspect of the matrix of a symbol, we mean the predisposition, preparation, or conditioning in the central nervous system of an utterer or interpreter that prompts him to use the symbol as he does. We need not dwell upon the proposition that the authorship of a symbol may be important to an interpreter. It goes without argument, for example, that it makes a considerable difference whether it was Khrushchev who said, "I have always worked for peace," or Rufus Jones. With a Quaker the symbol "work for peace" carries a sense or two scarcely to be found in the vocabularies of Little Russians. Let us call the authorship of an utterance its "identity."

If you, as an utterer, would communicate effectively, you must get in touch with the experience of your interpreter; speak his language; operate in his universe of discourse. The twenty-third Psalm is one of the world's greatest metaphors because so many people in so many places have at least a general knowledge of the relation between a good shepherd and his flock; but the full power of the poem is lost upon many an interpreter because he doesn't know that "anointeth my head" may have the sense in this textual environment of "puts on oil to prevent head-lice and ticks" and "spreadeth a table" may mean "spread a cloth upon the ground to prevent the loss of a single grain of precious fodder." We realize that "He spreadeth (or prepareth) a table before me, etc.," is usually interpreted as a shift from the shepherd-sheep metaphor to a host-guest metaphor. But, even if this is the better reading, it still may be regarded as a metaphor within a metaphor. Thus, "in the presence of mine enemies" would mean "I get to eat even with jackals around!" Some have even gone so far as to interpret "goodness and mercy" as faithful sheep dogs.

There is, perhaps, no better example in all literature of direct appeal to the verbal inheritance of the interpreter than the eloquent sermon of Father Mapple in Melville's *Moby-Dick*. Mapple is addressing a congregation of mariners on the subject of Jonah (the italics are ours):

"*Shipmates*, this book, containing only four chapters—four *yarns*—is one of the smallest *strands* in the mighty *cable* of the scriptures. Yet what *depths* of the soul does Jonah's *deep sea line sound*! What a pregnant lesson to us is this prophet! What a noble thing is that canticle in the fish's belly! How *billow-like* and boisterously grand! We feel the *floods surging* over us; we *sound* with him to the *kelpy bottom* of the *waters*; *seaweed* and all the *slime of the sea* is about us! But what is this lesson that the book of Jonah teaches! *Shipmates*, it is a *two-stranded* lesson; a lesson to us all as sinful men, and a lesson to me as a *pilot* of the living God."

. . .

He *dropped* and *fell away* from himself for a moment; then lifting his face to them again, showed a deep joy in his eyes, as he cried out with a heavenly enthusiasm, "But oh! *shipmates*! on the *starboard hand* of every woe, there is a sure delight; and higher the *top* of that delight, than the *bottom* of the woe is deep. Is not the *maintruck* higher than the *keelson* is low? Delight is to him—a far, far upward, and inward delight—who against the proud gods and *commodores* of this earth, ever stands forth his own inexorable self. Delight is to him whose strong arms yet support him, when the *ship* of this base treacherous world has *gone down* beneath him. Delight is to him, who *gives no quarter* in the truth, and kills, burns, and destroys all sin though he pluck it out from under the robes of Senators and Judges. Delight,—*top-gallant* delight is to him, who acknowledges not law or lord, but the Lord his God, and is only a patriot to heaven. Delight is to him, whom all the *waves* of the *billows* of the *seas* of the boisterous mob can never shake from this sure *Keel* of the Ages."[1]

Conversely, from the interpreter's point of view, the effective listener or reader must constantly be on the alert for environmental signs that give a clue to the utterer's linguistic heredity. If an Englishman asks you for a "biscuit," remember that what he wants is a "cracker"; if he asks for "packthread," get him some "string." Utterers naturally tend to use symbols as they have been taught (conditioned) to use them. The interpreter's problem is to detect the fact

[1] *Moby-Dick*, Chapter 9.

when their training has differed from his. And it *is* a problem, one that the educated user of English can solve efficiently only by the habitual employment of a good dictionary, and above all by the development of his capacity to employ the various techniques of definition. Since definition is simply an attempt at precise qualification, the direction of our next two steps is clearly indicated. We shall now make a brief survey of the psychology of qualification and then proceed to the basic theory and practice of definition.

STUDY QUESTIONS

1. (**A**) The basic communication situation depends upon what two complementary conditions? (**B**) Look up *communicate* in your dictionary. What aspect of the etymology relates to our two fundamental requirements for successful communication?

2. (**A**) Are we structurally identical? Similar? (**B**) Give an example of a communication situation in which the structures are not similar. (**C**) Why does the author assume the existence of adequate complementary structure?

3. Upon what factor does complementary experience depend?

4. What is a *conditioned response*? How does it differ from an *unconditioned response*?

5. (**A**) How are symbols *conditioned stimuli*? (**B**) As the utterer speaks, are his words conditioned stimuli or conditioned responses?

6. In order to communicate, the interpreter of our symbols must possess a set of conditioned responses. Give an example of an instance of failure due to inappropriate conditioning.

7. In Chapter 6 the author referred to the "perverted estimation of language." What does this concept have to do with the statement "Just as we find ourselves shouting at listeners who do not speak our language, so by a similar irrational impulse we assume that those with whom we attempt to communicate are equipped with complementary sets of conditioned responses to our own common stock of symbols"?

8. The interpreter's responses must be similar in the sensory, affective, and logical relations. Of the three, which would be likely to be most similar? Most different? Why?

9. (**A**) In the hat example, how was the concept of color conditioned? Of shade? (**B**) How did the need for the suffixes *-er* and *-est* arise? (**C**) How was the concept *in* learned? (**D**) When he utters the symbols *red* or *hat* without the things present, have the terms become learned? (**E**) If he is to communicate with another person about feathered hats, what must the other person have? (F) Is it possible for symbols to exist without direct experience of their referents?

10. Look up *macaroni* in the *O.E.D.* List at least four senses. With what sense of the term are you most familiar? What sense did the author of "Yankee Doodle" most probably have in mind?

11. (A) Give examples of the three general types of simple communication situations. (B) Why are they "simple"? (C) What is a *complex* communication situation? Why is it complex?

12. (A) Why are "emotions and conclusions relatively private," and why do they "present far greater problems of communication"? (B) Illustrate your answer by explaining why the "hat communication situation" would present fewer problems to the interpreter than the interpretation of Keats' "What is there in thee, Moon! that thou shouldst move my heart so potently?"

13. (A) What is the fundamental principle of symbolic meaning? State this principle. (B) What three synonyms have been given previously for this term? (C) Are some more inclusive than others? Is *textual environment* more or less inclusive than *context*? (D) Why did the author use *matrix* instead of *context*?

14. How are matrices limited?

15. (A) What was the matrix of Shakespeare's "To be or not to be" speech? (B) What is the matrix of your interpretation of this speech? (C) In view of your answer to (B), why must your matrix "always come to a stop short of the actual reference of the utterer"?

16. What is the difference between a *referent* and a *reference* in the following two statements? (A) "In complex symbols containing a high proportion of subjective referents, communication is a matter of chance unless the communicants are alert." (B) "So it is that the act of interpretation, when performed with conscious care, is largely a process of building up a theory of the matrix of the utterance. Such a process must always come to a stop short of the actual reference of the utterer."

17. What is the difference between a *complete theoretical matrix* and a *practical matrix*?

18. What is the etymology of *consider*, and how does it relate to Professor Heddington and Dr. Drystein?

19. What are the two principal aspects of a matrix?

20. Why is a written symbol harder to interpret correctly than a spoken symbol?

21. At what stage is a symbol "born"? Why is *born* in quotes?

22. (A) Are we considering the environment or the heredity of a matrix when we utilize the seven phases of meaning? (B) Can we apply

the tone or the referential effort of an utterance to written symbols?   (c)
How does tone differ from feeling?   (d) How does intention differ from
motive?   (e) Which of the seven phases of an utterance do you consider
to be most important to the interpreter? Why?

(f) What are the three sorts of symbols having secondary senses? If
our utterance is a metaphor, what will the plain sense be? Where would
this plain sense be placed on the conventional diagram—on the contextual
or the metaphorical side?   (g) Considering the seven phases of meaning, which would have meaning from symbol as well as meaning from
simple sign?   (h) Consider the utterance "Please pass the butter" as it
appears in the situation on page 90. Apply the seven phases of meaning
to this utterance.

23. (a) What are the environmental dimensions of an utterance?
(b) How does this relate to universe of discourse?   (c) How does knowledge of the environmental dimensions of an utterance help us to determine the sense of an ambiguous symbol?   (d) Give an example of a
case which demonstrates the possible difference in meaning of a statement
made in one universe of discourse and the same statement made in another universe of discourse.

24. How does consideration of only the textual environment limit
possible meaning?

25. "So much for the immediate environment of a symbol as embodied in the nonsymbolic phases of its meaning." How can symbols
have nonsymbolic meaning?

26. Who gives "birth" to a symbol? Who, then, gives "heredity" to
a symbol?

27. Why is it important to an interpreter to establish the identity of
an utterance?

28. How can an utterer "get in touch with the experience of his interpreter"?

29. (a) Why is the universe of discourse used by Father Mapple in
his sermon appropriate for his purpose?   (b) How would knowledge of
the environmental dimensions of an utterance help us in determining the
meaning of Father Mapple's speech?

30. The interpreter's problem is to discover when an utterer's training has differed from his. How can he solve this problem?

31. For review, define the following key terms from this chapter:
complementary structure, complementary experience, conditioned response, conditioned stimulus, law of matrix, complete theoretical matrix,
practical matrix, environment, heredity, environmental dimensions,
identity.

Awake your senses, that you may the better judge.

JULIUS CAESAR

10 THE PSYCHOLOGY OF QUALIFICATION

THE STAGES OF our discussion of qualification are determined by the structure analysis of the central nervous system presented in Chapter 2. That is, we will take up the subject in three stages, discussing the parts played by the sensory mechanism, the affective mechanism, and the logical mechanism of the brain. In suggesting the practicability of studying the behavior of the mind in the light of the known structure of the body, we necessarily take up a philosophical position unpalatably materialistic to certain minds. To these we can only offer the suggestion, with due respect, that if the not-so-firm firmament showeth the handiwork of God, the human c.n.s. declareth His infinite ingenuity. In Herrick's words,

> Even though we do not know how the brain thinks, we know as surely as we know anything in biology that it does so. And we know a great deal about the thoughts that it thinks. . . . These thoughts and their accompanying feelings can be attended to as they come and examined critically in retrospect, and this sort of experience makes up the greater part of the science of introspective psychology.[1]

We define a qualification as *a named response in the central nervous system* and we should perhaps remind you that our theory

[1] *The Thinking Machine*, p. 351.

of consciousness—and of course it is only a theory—is that consciousness exists when, and only when, some symbol, however private and peculiar to the individual, is being actively employed to relate the present moment to the past history of that individual. It is the act of making the present moment "of a sort"; the act of "sortance," to use a nonce-word of the Bard's. In fact, that is what the Latin word "qualify" literally means; and we present our theory of consciousness because we cannot conceive of the process of making something of a sort—of being "aware" of its relation to our past—without some kind of symbol to identify or signalize the act of recognition.

There is, to be sure, no such thing as a "pure" sensory qualification. The fact that a qualification is a qualification makes it a logical entity (entity is a Latin word for "thing"), because any name however "proper" is necessarily a genus term, and a genus term is a fundamental logical entity. Whenever you think of anything *as* a thing, its identity according to our theory is signalized or symbolized by the very act of naming it. Take you, for example; suppose your name is Hamilcar. By saying that Hamilcar is necessarily a genus term, we do not mean that you are of the same sort as the conqueror or the cat (Anatole France's cat, that is) but that Hamilcar is the name of the class of all experiences identified with or as you. Whenever anybody, including you, is consciously aware of you as you, Hamilcar or some other symbolic instrument of recognition must be at hand to unite the present Hamilcarian experience to the series that goes to make up your individuality in time and space. It is not only by means of genus terms that we designate our pigeonholes, but it is by genus terms that we create the pigeons that go in them. Of course, in some areas of our conscious life those terms are not definite public symbols like words, but are rather like the indescribable private symbols in which a blind musician thinks about music.

A sensory qualification, therefore, is a symbolic or logical act in which the essential or characteristic component is a sensation. The sensations themselves are rarely pure and simple, but if for no other reason but to call your attention to their complexity, it will be to our advantage to treat them as if they were. Here then is a simplified catalog of our more than twenty-nine types of sensory mechanisms, together with some illustrative words which may sometimes serve to symbolize and thus help us to conceptualize the accompanying sensory responses. Few of us have ever thought very carefully about what we mean by the word "sensation." It is quite natural to think of what our eyes do as one thing and what our ears do as another. And it is convenient for most of us to think of the left and right eye or the left and right ear as doing the same things because they are so much alike in outward appearance. It takes the careful observation of the scientist to discover the profoundly important implication of the fact that our left eyes look upon the world from a different point of view from our right ones. The perception of "depth," that is to say, the awareness of nature in the round or in its third dimension, turns out to be due not only to what the eyes have seen, but to the fact that the muscles that turn the eyes in their sockets have brought them into focus upon the same point. Hence our perception of depth in the scene around us is in part the result of a muscular sense which would probably have to be included in the ancient five-fold catalog under the sense of touch. Indeed, if we are to persist in the use of this ancient pentad, the category of touch will be the catch-all for numerous and various organs discovered or suspected by modern physiologists, such as the twenty-nine types defined in Herrick's *Neurology*.

We not only fail to take careful self-inventories of our marvelous machinery for keeping in touch with the world about us, but we are by no means always aware of the identity of the particular mechanism that is doing the job at any given moment. Take, for example, the use of the word "taste" in such an utterance as "nothing seems to taste right when I have a cold." In most instances such a remark would probably refer to the undifferentiated sensory responses of taste *and* smell; the fact that objects have to pass under our noses before they can get into our mouths makes it as natural and habitual to combine them as it is the sensations of both eyes or ears. This act of unconscious combination is even more pronounced in the matter of pure taste responses. Because our four sorts of taste organs are all not only in our mouths but on our tongues, it is difficult indeed to distinguish their operations; but a trained taster can develop astonishing skill in detecting the constituent flavors of food combinations, and it is interesting to note that any acquired refinement in the capacity to make nice distinctions will be accompanied and supported by an appropriate increase in the vocabulary.

Although it would be useless to attempt the abolition of the five-sense concept of sensation (at least until our dictionaries outgrow it), you will probably agree after studying the following list that the seven we here suggest is an improvement. A few moments of serious thought concerning the relationship between your bodily organs of sense and the vocabulary of sensation is almost certain to improve control in certain important phases of your language behavior. Here is our practical simplification of Professor Herrick's more elaborate inventory, together with a few illustrative terms that may perform the semantic duty of the sensation involved. This is not to say that they always do or even that they always should. It is rather to demonstrate that we knew all the time that we had more than five senses even though we didn't know we knew it.

(1) VISUAL. *Light, bright, dark, dull, dim,* and *red, blue, green, yellow* illustrate visual qualifications arising in the rods and cones respectively.

(2) AUDITORY. Noise and tone sensations of the ear produce auditory qualifications too numerous to mention.

(3) OLFACTORY. The sense of smell is comparable to vision and hearing in the high degree of discrimination of which it is capable. But, unfortunately, from an orthological point of view, there is no olfactory phenomenon like the rainbow (spectrum) upon which a systematic vocabulary of smell might be based. For this reason, olfactory qualification is either very general (*stink, fetid, fragrant, sweet, bad, aroma, bouquet*) or its nomenclature is borrowed (by concretion-abstraction) from the assumed *source of the odor* (rose, tea, sulphurous, etc).

(4) GUSTATORY. The language of taste derives from the activities of four sorts of organs in the tongue and pharynx. The so-called taste buds are specialized to produce the sensations which may be symbolized by simple terms like *sweet, sour, salty,* and *bitter* or complex terms like *delicious.* (It should be noted here that there is an instructive ambiguity in such words as *taste, flavor, relish.* When strictly used, they symbolize taste bud responses. But few of us take the trouble to hold our noses during the qualifying process, so that

in most cases undifferentiated smell responses are mixed in the symbolized experiences. Thus, we complain during a nasal cold that things don't "taste" good.)

(5) EQUILIBRATORY. *Balance, lean, stable, giddy, dizzy, poise, level,* etc., may symbolize sensations originating in the semicircular canals of the internal ear, although there is some question concerning our *consciousness* of canal function.

(6) SKIN. *Burn, itch, tickle, smart, titillate, caress, shudder, creep, tingle, smooth, rough, velvet* may symbolize various degrees and combinations of sensations arising in the end organs of the skin and the mucous membrane. *Hot, cold, cool, chill, warm, cozy,* and similar terms may symbolize responses arising in the so-called "warm spots" and "cold spots" of the skin and viscera.

(7) *Muscle.* Words like *squeeze, hug, jam, press, push* may symbolize sensations of deep pressure. *Heavy, heft, strain, stretch, cramp, twist, push, pull, taut, loose,* etc., may get their senses from the various end organs of tension in the muscles, tendons, and joints.

Professor Herrick lists nine sets of organs (some of which undoubtedly belong in our skin and muscle categories) which take part in the production of the more intimate sensations. Here are examples of the appropriate terms: *hunger, thirst, nausea*; the various terms which sometimes symbolize respiratory sensations, such as *stuffy, exhilarating, suffocating*; circulatory sensations, *blush, panicky, thrill, ecstasy*; sexual sensations, *lewd, wanton, voluptuous*; sensations of cavity distension, *full, stuffed, uncomfortable*; sensations of pain in stomach, heart, etc., *piercing, sharp, dull*; and, finally, the language which symbolizes those "obscure abdominal sensations associated with strong emotions of fright, anger, affection, etc., characterized (probably correctly) by the ancients by such expressions as 'yearning of the bowels,' etc."

Although the field of affective psychology, and therefore the semantics of affective qualification, is still a wilderness in which the lawless poet and the wayward mystic intuitively roam at will, we do have considerable reason to believe that the brain does include a mechanism or mechanisms for being angry, fearful, or in love. We do know that certain kinds of damage to the mysterious tissue within our skulls cause us to stop being curious about things, or feeling that they are funny. Or, conversely, that with certain types of damage we go right on being emotional, but lose the capacity to do so at the appropriate times and places. It is only, however, in surgical experiments with laboratory animals or medical observation and procedure in accident and disease that emotional behavior can, in any practical sense, be localized or isolated.

This makes the semantics of affective qualification a difficult and experimental enterprise when conducted by the method here attempted. The separation of sensation and emotion requires a kind of rigorous and disciplined introspection which is almost a lost art among the extraverted children of an age dominated by the so-called objective methods of nineteenth-century science; for that science was characterized by a justifiable distrust of the inward look. We are but slowly, not to say reluctantly, discovering that even science must be revitalized by the persistent and disciplined introspection carried on within the private laboratories of our souls. And we find that communication with regard to these complicated states we call emotions among us "windowless monads" requires that we identify these states with the various sensations which accompany them, and the logical— that is to say, physical—situations of time and space in which they occur.

It may be that sensation is the most primitive nervous activity, that in the evolutionary process certain sensations or combinations of sensations may develop the intensities which we know as *affects* and that those *affects* when connected with observed causes, or more properly with observations that are taken to be causes, become in the higher animals the complex patterns we know as emotional behavior. If such is the case, then an emotion is simply an intense sensation complex with a logical component. This would imply that only a symbol-using animal can have emotions. Of course, his symbols may be private symbols and even nonlingual. This is another way of saying that a given mind might have the capacity to be conscious without employing the tongue and the related vocal apparatus. But in man the process becomes discussable because of the public nature of language.

When the sensory mechanisms have done their work, the resulting sensations may themselves be the stimuli of moods or emotions which become conscious entities through the symbolizing process we here call qualification. To the redness and the odor with which we endow the rose, we may add the quality of loveliness. Of course, the redness, the odor, and the loveliness are all interpretations and, as such, conditioned responses. But learning to see color or smell odors is a relatively simple and restricted process, whereas the loveliness response is extensively conditioned by the more general experience of the individual. To two optically similar observers, a red rose is pretty sure to be similarly red, but its loveliness may vary absolutely. That is, for reasons of experience he may or may not recall, one of them might find the rose disgustingly red or treacherously fragrant.

It is probable that some readers may be troubled by an honest doubt about such thoughts as "learning" to see color or smell odors. The vital point to grasp here is that we do not refer to the mechanical and chemical (physiological) processes of seeing red as red and not as pink or purple. We are discussing the act of qualification. It is of no significance to us what an observer sees in the physiological sense, if he is unable to refer the present seeing experience to the proper series of past experiences.

Analysis of the statement "He can't tell red when he sees it" may be helpful. Here "tell" has the sense in which we are using "see." It means "to qualify as a visual response of a certain sort." "See" has the sense of "behold"—that is, "to fix the eyes upon."

A very interesting problem now arises. Suppose we parallel the idea of learning to *see* red with the idea of learning to *be* angry. Would it make sense to say "He can't tell when he is angry," or "He can't tell when he is afraid"? Now try these:

> He can't tell a fragrant rose.
> He can't tell a disgusting sight.
> He can't tell a good Limburger.
> He can't tell disgusting Limburger.

Most tasters do not have to be persuaded that the taste for Limburger is an "acquired" taste; we are simply suggesting that the capacity to *recognize* it is also acquired. And if you were to exclaim, "Yes, but it only takes once!" we would then bring up the recognition of grades or brands of Limburger.

In the light of present knowledge, it would seem that any apparent difference between sensory and affective qualification is due to two causes: first, the highly selective or discriminative senses of sight, hearing, smell, and taste have tended to set our notions or standards of qualification, but the emotional mechanisms are more like the sense of pain in being relatively gross or clumsy in operation; second, the result is a rich vocabulary of sight, sound, and smell, and a poor vocabulary of pain and emotion. Thus, the language we inherit does not promote training in discrimination. Until we see some considerable advantage in doing so, we are not likely to develop courses for learning to grade and classify our own aches and pains.

The qualification of emotion, however, presents a distinct challenge to semantic exploration. Though the poets have traveled widely and alertly in this realm of joy and sorrow, the scientist stands, for the moment, baffled upon the border. We may hazard the guess that this is probably due either to the fact that no specific organs of emotion exist in the brain, or that any which do exist operate only in connection with sensory organs too intimate for analysis. It may well be that emotions are simply the conscious aspect of what happens when a considerable portion of the brain is working under abnormally high or low tension.

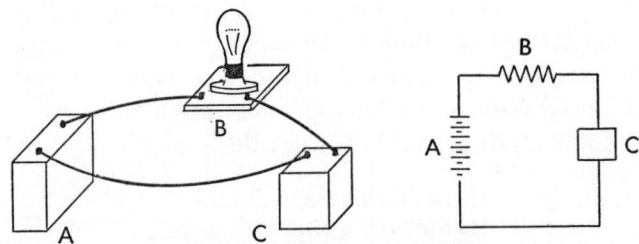

Perhaps we can make the point clearer with a simple electrical model. Suppose that we wish to operate a very delicate instrument, *c*, with a source of current, *a*, which is too strong for it. We therefore interpose the lamp, *b*. The slender filament of the lamp works as an "organ" whose function is to reduce (resist) the current flowing in the circuit through *c*. If the current from *a* is sufficiently increased in pressure (voltage), the filament will glow and thus might light our work. The filament, then, performs three functions. As part of the circuit, it is a conducting organ; as part of the current supply system, it is a resistor; as part of the total operation, it is a light. But we would not say that the apparatus had a special organ of incandescence.

Now, emotion may be comparable to the incandescence. The hypothalamus may be overheated, as it were, in the performance of other duties. And it is not difficult to imagine that if you were the lamp it might be difficult to distinguish your own incandescence from your own conductivity and resistance, particularly if you were hot. Even such basic emotions as fear, rage, love, and wonder confound the efforts of analysis.

But this does not mean that the semanticist is without methods of semantic control in dealing with the language of emotional qualification. Mindful that the hypothalamus, if it *is* the hypothalamus, works hand-in-glove (or axone to dendrite) with the sensory mechanisms and the cortex, he determines the senses of affective symbols by their accompanying sensations and logical relations. Take the word "snarl," for example. It may refer to the sound produced, the "feel" of producing it, the "feel" of curling the lip, or the sight of the curled lip and the bared teeth, all of which are sensory; or it might refer to the logical qualification of the bared teeth as a *sign* of imminent attack. Normally, affective symbols qualify certain sorts of sensory behavior, such as the sight and the sound of another's snarl or the feel and sound of your own, with certain sorts of situations such as attack with intent to bite.

The necessity of noting this double aspect of emotional language is easily seen by comparing the italicized words in these quotations:

> My tables,—Meet it as I set it down,
> That one may *smile,* and *smile,* and be a villain;
> At least I'm sure it may be so in Denmark:

> When Irish eyes are *smiling*
> Sure they *steal* your heart away.

> Thou shalt not *steal.*

In the first statement, the utterer, Hamlet, implies that a certain behavior of the lips is usually accompanied by a friendly attitude toward the stimulus, but in Denmark, where smiling uncles murder fathers, this is not necessarily so. The specific sense of "villain" here

is "my father's murderer," a logical qualification. Its affective component, evil, may be said to "infect" the sense of the word "smile."

The utterer of the second statement, an infatuated lover, plays a
similar trick with "smile" and "steal." Smile here has the sensory
denotation of the feel or sight of the facial area about the eyes not
usually associated with the intent to rob. In this utterance, however,
the affective component of *smiling* has "favorably" infected the vil-
lainous term "steal," which, in the third statement, bears its full affective complement of evil when translating the Hebrew engraved
on Moses' table of stone.

In conclusion, it may be emphasized that the identity and dimensions of the utterance are of special importance in the interpretation
of affective qualification.

We have already pointed out that all qualifications are logical
because for any given unit of experience to be meaningful, and thus
to be amenable to symbolic treatment, it must be of a sort. We have
already faced up to the fact that this position commits us to a particular theory of meaning which may or may not be true. We are
assuming that a sentient being can perform exceedingly complex
operations without the phenomenon we know subjectively as consciousness. The operations of a beaver or a weaverbird may be of
this sort, but it seems justifiable to assume that at some stage of purposeful behavior the higher animals develop recollected images which
serve to tie present experiences to similar past experiences. This
means that the first moment of consciousness takes place when the
meaningful moment is connected with previously experienced but
meaningless moments by the image symbol. It is therefore by no
means nonsensical to say that when we are conscious of any given
experience for the first time, we must be conscious of at least one
other experience similar to it, likewise for the first time. And our
most general sense of logical qualification is simply that first act of
signalizing the resemblance of the two now-meaningful experiences
to one another by what we have called a genus term. Obviously our
first genus terms will be either sensory or affective or both, and will
signalize the developing consciousness of our environment and the
affects which they arouse or accompany.

In this hypothetical evolution of consciousness, then, the type of meaning which derives from the genus-species relation would be the first to develop. One simple is recognized as similar to another simple, and the resulting complex is a genus symbol with its related species.

Next would come the realization that the simple could be taken apart into other simples, and the part-whole relation would produce a new complex composed of a named whole and its constituent named parts and the names of the relations among the parts, a tremendous advance in linguistic sophistication.

Observation of a complex whole in action with progressive changes in the relations among the parts would next lead to the concept of an operation, the constituent stages of which would depend for their identification upon the two preceding processes of classification and structure analysis. That is, the analysis of an operation, in addition to adding the fourth dimension of time, involves the concept of a changing structure and becomes so complex as to require the act of classification in dealing with its numerous aspects. Now a careful examination of the processes here briefly reviewed will disclose the necessary concepts that the intellect requires in order to consider them. In the first classification, there must be something to recognize as similar to something else, even though the latter is "realized" (made into a thing) for the first time. We thus need the name "something." If one substance is to be recognized as different from another the concept of "twoness" as well as oneness will be necessary, and thus the notion of *number* will be a primary requirement.

This awareness of difference in *substance* must lead in one way or another to the concept of *change*. Now it will be apparent upon persistent introspection that a simple thing can change only in *size*, whereas a complex thing can change both in size and *structure* where "structure" is the name for a whole made up of constituent parts. Either a change in size or a change in structure will involve the dimensions of time and space.

In our macroscopic universe, at least, change takes time, and something has to be somewhere to take it. Thus, the fundamental logical qualifications—that is, the essential instruments of analysis— are the terms: number, change, size, structure (shape), substance (energy, matter), space, and time, or their symbolic equivalents. And we may add that the discovery of those equivalents—those terms which we use from time to time as synonymous with those here used—is the necessary first step, the location of the site, so to speak, for the study of rational thought.

We may epitomize the evolution of such rational thinking thus: first you have to learn to recognize apples as apples, then you have to learn to take them apart, then you have to conceive of one of the parts—the seed, for example—as a stage in the operation of becoming an apple. As your comprehension of an apple as an organic, and therefore changing, entity develops, you have need of a larger and larger vocabulary. And whatever other terms it may include, unless you limit your thinking to your own private sensations and emotions, you will have to have symbols for conceiving of an apple at any given moment as one of a *number* of *changes* in the *magnitude* and *structure* of *substance* in *time* and *space*. And that moment conceived of as a moment of change will have meaning only in terms of the other six primary logical qualifications. Indeed, we may think of the six as "dimensions" of the seventh, which is change.

That is, unless you happen to be a modern theoretical physicist—in which case your concept of substance as matter and/or energy will be accompanied by a similar integration of the concepts of time and space into a so-called time-space continuum.

In summary, then, we may repeat that the observed structure of the c.n.s. suggests a working classification for sorting simple qualities and taking them apart when they are complex. For our conscious experience seems to be made up entirely of the stuff of sensation, emotion, and reflection, and we must conclude that any adequate theory of definition must be based upon this assumption.

STUDY QUESTIONS

1. A qualification is defined as "a named response in the central nervous system." Why does the response have to be *named* in order to qualify it?

2. Rephrase this statement, emphasizing the definition of the italicized words: "Our theory of consciousness is that consciousness exists when, and only when, some symbol, however private and peculiar to the individual, is being actively employed to *relate* the present moment to the past history of that individual."

3. Consider this situation: You experience a feeling in the pit of your stomach which we term "butterflies in the stomach." You have no such term for this feeling. All you possess is the recollection of the same feeling from a previous experience. Would the imprint in your mind of the remembrance of the feeling (with no word for such) constitute a symbol? Explain your answer.

4. Explain why designating a response as sensory rather than logical is a logical process. Which analytical process is it?

5. (**A**) Explain why "any name however 'proper' is necessarily a genus term." (**B**) Why is a genus term "a fundamental logical entity"? (**C**) Explain the statement "It is not only by means of genus terms that we designate our pigeonholes, but it is by genus terms that we create the pigeons that go in them."

6. Define *sensation* in the following sentence: "A sensory qualification, therefore, is a symbolic or logical act in which the essential or characteristic component is a sensation."

7. (**A**) Rephrase the statement "Any acquired refinement in the capacity to make nice distinctions will be accompanied and supported by an appropriate *increase* in the vocabulary." Explain *increase*.   (**B**) Define *nice* as used in the above sentence.

8. How would "a few moments of serious thought concerning the relationship between your bodily organs of sense and the vocabulary of sensation improve control in certain important phases of your language behavior"?

9. The author states that because "there is no olfactory phenomenon like the rainbow (spectrum) upon which a systematic vocabulary of smell might be based," quite often olfactory qualification is very general. How are the olfactory qualifications *stink* and *fragrant* more general than the visual qualifications of *light* and *dull*?

10. Considering gustatory qualifications, *sweet* and *sour* are considered *simple* terms, while *delicious* is *complex*. In what way is delicious *complex*?

11. By looking up *taste, flavor,* and *relish,* explain their "instructive ambiguity."

12. How do the skin qualifications of *hot, cold, cool, chill, warm,* and *cozy* illustrate the "nice distinctions" considered above?

13. Which of the sensory qualifications would most likely include temperature qualification?

14. Why do "we have considerable reason to believe that the brain does include a mechanism or mechanisms for being angry, fearful, or in love"?

15. (A) Why is the semantics of affective qualification a difficult enterprise? (B) How is emotional communication between us "windowless monads" possible?

16. (A) If an emotion is simply an intense sensation complex with a logical component, why would this imply that only a symbol-using animal can have emotions? (B) Give an example of how these symbols might be private and even nonlingual. (C) Can animals be afraid?

17. Explain the logical component in the emotion of fear.

18. (A) Explain the statement "the redness, the odor, and the loveliness (of the rose) are all interpretations and, as such, conditioned responses." (B) What is the difference between seeing a rose as red and seeing it as lovely? (C) Using the textual definition of *tell*, consider the following sentences: He can't *tell* when he is angry. He can't *tell* a good Limburger. (D) Can an animal *tell* when he is afraid?

19. Consider the following italicized words according to their sensory, affective, or logical components: "Most *tasters* do not have to be persuaded that the *taste* for Limburger is an 'acquired' *taste*; we are simply suggesting that the capacity to *recognize* it is also acquired."

20. Which universe of discourse has the most discriminating vocabulary: the sensations or the emotions? Why?

21. The author uses the electrical model shown on page 106 to illustrate what process may possibly occur in the brain during emotional behavior. With this illustration in mind, consider the statement "and it is not difficult to imagine that if you were the lamp, it might be difficult to distinguish your own incandescence from your own conductivity and resistance, particularly if you were hot."

22. (A) The physiological controversy over emotion does not prevent the semanticist from dealing with the language of emotional qualification. How does he do this? (B) What is the "double aspect of emotional language" referred to on page 107?

23. Why are the "identity and dimensions of the utterance" of special importance in the interpretation of affective qualification?

24. Considering logical qualification, why would "the type of meaning that derives from the genus-species relation be the first to develop"?

25. The evolution of the logical concepts has been illustrated in relation to their need in the growth of the three analytical processes. Trace their appearance in "learning to recognize apples as apples, then learning to take them apart, then conceiving of one of the parts—the seed, for example—as a stage in the operation of becoming an apple."

26. Which logical qualification is primarily involved in the following italicized words: (**A**) That lamp is *grotesque*.   (**B**) The noisy *crowd* pushed its way to the stadium.   (**C**) He feels he must *alter* the plan. (**D**) This *material* is too thin to use for the dress.   (**E**) The *huge* dog lunged at me.   (**F**) It was a *roomy* house.   (**G**) This *period* will be devoted to the study of mathematics.

Define, define, well-educated infant.

LOVE'S LABOUR'S LOST

11 THE THEORY
OF DEFINITION

A CHAPTER ON DEFINITION is a good way to close our remarks on the primary function of communication and open the subject of reflection. This is because appropriate definition is the best solution to most problems of communication and the necessary first step in the systematic solving of problems in general. Hence we may say that adequate definition is the last word in efficient communication and the first in the process of precise reflection.

The most important fact to know about defining, and it is the kind of fact that all seem to know and few seem to realize, is that there are two radically different sorts of objects which require defining: words and things. In Latin both "define" and "determine" mean to tell the ends or limits of something. When we determine a nautical position, for example, we are not concerned with the meaning of a symbol but rather with the end of a line on a chart, and hence the approximate location of a ship on the sea. When we try to "make out" a bacillus in a microscopic field, or a celestial constellation in a telescopic field, we are attempting the definition of a thing. This sort of definition is not the proper business of this book. We are concerned with words.

We are not, however, concerned solely with words as words; our chief concern is rather the relations of words with things. To say that in one statement the Latinism "locate" does the same semantic service as the more common word "place" in another is to deal with words as such. To say "this is the place that hurts" is to connect the word with a thing. Thus, there are two general types of definition of interest to us: definitions that connect words with other words, and definitions that connect words with the nonverbal experiences for which they stand.

Perhaps the most subtle manner in which words exercise their insidious tyranny over the mind is in the substitution of one symbol for another when accompanied by the pleasant sensation of enlightenment. *Definition by synonym*, which shall be our name for such symbolic substitution, is, of course, the most prevalent type of definition. It is the stock in trade of the lexicographer and the basis of that amusing game of "merry-go-round" that dictionaries habitually play with us. For example, Merriam-Webster tells us that "force" means strength, energy, or power; "strength" means force or power; "energy" means strength, force, or power; "power" means the ability to act; and an "act" is the exercise of power.

However treacherous and "circular" definitions by synonym may be, they are in practice indispensable in the field of communication; efficiency requires that communicants make sure that the substituted symbol does in fact make the desired contact with the relevant world of nonverbal experience. In the field of reflection, definition by synonym is a device for exploring one's vocabulary on the chance that experiences relevant to the solution of a given problem may be associated with terms other than those in mind at the moment. We shall illustrate this point in connection with the word "sort" in the chapter on problem-solving.

Definition by antonym, the second type of verbal substitution, is sometimes a more effective operation than definition by synonym. This is apparently because of the exceedingly ambiguous nature of the concept of opposition. When we attempt to define a term by identifying its opposite, we are reminded of several terms the applicability of which depends upon the circumstances, and the mind is thus challenged to make a conscious selection of the appropriate antonym. Definition of the word "rich" by antonym, for example, reminds us that among its many opposites are "poor," "lean," "plain," "sparse," "weak," "cheap," "thin," "bright," and so forth. Thus in defining "rich" in the expression "a uniform of rich blue" we would say that rich is the opposite of bright, but not in the sense that dull is the opposite of bright. There is an instructive note in the old Century Dictionary that betrays the lexicographer in the very act of confessing the inadequacy of definition by synonym and the somewhat more effective substitution of the antonym principle. "Rich," he complains, "as applied to colors in zoology has a restricted meaning, which, however, is very difficult to define. A metallic, lustrous, or iridescent color is *not* rich; the word is generally applied to soft and velvety colors which are pure and distinct, as a *rich* black, a *rich* scarlet spot, etc., just as we speak of *rich* velvets, but generally of bright or glossy silks."

When our lexicographer uses "velvety" he is substituting a synonym; when he implies that rich colors are *not* glossy he is using the antonym route very much as Shakespeare's Polonius does when he suggests that his son's apparel should be "rich, not gaudy."

Little need be said of a theoretical nature about either of the types of verbal definition except to emphasize the superiority of definition by antonym and to present in some detail the theory of opposition. For in considering the ambiguity of the term "opposition" we move logically to think about the connection of words and things. When we define "blonde" as the opposite of "brunette" we offer a mere verbal substitution, but when we set up a scale and appropriate symbols for the check points on it, its meaning derives from the physical objects which it is designed to qualify.

In his essay on the subject, C. K. Ogden concludes that all ideas of opposition derive directly or metaphorically from subjective directional responses based upon the mind's awareness of the normal structure and position of the body. If you were a perfectly spherical eye, uniformly sensitive all over and free to roll about upon a perfectly smooth plane, the only oppositions possible to you would be— well, what would they be? Lacking head and foot, you would not be able to conceive of up or down; front and back would be senseless without a forehead; left and right, without sides. Nor would the possibility of being turned inside out be likely to occur to you. What you would turn over in your mind while rolling on a mirror is too difficult to contemplate. All of these relations, which are the very substance of rational being, may be analyzed in terms of position or progress upon a scale, or position or progress with reference to a mid-station or "cut," or both.

Opposites, like black and white, top and bottom (head and foot), front and rear (head and tail), when diagrammed, yield vertical or horizontal scales that grade from minimum to maximum. The extremes or ends are opposites. When we work from the common end of two scales, the mid-point of reference (historically, the station of the body) is called a "cut." Thus, left and right, above and below, forward and backward, past and future, are directions on the opposite scales of a cut. The natural estimation of hot and cold is based upon the cut of bodily temperature (tepid or lukewarm). There are four standard artificial scales, three of which are double. The Fahrenheit is based upon the cut of the temperature of mixture of equal parts of snow and salt; the centigrade and Reaumur, upon the freezing point of water. The "absolute" scale is based upon the theoretical point at which molecular motion is suspended. Obviously this point is not a cut but an extreme—the absolute absence of heat.

There are several types of cuts, and they go by such names as medium, median, mediocre, middle, neutral, indifferent. Thus, we get such oppositional scales as: blonde-medium-brunette; red-median gray-green; excellent-mediocre-poor; left-middle-right (radical-liberal-conservative); bright-neutral-dark; and acid-neutral-alkaline.

The cut analysis is also applied by Mr. Ogden to the opposition of reversed forms (enantiomorphs), such as shoes, gloves, and mirror-images. He suggests that the cut is the mid-station through which the one must pass as it turns inside out to become the other. We may rationalize this type of opposition with fewer mental gymnastics, however, by saying that the left glove is the opposite of the right because the left hand is opposite the right; or that the image is the opposite of the object because its left is the object's right. In doing so we are, of course, shifting the sense of the word "opposite."

The analysis of scalar opposition is vitally important for two reasons. It calls attention to the illogical character of the natural semantic development of language, and lays the foundation for accurate definition. Accurate definition depends upon those processes in the central nervous system that we have called qualification; this, as we took pains to point out, is a treacherously relative phenomenon. Take, for example, the estimation of hot and cold by means of the unaided sense of touch. Two sworn witnesses could contradict one another on the stand without perjuring themselves, if the one had just come from a refrigerator and the other from a boiler room. The first might swear that the corpse was warm, the second that it was as cold as any stone. Under such circumstances, could it be said that they gave "opposite" testimony? And if their depositions were symbols, were the referents "opposites"? And if so, what is the sense of "opposite" here? You say "Laughing is the opposite of crying." Is laughing for joy the opposite of crying for joy? You say "Love is the opposite of hate." Is love-resentment the opposite of hate-resentment? Perhaps, but how? Some of our verbal oppositions turn out to be so vague and conventional as to rank with out-and-out psittacisms in meaninglessness.

Fahrenheit calibrated his scales by dividing the stretch from the temperature of snow and salt to the boiling point of water at sea level into two hundred and twelve equal parts; Celsius divided the stretch between the freezing and boiling points of water into one hundred equal parts; Reaumur divided the same stretch into eighty parts. What a delightful comedy of errors those learned gentlemen might enact in a simple conversation about the weather! Fortunately, we have neat mathematical formulas for equating such scalar symbols.

But in the more vital fields in which men are ready to fight and die, we operate with a thousand scales whose cuts and calibrations are as varied as Hedda Hopper's hats. "There never was a good war nor a bad peace," says one. "Better to die free than live enslaved," says another. Good and bad, war and peace, life and death, slave and free, are opposites, and the intelligent determination of their scales and cuts is the basic operation for establishing a theory of social sanity.

Obviously there is no point in discussing theories of social sanity without knowing what we are talking about. Knowing what you are talking about is but another way of referring to the essential connections between words and things. And the types of definition we next propose to review are simply the different forms that the statements of such connections may take.

The first type is simple and obvious. It is *definition by identification or exemplification.* We point to a five-cent piece and say, "This is Monticello," or, "This is Thomas Jefferson." Or, pointing to the same coin, we say, "A nickel is one of these." If we think of this type of definition in terms of the genus-species relation we may say that a term is identified when its referent is the only species in its genus, and that a term is exemplified when any of several species is used to define the term. Now if we stop and enjoy a second thought about the Monticello and the Jefferson on the coin we must revise our statement and say, "This is a representation of Jefferson or Monticello," and such a statement becomes definition by exemplification of the term *representation of Jefferson* or *representation of Monticello.* Obviously we should have to journey to the mansion or the tomb for a true definition by identification.

Further consideration will bring us to the discovery that we use the term "example" in two senses: "species" and "specimen." White is an example (species) of color in the most general sense of the word "color." This page presents a specimen of white. This page also presents an example of white. The fact that a specimen name stands in the same relation to its species term as a species term does to its genus term accounts for the ambiguity of the word "example." To define color as "what red is" is more like what we have called definition by synonym than what we here mean by exemplification.

When unable to define by exemplification, we frequently make use of objects that resemble the referents of the terms we would define. *Definition by comparison,* however, usually involves some indication of the way in which the comparable objects differ. When an Australian asks an American to define "Teddy bear" and the answer is "It's like a koala, but it's just a doll," you have a typical definition by comparison involving a genus-to-genus relation. If you define "koala" by saying "A koala resembles this Teddy bear, but it's alive," you are comparing by a specimen-to-genus relation.

There now remain the three types of definition that characterize our most systematic efforts to see and think clearly. We might deal with them jointly under the heading "analysis," but by taking them severally we neatly complete our customary tale of seven and emphasize once more the eternal relevance of the three basic operations of logical behavior.

Both exemplification and comparison are rudimentary forms of definition by classification, to be sure. But under *definition by classification* we would include only those completely developed forms in which the mind deliberately selects the appropriate genus term and carefully differentiates the species to be defined from all other species in the genus. The type of definition that performs this operation is called the logical definition by logicians. Perhaps we should add that the logician's senses of "genus" and "species" differ from those of the biologist. In logic, a given species term may belong to any number of genera, for genus is simply the name of any class, however determined, that includes the species as a member. And a term that is a species in one classification may be a genus in another, whereas in biology the level of abstraction at which the term "genus" operates is fixed.

Thus, in the sentence "He was sitting in a chair," a logical definition of "chair" would be: a chair (species term) is a single seat (genus term) with a back (differentia). In the sentence "The Queen Anne should be placed by the fire," the logical definition of "Queen Anne" would be a chair (genus term) with a high upholstered back (differentia) and wings (differentia).

The formula for the logical definition that we here call definition by classification is as follows: state the genus of which the term to be defined is a species, and then differentiate it from all other species of the same genus. Here are the traditional rules for a good definition by classification:

1. The genus and differentia terms must not be mere synonyms of the species term; e.g., a cow is a bovine ruminant.

2. The genus and differentia terms should belong to the appropriate universe of discourse. The classic horrible example is Dr. Johnson's definition of network as "Anything reticulated or decussated, at equal distances, with interstices between the intersections."

3. The differentia must exclude all other species of the genus.

4. The definition should state what the species is, not what it is not.

Attention may also be called to the fact that the limits of the genus and differentia are arbitrary. When we define a koala as a small, tailless, arboreal, herbivorous, Australian, marsupial mammal, we have practically left it to the interpreter to decide upon the scope of the genus term; it might be "mammal," "marsupial mammal," "Australian marsupial mammal," and so on. And finally we may note that when exhaustively applied in a given universe of discourse, this type of definition produces the sort of systematized body of knowledge that we call a "science" in one sense of the word.

When the term to be defined is related to a structure, adequate definition will deal with the basic structural relations by means of *structure analysis.* If, for example, the term is the name of a part, the definition of it will contain the name of the whole to which it belongs and a statement of its relation to the other parts; by such a definition it may be clearly distinguished from the other parts, and its articulation with the adjoining parts may be understood.

For example, in the sentence "The chair was undamaged except for a broken stretcher," a definition of "stretcher" by structure analysis would be as follows: A stretcher is a brace between the rungs of a chair. An analytical definition of the name of a structural whole would contain the names of the principal parts and a statement of their articulations with one another. For example, a definition by structure analysis of the word "chair" in the sentence "Chippendale designed admirable chairs" would be this: "A structure usually composed of a platform supported by four legs, two of which are extended to form a back. The legs are mortised to four rails which support the platform or seat and are braced by rungs that reach from back leg to front leg and are themselves braced by a stretcher from rung to rung. Between the top back rail and the back seat rail, which extend from one extended leg to the other, there is sometimes a vertical member or members called splats, which are mortised into the rails."

Definition by operation analysis is the device by which we define terms that have to do with structures in action. Just as the basic structural relation is that of part to whole, so the basic functional relation is that of stage to operation. We may define "operation" as a set of movements with an assignable purpose, and a "stage" as a movement or set of movements that make up a meaningful unit in an operation. A structure or set of parts moving in an operation is a system. Systems have purposes. The performance of any part of a structure in an operation is a function. Hence we employ operation analysis in the definition of functions, purposes, systems, and their moving parts and stages.

A watch, for example, is an operational structure. When running, it is a system or dynamic structure. On a certain watch there are four hands. They are functional parts. The red one is called the calendar hand. The definition by operation analysis of a "calendar hand" as used in the foregoing sentence would be this: a red hand that makes one complete revolution of the dial to sixty-two revolutions of the hour hand and that also (when properly adjusted) makes two revolutions to one revolution of the earth with reference to the sun. Thus, when properly set, the calendar hand tells the day of the month. Terms like "operation," "purpose," and "function" are, of course, relative. We might define the operation of a watch as its entire useful life, or its running from one winding to another, or its running during a complete revolution of any one of its hands. Similarly, the concept of its purpose might vary from telling seconds to telling days of the month.

If we were to regard the ordinary watch as a device for telling seconds, the function of the second hand might be to number seconds below sixty; the readings of the other hands would then be used for calculating elapsed seconds above the number sixty. If our purpose did not involve keeping track of the number of seconds above sixty, then the other hands would be functionless and not, strictly speaking, a part of the system for telling seconds.

As you may have discovered in your own private attempt to trace examples of semantic growth, the same word or phrase may subtly shift its sense while the mind is busy using it to think. Let us take the definition "a stretcher is a brace between the rungs of a chair." Clearly this statement takes the form of a definition by classification. "Brace" is the genus term and "between the rungs of a chair" is the differentia. But from our point of view, it *is* a definition by classification only if the mind that formulates it is first answering the question "What is the stretcher a sort of?" and then "How does it differ from all other sorts of brace?" If the mind is concerned with the location of the stretcher in the whole assembled structure of the chair and its articulation with each opposing rung, then the mind is *not* sorting but anatomizing, and the statement is what we have called a definition by structure analysis. But suppose the word "stretcher" occurs in a sentence like this: "The trouble with those chairs is that they lack stretchers. They get rickety under constant use." Now, the relevant definition might well be "a stretcher is a member of a chair which, by rigidly connecting the side rungs, counters a lateral strain upon the front and back rail joints." It will be seen that the expression "by rigidly connecting" in this instance means something more than mere location or articulation. We are here thinking of what the stretcher *does* by being where it is. We are therefore defining it in terms of function that is dynamic, and if we were to equip our chair with devices for registering local stress, when the chair was put to use we would observe that parts of it did in fact move. Our indicators would rise to a maximum point with the first contact of the user and would then stabilize, showing the slight variations accompanying the slight shifts of the body. There would probably be a new high indication as the occupant arose, and finally a return to zero. In these successive stages of Operation Chair, the stretcher would perform its function. If we shift attention from the stretcher as a part to the stretcher as a whole, then we consider *its* constituent parts—in this case the two ends and the shaft between. To brace the rungs against thrust would be the function of the shaft, and to prevent their separation would be the function of the ends.

Thus far we have attempted to distinguish among three types of logical thinking, even though the thoughts involved in them are expressed in the same or similar language. We have insisted that it is one thing to think of membership in a group in the sense that chair is a species of the genus furniture, another thing to think of constituent parts in their proper places in structural wholes, and still another thing to think of steps or stages in operations and the moving structures that enable us to determine them.

It should perhaps be observed that a classification analysis cannot be made of a genus that contains but one species. Similarly, a structure term cannot be literally defined by structure analysis unless it stands for a complex object, and an event term cannot be defined by operation analysis if the event is instantaneous. At the present moment, for example, so far as our dictionaries are concerned, the term "electron" apparently stands for an unanalyzable object or event, and it makes no sense to say "What sorts of electrons are there?" or "What are the parts of an electron?" or "What are its stages?" But some of our physicists seem now to find reason for talking about two sorts of electrons: positrons and negatrons, or positive and negative electrons. Thus we have an interesting sense growth (probably a generalization), and we may say of electrons in the new generic sense that there are two sorts. As particles, if they are particles, they are simple—that is to say, they have no parts; but as "wavicles," if they *are* "wavicles," they would be composed of two "stagicles"; let us say, for example, from "troughicle" to "cresticle" and "cresticle" to "troughicle."

To summarize briefly, when we define symbols by classification we tell what sorts their referents belong to and/or what sorts of referents they include and how they differ from other sorts of the same sort. When we define by structure analysis we name relevant wholes or parts and tell how they fit together. When we define by operation analysis we tell what things are for and how their parts work together, stage after stage, to achieve their purposes.

In closing this chapter we would not give the impression that definition is a simple matter of choosing a method and banging away. We are in fact dealing with the most difficult and subtle operations of the mind, and the attempt to throw light upon our own thoughts by further thinking of our own may resemble the attempt to lift ourselves by our own bootstraps. Any considerable success in the definitive process will depend not only on the will to do and the practice in doing, but upon a clear understanding of the distinction here made between words and things and objects and ideas.

When we define or give meaning to a word, we are not necessarily connecting it with an experience of the nature of Gibraltar or the Empire State Building. The experience for which it stands may be that kind of experience for which words like "strength" and "height" stand. It is customary to symbolize this distinction with the words "concrete" and "abstract." The Empire State Building and Gibraltar are concrete. One of the qualities they have in common, height, is abstract. Now in actual practice, adequate definition requires a well-developed alertness to the fact that our thoughts shift endlessly back and forth between the concrete and abstract worlds of our consciousness.

We have not, for example, dealt with definitive metaphor, because it tends to create rather than clear the very confusions that definition attempts to dispose of. When we define with dead metaphor we merely define by synonym; when the metaphor is alive we are defining by implicit comparison, whereas the very business of good definition is to be explicit. We cannot leave it to the interpreter to abstract from the "scene" of the metaphor the relevant quality of relationship; it is the very thing we are most concerned to point out. Aristotle was right when he warned us to beware of metaphor, although we should have to admit, as he himself undoubtedly would, that the right metaphor at the right time might well be the best of all possible definitions.

Be this as it may, the successful use of either definition by metaphor or definition without it involves making the necessary connection between the right abstraction and the right concretion, the right concept and the right object. In the next chapter we shall therefore continue the subject by demonstrating the more elaborate and complex processes necessary to understand clearly the connection between complex thoughts and complicated objects.

STUDY QUESTIONS

1. How does appropriate definition relate both to the communication and problem-solving functions of language?

2. The author states that there are two different sorts of objects that require defining—words and things. This implies that things, too, are ambiguous. Consider the difference between defining the word *brick* and the thing *brick*.

3. The author goes on to say that we are concerned with the definition of words in this chapter. There are two different general sorts of definitions of words: definitions that connect words with other words, and definitions that connect words with the nonverbal experiences for which they stand. Classify each of the seven specific sorts of definitions given in this chapter as either (1) a definition that connects words with words, or (2) a definition that connects words with the nonverbal experiences for which they stand.

4. Give an example of an instance in which definition by synonym is inadequate, and another in which it is adequate.

5. (A) How is definition by antonym sometimes more effective than definition by synonym?   (B) Look up *opposition* in your dictionary. (C) What is a "cut"?   (D) What is the cut when we speak of left and right, above and below, hot and cold?   (E) In defining such words as *medium, middle,* and *neutral,* would you be likely to define them by antonym? Why?   (F) How are we shifting the sense of *opposite* when we say that the left glove is the opposite of the right because the left hand is the opposite of the right?

6. Why is the analysis of scalar opposition important?

7. (A) How does the "treacherously relative" process of qualification interfere with accurate definition?   (B) In the example of the two sworn witnesses, given on page 118, did they give "opposite" testimony? Were their referents "opposite"? What does *referent* mean here?   (C) Consider whether "laughing for joy as the *opposite* of crying for joy" is the same opposite in "laughing is the *opposite* of crying."   (D) In the sentence, on page 118, "Some of our verbal oppositions turn out to be so vague and conventional as to rank with out-and-out psittacisms in meaninglessness," could we use *arbitrary* as a synonym for *conventional*?   (E) What is a *psittacism*? If it isn't in your desk dictionary, and you don't have an unabridged dictionary available, how would you go about determining its meaning?

8. "In the more vital fields in which men are ready to fight and die," why is the intelligent determination of scales and cuts essential?

9. (A) There are two sorts of definitions by exemplification. Name and illustrate these.   (B) What is the difference between a *species* and a *specimen*? In a classification, which of the two would be more general? Which would be placed in a pigeonhole?

10. What is the essential difference between definition by example and definition by comparison?

11. "It's like a koala, but it's just a doll" is a definition by comparison of *Teddy bear* involving a genus-to-genus relation. "A koala resembles this Teddy bear, but it's alive" is a definition by comparison of a koala involving a specimen-to-genus relation. In view of your previously established definitions of *specimen* and *genus,* consider the differences between the two definitions by comparison.

12. The last three types of definition are related to the three sorts of analysis. Would you say, then, that they will be more logical and systematic than the preceding four? Why?

13. How are definition by exemplification and definition by comparison rudimentary forms of definition by classification?

14. In what way do the logician's definitions of *genus* and *species* differ from the biologist's?

15. (**A**) To what genus does *man* belong, and what differentiates him from all other species in that genus? (**B**) Define the following by classification definition: alfalfa, Kleenex, lipstick, talk, love, closet, fir, whole, path.

16. (**A**) Define the word *wing* by structure analysis. What is the name of the whole to which it belongs? What are the other parts to which it is connected? (**B**) Which of the following terms would you be most likely to define by structure analysis: house, fibula, past, petal, honor, roof, gear? (**C**) Define your choices, and explain why you didn't define your rejections by structure analysis. (**D**) In defining *arm* (of the body), would you define it as a whole or a part?

17. What is the difference between definition by structure analysis and definition by operation analysis?

18. Define the following terms by operation analysis: murder, clock, shooting, sail, yesterday, college.

19. Identify the following definitions by designating them as classification, structure analysis, or operation analysis: (**A**) A *bevel* is a tool used in measuring or marking angles and in fixing surfaces at an angle. (**B**) The *hand* is a structure consisting of the phalanges, which are connected to the metacarpus, which articulates with the carpus. (**C**) A *feather* is one of the light, horny, epidermal outgrowths which together make up the external covering of birds. (**D**) *Morning* is the part of the day beginning at 12 midnight and ending at 12 noon. (**E**) A *girl* is a young woman. (**F**) *Sprouting* is the point in the development of a plant when the germinating seed has pushed the blade of the plant above the surface of the ground and before the plant is fully developed. (**G**) *Crustacea* is a class of invertebrates that usually live in water and breathe through gills. (**H**) An *iris* is the round, pigmented membrane surrounding the pupil of the eye, having muscles that adjust the size of the pupil to regulate the amount of light entering the eye.

20. (**A**) What determines which sort of definition you will use in a given instance? Illustrate your answer. (**B**) Consider this situation: Three different scientists—a taxonomist, an anatomist, and a physiologist

—are faced with the problem of defining *hand* in the sentence "The hand is quicker than the eye." If they act characteristically, determine how each might define the word.

21. (A) What procedure do we follow in defining abstract terms like *strength* and *height*?   (B) How is the definition of abstract terms related to definitive metaphor?   (C) Why isn't definitive metaphor included among the seven sorts of definition?

Definitively thus I answer you.

RICHARD III

I have studied eight or nine wise words to speak with you.

MUCH ADO ABOUT NOTHING

12 THE PRACTICE
OF DEFINITION

LET US TAKE THE TERMS "subjective" and "objective" and see if we can make up our minds what we mean by them in some such statement as this: "Philosophers and artists are subjective; scientists, objective." First of all we must point out that the two terms make up a semantic pair. The one has no meaning without the other. We may define each by antonym with the other. We may define them by synonym by translating the last syllable and say that "subjective" pertains to a subject, and "objective" pertains to an object. By operation analysis we may say that subjects perceive or conceive objects in the process of knowing. The word "knowing" reminds us that we are talking about the c.n.s. and should waste no time in examining our terms for their sensory, affective, and logical components. It is easy to see from the following discussion that no particular sensory mechanism is necessarily involved and that although the sentence might be uttered with some considerable emotional content, it is used here entirely without feelings of praise or blame. The terms are primarily logical. What, then, is the basic logical relation that establishes whatever meaning they have? What goes on in the world when a poet is being subjective, and how does it differ from what goes on when a scientist is being objective?

When the poet sings "Drink to me only with thine eyes," he is responding immediately or in retrospect to an object, his beloved, outside himself; but he is fundamentally concerned with the sensations and emotions which that object stimulates in him; and whether the object justifies his praise in the opinion of others, or indeed whether there actually is such an object, is quite irrelevant to his purpose, which is the weaving of a beautiful pattern of sound and imagery into a richly affective concept of feminine loveliness. This it is to be subjective.

Now the scientist is primarily concerned with the identity and continuity of the external object that stimulates his response. Scientists characteristically have been rather unphilosophic about these objects that they observe so objectively, and philosophers have been characteristically unscientific about them. I must point out that here the word "philosopher" has shifted its sense from the one set up for it in Chapter 1; here it means that special sort of theoretical scientist who tries to make up his mind what he means by meaning—philosophers call him an epistemologist. Epistemologists Ogden and Richards in the youthful, rebellious days of *The Meaning of Meaning* seem not to have thought through this problem of the object. At least the following footnote gives that impression.

In particular, by using the same term "meaning" both for the "goings on" inside their heads (the images, associations, etc., which enabled them to interpret signs) and for the referents (the things to which the signs refer) philosophers have been forced to locate Grantchester, Influenza, Queen Anne, and indeed the whole Universe equally inside their heads— or, if alarmed by the prospect of cerebral congestion, at least "in their minds" in such wise that all these objects become conveniently "mental." Great care, therefore, is required in the use of the term "meaning," since its associations are dangerous.[1]

It need not seem absurd to locate the Eiffel Tower, or Everest, or the Grand Canyon for that matter, "in the mind" because it is so perfectly obvious that they can exist *as* the Eiffel Tower, Everest, or the

[1] *The Meaning of Meaning*, p. 22.

Grand Canyon nowhere else. Perhaps we can take a step toward clarification of this puzzling state of affairs and move a little closer to our definition of "objective" by suggesting a distinction between an object and a thing. Let us define object as the external cause of a thing. Whether objects "exist" is obviously not discussable, for the word "object" as used here must necessarily stand not for a thing but for a hypothesis. There is, for example, no way of telling whether objects are singular or plural, whether one should say the stimulus of the Eiffel Tower experience or the stimuli of the Eiffel Tower experience. If, then, it is impossible even for the scientist to escape the essential subjectivity of his sensations, generalizations, and deductions, what do we mean by calling him objective?

Perhaps the essential logical qualification that we somewhat casually call "objective" is simply a special sort of subjective behavior called corroboration. To be objective is simply to test and retest your original observations. For scientists, properly so called, do not trust senses—not even the highly discriminative senses of the trained artist. They therefore contrive to base their observations upon the operation of ingenious mechanical, electrical, and chemical devices that may be "read" by a logical process like counting and by the exercise of such low-grade sensory discriminations as those required to note the position of a black index on a white dial or the gross change in the color of litmus paper. The logical component of a scientific qualification is, therefore, very great. It is represented by the operator's understanding of the structure of his instrument (a highly logical consideration) or by his "faith" in its designer and the integrity of the mechanic who followed the design. Further "accuracy" may be sought by averaging (also a logical process) the results of several readings.

Thus, for the modern scientific mind, seeing is not believing. The scientist must deduce to be sure; and there is nothing of which he was more "certain" than that the other side of the moon was also convex before the Russians proved it so. With the scientist, we who are studying semantics reach the paradoxical position of attaining objectivity by being more and more subjective.

Does all this mean that life is an illusion, that things exist only in the mind? Yes, and no. It all depends on the senses of "thing" and "exist." We have no choice but to conclude that the world is full of a number of things that "exist" outside the mind, but they are meaningless. To have meaning, to be a "thing" in a meaningful sense, to be an object of attention, a thing must be "of a sort." It must, at least, be of the "thing" sort. But to be "of a sort" is to be "in the mind," or subjective. Thus we conclude that the word *objective* may have two senses for us: "meaninglessness," and a far more useful sense, "the subjective quality of being the logical product of corroborated experience." Thus *subjective* has an ordinal ambiguity that will bear watching, for we may say that there are two sorts of subjectivity—objective and subjective.

Our final definition of objective as characteristic of one who consciously attempts to corroborate experience is a definition by classification wherein the genus term is *characteristic of conscious experience,* and the species term is *corroborated.*

For our next demonstration we shall attempt to define the name of a sort of complex physical structure to be found in most automobiles: the name is *differential.* This particular thing is recognized at least in part by all of us, known intimately by many of us, but understood by very few, even among mechanics. We are therefore about to define the term "differential" as it appears in such sentences as "Racing cars have no differential."

In this demonstration we shall introduce a rather elaborate but effective combination of several defining processes; that is, any or all of the seven forms just reviewed that seem to be useful at the moment. Let us call this type of complex definition *definition by conceptual model.* For in it we shall construct an imaginary device that will enable us to think clearly about a whole group of actual devices—the differentials in our automobiles so far as some of their essential characteristics are concerned. We are going to get clear about a complex abstraction, the differential, by means of an imaginary concretion.

The most common way of aiding in this process is to use a diagram, and the figure in the accompanying diagram is the simplest possible picture of the relationship—the abstraction—that we have in mind (except that $p\ q$ is an unnecessary repetition of $p\ d$). You must not think that any part of your car looks like the diagram. That is why we call it a "conceptual" model. We are attempting to define the *concept* of the differential, that set of essential relations which make any particular differential what it is. Thinkers engaged in highly theoretical study sometimes find that their minds are incapable of grasping the implications that the logical manipulations of their symbols produce. Therefore they devise analogous concrete models so that they can literally see what they are thinking. Physicists and chemists, for example, assert that their conceptual models of various molecules have played a vital part in the progress of modern science and industry.

We begin with a working definition designed for the person who doesn't know what we are talking about. It is a very simple definition by classification: the differential is the device inside the fat part of the rear-axle housing of your car that enables it to round a corner without grinding the inside tire on the pavement.

From the point of view of structure analysis we have here the relation of three revolving wheels or gears *l, m,* and *r.* They may turn on the same axis and are so connected that their relationship is expressed by the algebraic statement $m = \frac{1}{2}(l + r)$ where *m* represents the revolutions of the middle gear and $l + r$ the revolutions of the left and right rear wheels or the gears rigidly connected with them. We say this in the hope that you not only do not understand the mystery of the rear end of your car, but that you are in a state of perplexed but painless confusion brought on by the emotional component of the terms *gear, algebraic,* and $m = \frac{1}{2}(l + r)$. This is because we also wish to demonstrate that our habitual fear of technical language is unnecessary and sometimes easily overcome.

One of the most unfortunate (not to say dangerous) results of our inadequate educational technique is the number of us who are frightened by mathematics and "English." One reason for this is that learners are often required, or at least permitted, to learn symbols without learning the meanings of the symbols. We do not mean to imply that mathematics and "English" need not be "hard" subjects, but rather that the hardness need not produce fear and frustration.

The device inside the housing between the rear wheels of your car does not look like the sketch, but it works on the same principle. Cones *l* and *r* behave like the left and right rear wheels. In your car

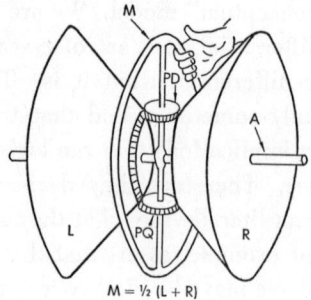

$$M = \tfrac{1}{2}\,(L + R)$$

m is a gear driven by the shaft from the motor. Thus, *l*, *m*, and *r* are free to turn on *a* (for axle). *Pd* and *pq* are free to turn on *m*; they are called pinions. If you can add and subtract, and if you have some patience, you can see how they work. Here are the "laws" of the differential:

(1) When *m* turns once, *l* and *r* do the same and in the same direction. *Pd* and *pq* turn with *m* but not on it. They drag *l* and *r* around together: hence we get $1 = \tfrac{1}{2}\,(1 + 1)$.

(2) When *l* is still and *m* turns once, *pd* and *pq* chase one another around the teeth of *l* one trip. Since they are in mesh with *r*, they force *r* to make one extra turn in addition to the one it gets from *m*: $1 = \tfrac{1}{2}\,(0 + 2)$.

(3) When *m* is still and *l* makes one turn, *pd* and *pq* turn *r* one turn in the opposite direction: $0 = \tfrac{1}{2}\,(1 - 1)$.

You must study this arrangement until it is quite clear to you that whenever the behavior of one cone (wheel) *differs* from that of *m* (transmission gear) the pinions make an exact complementary adjustment in the behavior of the other cone (wheel). Hence the name *differential*.

We have now acquired a model with which to embody the complex concept of the differential and since it is a structure in action we must use the terminology of operation analysis. The whole system is composed of the following parts: axle, wheels, differential gears, transmission gear, and pinions. Remember that it is a whole system made up of parts that change in relation to one another. The definitive property of a part in this system is that it is free to rotate upon or within one of the other parts and is indispensable to the purpose of the whole. The purpose in this instance is the progressive adjustment of the speeds of the differential gears, in relation to the transmission gear. It is instructive to note that one of the pinions is not necessary to the operation of the whole. Therefore, in this particular whole the two pinions constitute but one part. Now, if the sense of *purpose* is shifted to "strength and reduction of vibration," the function of the two pinions becomes the distribution of stress through balance. Each pinion is then a part.

The most important fact to note in connection with the study of definition is that an adequate definition of a whole or system as here understood requires the statement of its purpose and of the function of each part. An adequate definition of a part requires a statement of its relation to each of the other parts and to the purpose of the whole. Insofar as you have succeeded in relating the words on these pages to the diagram and the algebraic equation, you will be able to grasp the following definition by classification: a differential (species term) is a mechanical device (genus term) in which three revolving gears are so connected that the average rate of revolution of two of them is always equal to the rate of the third (differentia).

Our third and last demonstration may be called a multiple definition, or perhaps better still, a lexicographer's definition. For it is the dictionary-maker's business to give us as many established senses of a word as the scope of his dictionary permits. But let us hasten to add that the utility of the lexicographer's definition is not limited to the making of dictionaries. For in respect to some words—the most important ones—whether we are using them for communication, reflection, or emotional adjustment in some particular context with some particular sense, it is highly profitable to consider the other senses in which they may be used in other contexts. The process of multiple definition tends to increase the likelihood of adequate communication, to clarify the act of reason, and to enrich the content of the poetic moment.

We think for example that if you have never given careful thought to the term *balance*, which is the subject of our final definitive exercise and which we regard as the most important concept in the vocabulary of a civilized being, that you may be able to realize to some considerable degree this threefold profit.

To begin with, "balance" is the name of the basic mechanical instrument of civilized intercourse and scientific progress. Indeed, civilized man has selected this instrument as the symbol of his noblest social virtue, justice. It might just as fittingly serve as the symbol of science, for it represents the fundamental scientific process of nice comparison, measurement, and quantification. Commerce, justice, science, and, as we shall demonstrate, art, all find their most fundamental representation in the simple but infinitely suggestive mechanism of the balance. Let us survey the sensory applications of the term as the first step in a component analysis.

SIGHT. (1) The balance itself yields the concept of visual symmetry. (2) The rod response in the eye yields the concept of chiaroscuro, the balance of light and shade. (3) The cone response in the eye yields color balance, small bodies of strong color with larger bodies of weaker color, etc. (assuming that the cones are color response organs). (4) "Design" is the product of (1), (2), and (3) above, as expressed in balanced patterns of color, line, and mass.

POISE. Equilibratory and kinesthetic (muscle sense) balance frequently symbolize those complex responses deriving from the end organs of the inner ear and the muscles, joints, and tendons. We not only "feel" in or out of balance, but respond sympathetically when we see objects that appear so. As a critical term, it would figure prominently in an analysis of the delight we take in riding, dancing, juggling, and certain forms of acrobatics.

SOUND. By metaphor, balance becomes a useful term for the consideration of music, drama, and rhetoric. Harmony, counterpoint, and the play of instrument against instrument, choir against choir, in symphonic composition may all be referred to as forms of auditory balance.

TASTE and SMELL. Again by metaphor, balance is the term by which is symbolized the aesthetic or medicinal adjustment of complex gustatory and olfactory responses. Words like "flavor" and "bouquet" may sometimes be defined in terms of the balance of sweet and sour, bitter and sweet, etc.

PAIN. In the application of a so-called counterirritant, we even may speak of a balance of pains.

In the field of affective behavior, "balance" has long been a basic term. We use it not only as a synonym for emotional stability in the individual, but also in the analysis of complex art forms. We speak, for example, of the balance of mood in Shakespeare's skillful adjustment of moments of tragedy, humor, pathos, wit, or grotesquerie. One might well define the basis of Aristotle's idea of "catharsis" as the balance of pity and terror, and the cathartic process itself as the balance of aesthetic delight against the pity and the terror.

"Balance" is, of course, primarily a logical term. A glance at the extensive dictionary entry will display its wide use in physics, mechanics (our differential, for example), chemistry, biology, dietetics, accounting, and so on. The algebraic equation may be described as the mathematical expression of a logical system in balance—a balance that could have no better concrete representation than the device that was once called *libra bilanx*, a scale with two pans.

"Art," said Robert Henri, "tends toward balance, order, judgment of relative values, the laws of growth, the economy of being—very good things for anyone to be interested in."[2] Here are Claude Flight and Edith Lawrence struggling with the same thoughts in Basic English:

And, in addition, your natural impulses, which you get from your father, and your father's father, make you have tendencies in certain directions which give a twist to your outlook.

In fact, you may take it that in every-day living you are only half awake. Now do not get angry; men of learning have made it clear that this is so.

But an artist is different. He would not be an artist if his feeling were not free, and if he had not a very open mind. In seeing and experiencing, his mind and his feelings are not chained to certain special interests, and he is able by the power of his art to make his experience clear. He does this in the ways you have been reading about, with the help of "formal order" and in a special degree by putting the mind in a condition of balance. So you are able to get great value from his art, because it makes clear to you things you had not been able to see before. You have the experience of being free, of being truly awake, for a time at any rate, and you get the sudden sense of the beautiful which only comes when your feelings are in complete balance—an effect which only the greatest art is able to give.[3]

[2] *The Art Spirit*, p. 5.
[3] *A Little About Art*, p. 63.

In comment, we need only to point out that "balance" in these passages symbolizes a rich and dynamic synthesis of the full range of the sensory, affective, and logical uses of the word. Indeed, one may go as far as to say that Henri's terms "order," "judgment of relative values," "the laws of growth," and "the economy of being," are but progressively complex and inclusive applications of the principle of balance, that same principle of controlled self-realization that I. A. Richards has called "psycho-politics," the government of the soul.

The demonstrations in this chapter have been intended to balance the deceptive simplicity of the view of definition presented in the previous chapter. A brief statement in one of the seven forms there outlined is not always adequate if one really means business. A precise understanding of a term like "parts" as used in connection with the differential may require patience and perseverance on the part of both utterer and interpreter. On the other hand, a term like "balance" in the Henri quotation cannot be defined with precision. Its dynamic implications must grow within the mind, and the definer can do no more than plant the seeds of thought and encourage their development. To share with Henri the meaning of "the economy of being" is to share with Herrick the meaning of "the knowledge of good and evil" (cf. p. 19).

Hence we come to recognize the utter inadequacy of dictionaries. But they are indispensable, nevertheless, to the user of an overextended vocabulary like English, and we must now move on to a consideration of their virtues and their limitations.

Let us repeat; a good dictionary is essential to civilized living in English. Its habitual use increases the scope of one's intelligence; promotes communication with one's fellows; and fosters a wholesome sort of humility—one finds himself so frequently either ignorant or mistaken. There are several excellent portable dictionaries. We recommend the *American College*, the *Merriam-Webster Collegiate*, the *Funk and Wagnalls College Standard*, the *Winston Encyclopedic*, and the *Webster's New World Dictionary*, which, by the way, contains Ogden's *Basic English* word list.

A "handy" dictionary is by no means entirely adequate, however. One must have easy access to an "unabridged," preferably

Merriam-Webster's New International; and one should make an occasional pilgrimage to *Murray's New English Dictionary* (the unabridged *Oxford*) just to maintain contact with the world's greatest.

It is in the investigation of these so-called "unabridged" dictionaries that one discovers the skeleton in the lexicographer's closet. Comparison of the entries under the noun "pass" in the *Oxford*, the *International*, and the *Standard* discloses the following somewhat disconcerting information: about fifteen senses that are clearly or possibly the same in all three dictionaries; about fifteen more senses given by the *Oxford* and *Webster's*; three given only by the *Standard* and the *Oxford*; two given only by the *Webster's* and the *Standard*; eight in the *Oxford* alone; and four in the *Standard* alone (if nos. 7 and 17 are really separate senses). Hence, there are at least fifty-three recorded senses, of which the *Oxford* cites forty-two, *Webster's* thirty-eight, and *Standard* twenty-four. The noun *pass* was chosen at random, but similar words would yield similar results. All of which suggests that lexicography is a very difficult science and that lexicographers are human.

And now by way of closing our discussion of definitions and definition makers, we pray you, we do beseech you, to *read carefully the critical apparatus in the front and back of the dictionaries you are accustomed to use!* Most people who have dictionaries do not know how to use them. Yet an hour or two of amusing inspection will increase forever after the daily dividends from one's investment in a dictionary. For a dictionary *is* a stock certificate in the gigantic enterprise of human communication.

STUDY QUESTIONS

1. What is the difference between *theory* and *practice* as illustrated in Chapter 11, "The *Theory* of Definition," and Chapter 12, "The *Practice* of Definition"?

2. (**A**) Why does the author talk of *subjective* and *objective*? (**B**) The author says that *subjective* and *objective* make up a semantic pair. Would *hustle* and *bustle*? Define "pair" as used here. (**C**) Are subjective and objective *opposites* in the sense that blonde is the *opposite* of brunette? In the sense that left is the *opposite* of right? In the sense that outside is the *opposite* of inside?

3. After applying several forms of definition, the author considers *subjective* and *objective* through their sensory, affective, and logical aspects. They are both primarily logical. What basic logical relation allows both terms to be placed in that category?

4. What goes on in the world when a poet is being subjective, and how does it differ from what goes on when a scientist is being objective?

5. How has *philosopher,* on page 130, changed in meaning from the definition set up in Chapter 2?

6. What is an *epistemologist*?

7. How didn't Ogden and Richards think through the problem of the object?

8. (**A**) Considering the definition of *objective* more thoroughly, the author makes a distinction between an *object* and a *thing*. What is this distinction?   (**B**) Explain the statement on page 131, "Whether objects 'exist' or not is obviously not discussable, for the word 'object' as here used must necessarily stand not for a thing but for a hypothesis."

9. How is "objective" a special sort of subjective behavior?

10. What is corroboration?

11. (**A**) The author states that the logical component of a scientific qualification is "represented by the operator's understanding of the structure of his instrument or by his 'faith' in its designer and the integrity of the mechanic who followed the design." Why is *faith* in quotes?   (**B**) Since the semanticist is a scientist, what is his "instrument"?   Who *designed* it?

12. (**A**) What does *deduce* mean in "The scientist must deduce to be sure; and there is nothing of which he is more 'certain' than that the other side of the moon is also convex"?   (**B**) Is *deduce* one of a semantic pair? If so, what is the other member of the pair?   (**C**) How do these terms relate to *subjective* and *objective*?

13. (**A**) Explain the statement "With the scientist, we who are studying semantics reach the paradoxical position of attaining objectivity by being more and more subjective."   (**B**) What does *paradoxical* mean here?

14. (**A**) In the sentence "Thus, *subjective* has an ordinal ambiguity that will bear watching," what does *ordinal* mean?   (**B**) How would an *ordinal* number differ from a *cardinal* number?   (**C**) How are ordinal numbers more *complex* than cardinal numbers?   (**D**) In applying these concepts to classification, let the cardinal numbers designate the same order of the species (vertical factors) at any level. Let the ordinal numbers designate the order of the horizontal factors at the different levels.

In the following classifications, indicate whether *animal* has ordinal or cardinal ambiguity:

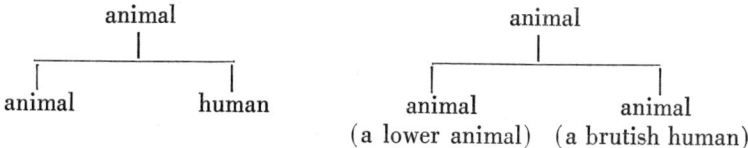

(E) Would *sign* and *logical* as used in this book have ordinal or cardinal ambiguity? (F) With these definitions in mind, explain the statement given in 14 (A) above.

15. (A) Define *definition by conceptual model.* (B) Should definition by conceptual model be added to the list of seven definitions in Chapter 11? Why? (C) What does definition by conceptual model have to do with definitive metaphor as discussed on page 125?

16. (A) What do we mean when we state that the diagram on page 134 is a picture of an "abstraction"? (B) How is the diagram a *concept* of the differential?

17. The differential is a mechanical system of five functional parts so arranged that their relation to one another may be expressed by the equation $m = \frac{1}{2}(l + r)$. (A) Name the five parts. (B) Using the five names, describe a differential symbolized by the equation $m - l = -m + r$. (C) Which of the following three statements is the best description of a differential? (1) Three gears rotating on the same axle so connected by a pinion rotating on the middle one that whenever its speed is caused to exceed one of the other two, the other will correspondingly increase. (2) Two gears so related to a third on the same axle that a decrease in the r.p.m. of one with reference to the third will be added to the r.p.m. of the other with reference to the third. (3) Two gears so related to a third that when one is turning clockwise the other is turning counterclockwise.

(D) What should be added to make the best description completely explicit? (E) Is this the same differential as in (A)? (F) In *arithmetical* terms, what is the function of the pinion gear? (G) What sign in the equation $m - l = -m + r$ corresponds to the function of the axle?

18. How is the name *differential* an apt one to describe the behavior of the device inside the fat part of the rear-axle housing of your car?

19. Reviewing our definitions of the terms *system, purpose, function, whole,* and *part* established in Chapter 2, apply each to the concept of the differential.

20. How does each pinion become a part when the purpose of the differential is shifted to "strength and reduction of vibration"?

21. Adequate definition of a whole or system requires what explanation?

22. The third demonstration of definition utilizes multiple definition. Describe this process, and discuss its value as applied to the functions of language.

23. (**A**) How did the consideration of *balance* by component analysis lead toward your greater appreciation of that term as used in Henri's statement "Art tends toward balance, order, judgment of relative values, the laws of growth, the economy of being—very good things for anyone to be interested in." (**B**) Is the term *balance* affective or logical, as used in the above quotation?

24. The author has demonstrated the practice of definition by three illustrations. (**A**) In reviewing, describe the methods used in each. (**B**) What will determine which method will be employed in any given instance?

25. Describe the faults and assets of dictionaries.

26. Look in your desk dictionary and determine where the following information would be found: (**A**) Key to pronunciation. (**B**) Under the entry for "deduce," you see "*Cf.* induce." Where will you find what the symbol *cf.* means? (**c**) Some dictionaries present the earliest meaning of a word first; some present the most commonly used meaning first. Which procedure is employed in your dictionary? (**D**) Does your dictionary give you any rules for spelling? (**E**) You have run across the name *Thomas Cranmer* in your reading. Where do you find information concerning him in your dictionary? (**F**) A friend of yours is going to Cornell College and you wish to write to her. How will your dictionary give you this information? (**G**) In the light of information presented in this course, would you prefer the etymology of a word to be listed first or last? Why?

27. Diagram the metaphor on page 139, "A dictionary is a stock certificate in the gigantic enterprise of human communication."

In the quick forge and working-house of thought . . .

HENRY V

13 SYMBOLIC INSTRUMENTS

WE NOW EMBARK on the second leg of our semantic voyage, the consideration of language as an instrument of reflection; that is to say, of reason or problem-solving. It should be apparent, however, that the processes of communication and reflection are not mutually exclusive. When we reason over considerable periods of time about complex problems involving numerous units of thought, our first requisite is some system of notation that will enable us to record our progress. The artificial systems we call "mathematics" and "musical notation" make possible a metropolitan telephone exchange or a Fifth Symphony. For most of us, however, the process of recording depends chiefly upon the more or less systematic use of natural language symbols by means of which from moment to moment and year to year we communicate with our developing selves. It would be very difficult, for example, to compose a chapter like this without reading it over and over as it grows.

But communication, however necessary, is only incidental to the linguistic operations we now propose to study. Our present object is to get clear about what goes on in our heads when we make up our minds. What language tools do we use, and how do we use them? Can we identify and describe a minimum essential set of reflective operations the understanding of which will help us solve more efficiently the problems we now solve, or even enable us to solve problems now beyond our skill?

The answer, of course, is that we *can* set forth "the basic rules of reason," and that we *can* make a marked improvement, both in scope and efficiency, in the thinking of any person who has heretofore depended upon the intuitive and irregular procedures characteristic of human thought outside the exact sciences. We have already suggested that the necessary first step in the reflective process is definition, or what the engineer calls "setting up the problem." We must therefore explain what we mean by reflection or the problem-solving process. What do we mean here by the word *problem*?

For us a problem—the thing, not the word—is a state of mind characterized by the momentary awareness of a need to know something that is not then in the consciousness. It is an instant of uncertainty concerning what is to happen next if the event is to be one of our own choosing.

There are two sorts of problems: the kind that, for all practical purposes, are solved when clearly formulated, and the kind that we call puzzles. As we use the term, a puzzle is a problem the statement of which confronts the mind with two or more avenues of solution. We may say in conclusion, then, that reflection is the process of consciously meeting an experienced need by the exercise of applicable linguistic operations, the first of which is definition.

Now we have already answered the question "What sorts of definitions are there?" in two different ways. We have suggested a sevenfold sorting of definitive forms and the fundamental desirability of component analysis, but we have not put the question "What sorts of word tools are used in defining?" Indeed, we find ourselves in the middle of the study of how words work without having asked or answered the question "What sorts of words are there as determined by the sorts of work they do?"

For hundreds of years grammarians have been telling us there are eight sorts of words, but that bit of information has contributed very little to the clarity of our thought. This is partly because so many words occur in our natural language simply out of custom and not because they are necessary to the thinking process in which they are employed. What we here require is a classification of language symbols not according to the way they are used in the sentence but according to the sort of thought they represent. "Gold standard" and "standard of gold" are different grammatically, although their semantic function may be the same. But the function of "gold" and the function of "standard" are vastly different. Gold as gold may be said to exist only in the mind insofar as it is something that is yellow, heavy, and precious. We feel, nevertheless, very certain about the "existence" of some external stimulus with which the conscious event originates. "Standard," on the other hand, stands for something going on in our heads that may be connected with concrete external realities only after due consideration, and we might add (somewhat paradoxically) that although gold is an exceedingly durable substance, from our point of view, it is decidedly not one of "the eternal verities," whatever *they* are.

Let us attempt a classification of symbols that aid all kinds of semantic navigation, whether our thoughts are moving upon the face of the good earth or zooming into the stratosphere of the imagination. Let us sort symbols according to the apparent relation between the thought they symbolize and the demonstrable contacts with "external reality" which have in part determined those thoughts. *Demonstrable contact with reality* is, of course, simply a synonym for what we have called elsewhere the process of corroboration. We have excellent precedent for founding our present enterprise upon a rock.

We must ask you to select your own rock—one that you can see, touch, heft, and name. Now watch us and do as we do, think as we think. We see one rock; it is an egg-shaped boulder from a river bed, smooth and hard; it seems to weigh about a pound. We shall name it "Pete," with a capital P. Now, the symbol *Pete* symbolizes our thought of this particular egg-shaped, smooth, hard, sixteen-ounce boulder. We give it a proper name because it is the very own name of that boulder and only that boulder. It does not stand for anything that that boulder has in common with anything else, but only for the respect in which that boulder differs from everything else; that is, the respect of being its peculiar, particular, especial self.

Now remember that the boulder can be its peculiar, particular, especial self only in respect to its being *so* egg-shaped, *so* smooth, *so* hard, *so* heavy only in our c.n.s. Its egg-shapedness derives from our experience with eggs—peacock eggs, as a matter of fact—a little matter you wouldn't understand if you don't know your peacock eggs, or rather *our* peacock eggs, which, of course, you can never know. (Indeed, some question the existence of *peacock* eggs.)

We are trying to express the idea that a proper name is the name of a very, very special sort; but with a little careful thought you will see that it *is* the name of a sort and not a thing; for if Pete can exist as Pete only in the c.n.s., the symbol "Pete" must stand for a class of Petrine events in experience. It is for this reason that the most proper of proper names is in fact a generalization and may be defined as the name of a group of interpretations assumed to be caused in part by the same external stimulus.

Operationally, a proper name may also be viewed as the name of an undefined operation, and/or the structures that perform it as identified by the utterer during one or more of its stages. That is, the name "Pete" stands not for the class of all Pete experiences but for the total Pete operation, Pete being Pete in time and space as connected with any or all specific Pete experiences.

Now when we call your attention to Pete, introducing him, as it were, and the symbol *Pete* becomes an instrument of communication as well as of reference, the symbol takes on a subtly new and different significance. For we will find ourselves using it again and again, as if it stood for the same thing as distinct from the same hypothetical stimulus. That is, when we use Pete to refer to *our* reification (*reification* means thing-making) it has the shape, texture, and weight with which *we* endow it. Your reification may differ materially if one or the other of us is color-blind, or has no fondness for peacock eggs, or is paralyzed so as to be unable to estimate by sensory means the heft of the boulder.

Now if we operate with the word in full consciousness of these things, knowing that your Pete is not our Pete when we use that word to refer to Pete, it is performing a different function from the proper name as we have just defined it, for we must assume that at least some of our responses must be adequately similar, that Pete affects us in some respects in the same way. We might distinguish the two by calling the one a private proper name and the other a public one.

We would therefore define a public symbol as one referring to a public object, and then define a public object as the sum of the responses to an external stimulus that appear to be common to two or more interpreters. In this sense Tom might be said to use a public name because he assumed that Dick and Harry had enjoyed common responses to the stimulus for which it stood. To us, for example, the Rock of Gibraltar is a public name whose meaning for us is based entirely upon hearsay and projection (photographic representation). The writer remembers having enjoyed a conversation at a supper party while seated next to an engineer. A relative had recently returned from Mexico City with a most interesting account of the National Theatre. We had been enthusiastically informing the engineer about the great multiple stage and its magnificent glass curtain. There was an amused look in his eye from time to time, which made sense when he finally remarked, "Yes, I know; I built it." There was no embarrassment because there had been no pretended firsthand knowledge, but since becoming professionally concerned with the psychology of language, the writer has often thought how much more his words must have meant to the engineer than they did to himself. For the engineer the proper name, National Theatre of Mexico, was both a private and a public symbol. For the writer it was entirely public. Few of us indeed ever become appropriately cautious with the numerous public symbols for which we possess no private counterpart.

Our first type of symbol, then, sorting from the point of view of semantic function, is the type of proper name that we use both at first and second hand. Of course, we do not use the term in the loose sense of "capitalized noun" but in the sense for which most of us would use the expression "given name." We do not usually regard proper names as generalizations, but we hope you will realize that in fact they become so a split second after their creation.

Our second type is the recognized generalization. We may define *generalization* as the name of what two or more things, real or imagined, have in common. Just as we distinguish between private and public or first- and second-hand proper names, so we may distinguish between real and imaginary generalizations. Thus the symbol *bivalve oyster* is a real generalization. The symbol *tree-climbing oyster* is an imaginary generalization—it is an imagined genus with no actual species. If, however, we compose a fairy tale about the three little oysters that climbed a tree, then it would be an imaginary species with three imaginary specimens, and the implication of the imagined situation might involve innumerable imaginary tree-climbing ancestors. But if someone were to ask, "Do tree-climbing oysters have spurs?" we could not answer the question by examining one. We should have to invent the new imagined genus *oyster spurs*.

Real generalizations are inductions. That is to say, the terms *induce* and *generalize* are synonyms, for an induction is a statement of the common characteristics of a group of objects or events recognized upon examination.

This suggests our third type of symbol, the deduction. A deduction is simply the reverse of an induction, the reverse of the genus-species relation. Its explicit formulation is called *Aristotle's dictum*, which simply states that a species has the qualities of its genus. The symbol *the other side of the moon is round* used to be a deduction; in fact it still is if you stop to think it over. The complete explicit formulation of a deduction is called a syllogism. In this case the relevant syllogism might be this: "Objects that appear to be round and appear to belong to a class of objects known to be round are round; the moon appears to be round and apparently belongs to such a class (revolving celestial bodies); therefore the moon is round." A little thought will convince you that in order to be sure that a given species belongs in a given genus, you must know *all* the qualities of the genus and must have examined the species for all qualities of the genus.

We seem to discover new knowledge by the syllogistic process when we say, for example, "All men are mortal; Socrates is a man; therefore Socrates is mortal." But the fact is that if all men are mortal we cannot tell whether Socrates is a man until we have determined his mortality—in other words, until we find him dead.

It is, of course, a great convenience to assume that Socrates is a man because he looks like one, but this is just a deduction. Let us go back and examine it. Its formulation would be: "Objects that resemble men in most respects are men; Socrates resembles men in most respects; therefore Socrates is a man." Now, it is obvious that if he is a man he resembles men in *all* necessary respects. So it is obvious that we are right back where we started. We must know all the characteristics of men, and that Socrates has all of them, before

we can be sure. Hence it becomes clear that in deductive thinking
we are simply reminding ourselves of the implications of our generalizations. Formal logic, so-called, is simply a set of exercises that
leads the mind to an understanding of such concepts as *all, some,* and
none. A deduction may therefore be defined as a term that symbolizes an implication. And unless you have followed us very successfully, it is difficult to see how we have achieved much more than
another definition by synonym. *Implication* is a synonym for *deduction* in such a sentence as "The conclusion of a syllogism is an
implication of the premises." One of the senses of deduction is "the
conclusion of a syllogism."

Incidentally, the word *premise* suggests our next step. Thus far
we have mentioned three types of symbol as classified according to
semantic function. Each type included two subtypes when classified
according to the cause or the immediacy of the utterer's experience:
first- and second-hand proper names, original and borrowed generalizations or inductions, and finally conclusions based upon premises
that have been privately corroborated or conclusions based upon
borrowed premises.

Now a deduction, implication, or conclusion is not necessarily
derived from such premises, and a question concerning the nature
of premises is therefore in order. In the syllogism "All centaurs have
hoofs; Chiron is a centaur; therefore Chiron has hoofs" the conclusion is quite valid even though untrue in actuality. That is, centaurs are nonexistent and hence one named Chiron could not have
hoofs. A relevant question is, therefore, what sorts of premises are
there besides those in which real proper names and generalizations
are employed? What sorts of thoughts do we have that are not
directly traceable to corroborated sensory experience or indirectly
traceable by way of public generalizations or proper names to the
private experiences of others?

What about the word "standard" in the expression "gold standard," for example? Here we are not using a word to symbolize a
thing, a group of things, a thing or one of its parts, or a thing in
operation or in one of its stages, but are rather symbolizing the relationship between two or more things. When relation words take
the form of prepositions, conjunctions, relative pronouns, and con-

junctive adverbs they are sometimes called *symbolics*, but we wish
to emphasize the fact that the meaning of words like *above*, *beyond*,
over, *into*, and *of* is unchanged by altering their grammatical function. We may say that this letter is for you, this is your letter, you
are its owner, the ownership is yours. It is the concept of that ownership to which the symbol refers.

If you will think about it carefully you will see that relation words,
whatever their grammatical form, symbolize the relations of genus
to species, part to whole, part to part, whole to whole, whole to part,
stage to operation, structure to operation, etc., or generalizations of
these relation concepts. That is, we may use a relation word in particular, as in the ownership of this or that hat, or to symbolize the
general ownership of hats in general.

Now since language gives us this most convenient ability to
distinguish between the owner and the things owned, and even to
symbolize the relation between them in order to analyze our natural
experience, it becomes possible through the artificial reversal of this
process to put things together with words that have never been found
together in natural experience. With the generalization *horse* and the
generalization *man* and the relation term *half* we may synthesize the
concept *half-man–half-horse* and arrive at the concept of a monster
without having visualized its physical appearance. Semantically, the
"notions" Chiron, Alexander, and Bucephalus are very much alike,
and for most of us one is as "real" as the others because we learned
about them all solely from books and pictures; but they differ radically from concepts arrived at by the experimental combination of
language symbols as such. This is because presumably the thing and
its name were presented to us more or less simultaneously—the one
as the proper name of the other.

But when we start with a name already possessing some more or
less definite sense, apply it somewhat arbitrarily to some thing or
experience, and then seek some reasonable ground for applying the
name to such an experience, new insights may occur, novel ideas
may be born which may be of vital significance to our well-being.
Perhaps the best term for the sort of operation we have in mind is
assumption. When we make an assumption we use a symbol that has
a reference—that is to say, a corresponding thought—but no referent, no percept to which the thought refers.

Keeping in mind that we are sorting our symbols according to their relation to the so-called real world, we may determine three sorts of assumption. There are the symbols known to be false because they do not have the usual referent but are found to be expedient. Then there is the symbol that is unverifiable in respect to a referent although one might conceivably exist. And finally there is the symbol for which the referent is assumed for the very purpose of verification. In illustrating the different types of assumption we are advancing into a semantic mine field and must move with extreme care. It is dangerous to meddle with the other fellow's assumptions or even to suggest that they *are* assumptions.

If we refer to the legal fiction of regarding a corporation as if it were a person as an example of the first type, no one will be outraged, for we all know that corporations are not persons. But when we speak of human rights as if they were forces that can be identified very much as we might identify magnetism by means of iron filings, many of us resent the challenge to perform the identification. And when the connection between reference and referent of such a symbol as *Jehovah* or *Jesus* is questioned, we are outraged if we are Jews or Christians. Now it is not our intention, nor would it be to our purpose, to question the proposition that there is no god but God, or even the proposition that Mohammed is His prophet. The object here is simply to note that the word *God* and the word *prophet* are different sorts of words from the word *Mohammed*, and that the descriptions of the relations between the symbols and their referents will differ, although all three descriptions will involve assumptions.

The connection between the symbol *Mohammed* and an external public object is a so-called "matter of history," and whatever doubt or certainty we may enjoy concerning it we express in terms of "the relative historicity" of Mohammedan biography. Now if the symbol *prophet* refers to the professed capacity of Mohammed to reveal the will of Allah, then we are not dealing with the connection between a symbol and a public object, and our interpretation involves the presence or absence of an emotional component for which we customarily use the term *belief*. There may or may not have been direct communication between the One named Allah and his Prophet, but the believer assumes that there was.

Now when we move on to Mohammed's assertion that there is

no god but God, a connection between the symbol God and a public object is not only implied; identification of the object involves the repudiation of a vast class of allegedly similar connections. The acceptance of the Allah assumption automatically involves the rejection of the Mumbo Jumbo assumption and all the other gods of the Congo. We might well call this semantic operation the Great Assumption, forming as it does the major premise of the great religions.

Semantically, there seems to be no analytic method by which the authenticity of divine names may be established. They must be matters of belief or direct personal revelation. If matters of belief they are clearly assumptions as here defined, and if matters of direct personal revelation they are subject to the same semantic discipline as other public objects. For illustration, when the night watch, including the skeptical Horatio, all testify to the true avouching of their own eyes, the ghost of King Hamlet becomes a public object for the three of them. When Hamlet sees him while Queen Gertrude, gazing into emptiness, assures her son that she sees all there is to see, King Hamlet is a private revelation.

Now we are fully aware that this attempt to define assumption brings us face to face with the phantom of extrasensory perception. We know that persons of high intelligence allege the demonstrated actuality of foreknowledge, clairvoyance, and telepathy. It is clear that for those for whom they are realities, the theory of meaning that we here expound is about as adequate as a two-legged horse. We must frankly confess a vigorous skepticism about extrasensory perception. Such skepticism to the contrary notwithstanding, we leave the theories of it to Dr. Rhine and Mr. Huxley and their followers, and we hasten to add that we are not in the least troubled by any inability to justify scientifically the Christian faith by which we live. The point we would like to make is that it is in the interests of international, interracial, and interdenominational amity and is the very basis of personal probity for us to learn to recognize our assumptions as assumptions and for the kind of assumptions they are. We need render unto science the things only that belong to science; and it is the function of assumption in scientific thought that is our next concern.

In science, as elsewhere, we meet the assumptions of convenience and expedience, such as equations that assume frictionless machines or chemicals in a pure state. But by far the most important function of language in the development of scientific understanding and control of the world about us is the use of a kind of assumption called *hypothesis* at first, *theory* in a more developed state, and *law* when its implications have been extensively corroborated. A hypothesis resembles other assumptions we have discussed in that it may be either true or false and may be used as the premise of rational action; otherwise it differs radically as to function and purpose. Hypotheses are employed experimentally in the search for truth. Without them the so-called scientific method is not possible. The reason for this is not always readily grasped and will now be illustrated in some detail.

Suppose, for example, that you are about to prepare an account of some fairly complex subject, such as the history of marriage. As soon as you have arrived at a clear working definition of your topic, you begin the collection of data. Now a *datum* is an item of some sort regarded as relevant to your problem. But everything is in some way related to everything else, and since you cannot possibly consider all the facts related to marriage, you must limit the field of relevance in some practical, arbitrary manner. Let us assume that you are at work on the status of marriage in modern urban society; perhaps you may attempt to discover to what extent the institution persists because it is biologically useful, economically expedient, socially convenient, religiously compulsory, or merely psychologically traditional. To proceed thus is to set up a fivefold hypothesis that enables you to gather from the innumerable items cast up by the sea of experience upon the shores of your observation only the limited number of relevant data—relevant, that is, to one or more of the five factors of your hypothesis. The hypothesis (the reference of the symbol *hypothesis*) is like a light by means of which we search for truth; but it is a colored light that may render invisible the very object we seek. That is why, after a fair trial, we must not hesitate to abandon one color for another. When our hypothesis possesses the proper color and intensity, it will reveal some of the facts as data, which may then be further studied and verified as signs of truth.

As the evidence in favor of a hypothesis (the thing again, not the word) accumulates to a convincing degree, we frequently symbolize the fact with the term *theory*. Thus, semantically, a theory is the name of a hypothesis that has outgrown its experimental short pants. With Charles Darwin, *biological evolution* was a hypothesis; in contemporary science it is a theory that no rational observer, however cautious, hesitates to accept.

When predictions based on the implications of a theory are continually borne out by observation, the relation symbolized is still further elevated to the status of a *law* or *natural law*. The abstraction "law" is a dangerous one to employ because it implies that the mind has finally arrived at the truth, ultimate and eternal. Thus, the eyes of science become myopic and lose the power to discover old errors and discern new truths.

"'What is truth?' said jesting Pilate and would not stay for an answer." "It's just what I can't seem to find out about Santa Claus," said the little boy. Fortunately, we need share neither the skepticism of the one nor the perplexity of the other. For us *truth* is a symbol, and our problem can never be greater or less than the process of finding out what, in any given utterance, we are doing with it. In the present discussion, *truth* has the sense of *a logical qualification that cannot conceivably be refuted at the moment because it appears as an implication of some permanent relation in the universe independent of the qualifier.* By "permanent relation" is meant one that *must* obtain whenever a given set of factors is present. Truth in this sense can *exist* (that is, be predictable) only in a symbolic universe of our own making, for only in our own self-constructed universe can we be conscious of all the factors. Thus, we may construct the artificial universe of the right triangle and discover (deduce) that the square of the hypotenuse is equal to the squares of the other sides. If we allege a qualification as true of a universe not of our own construction, truth (that is, the term *truth*) can only function as a hypothesis.

This fact is a corollary of what we learned about a part functioning in a system. We found that a part can be adequately defined only in relation to all other parts. Thus, if any part is not known, the complete function of any other part can only be guessed. Says Sir William Dampier:

The critical examination of the process of induction has shown that inductive science can only draw conclusions which are more or less probable. Sometimes the probability in favour of a generalization is enormous, but the infinite probability of certainty is never reached. A few years ago, the exact accuracy of Newton's law of gravity and the permanence of the chemical elements were thought to be quite certain and, in fact, the probability in favour of those principles was so great that we all should have been willing to bet our last shilling at long odds on their truth. Yet Einstein and Rutherford have proved that we were wrong, and our money would have gone to that rash gambler who had the apparent (nay real) folly to take our bets.

Thus experience confirms modern theories, and goes to show that the generalizations or laws established by induction, even when universally accepted as true, should be regarded only as probabilities. Since much of the evidence for philosophic determinism rests in a belief in the universal validity of natural laws, this question is of importance. Indeed the word "law" used in this connection is misleading, and has had an unfortunate effect. It imparted a kind of moral obligation which bade the phenomena "obey the law" and led to the notion that, when we have traced a law, we have discovered an ultimate cause.[1]

By way of defining *ultimate cause,* as used by Sir William, we may again appeal to our differential. Suppose that you see the left wheel turning clockwise while you are twisting the right one counter-clockwise. When you have "traced" the relation of each of the parts to all the others, you then interpret your twisting as an "ultimate cause." The "law" of the differential is $m = \frac{1}{2}(l + r)$. This complex relation may likewise be a referent of the term *cause* and would also fit the passage as the sense of "ultimate cause." That is, we may also say that the left wheel turned *because* of the law.

Perhaps the most important thing we can do in a study of this sort is to relate the concept of hypothesis to the creative function of metaphor. Hypotheses are frequently metaphorical. Lancelot Hogben, for example, has pointed out in his *Science for the Citizen* how the knowledge of fluid mechanics was brought to bear upon the field of sound by importing the wave concept as a working hypothesis, and how the elaboration of that hypothesis in the science of sound made possible, upon a second transfer, the modern science of electrokinetics.

But it is now high time to remind ourselves that our classification of linguistic functions was brought in to help us understand the nature of the defining process—the first step in solving a complex

[1] *A History of Science,* p. 460.

problem. In problem-solving, it should be apparent that in defining our key terms as we formulate our problem it is vitally important to note whether our terms are proper names, imaginary or real; or generalizations, imaginary or real; or deductions, valid or true; or assumptions, and if assumptions whether they are false but expedient, practical guesses, or symbolizations in some stage of the hypothesis-theory-law series.

Once our problem is adequately stated, we can tell whether it is a puzzle or immediately amenable to the processes of analysis. If it is a puzzle, our next step is the selection of a working hypothesis, after which we may proceed with the regular analytical processes; that is, to the construction of such working classifications or structure or operation analyses as may be relevant.

We must now speak in greater detail, therefore, concerning the three types of systematic procedure—classification, structure analysis, and operation analysis.

In classifying we count or sort for a purpose. A gardener, for example, sorts plants according to the esthetic effects they produce at any given time of year; a botanist sorts them according to structure; an herbalist according to their medicinal or gustatory properties; and a farmer according to their relation to his agricultural requirements. There are three good reasons for classifying the data of complex problems: ease of reference, as in the case of alphabetical or numerical sortings; as an aid to memory; and for comprehension. By classification we may organize vast systems of facts into patterns simple enough to think about and hence to control, for in an adequate classification any item under consideration may be seen in its multifarious relations to all the other items in the classification. By means of classification we do for the facts of any given problem exactly what the Dewey decimal system does for the books in a library. An English-style rider finds it expedient to control his mount by means of four separate reins. An American mule skinner with a team of twenty would have his hands full indeed if he had to manage eighty separate ribbons of heavy leather. He achieves control over his obstreperous charges partly, of course, by his blacksnake and notorious profanity, but principally by an ingenious system of connecting the many bridles so that a few reins do the work of many.

In similar fashion, the mind simplifies the control of thoughts by means of the rein-symbols we have called generalizations. Groups of individual thoughts are recognized as similar by virtue of some specific quality that then becomes a *sorting factor* by which they may be tied together.

A sorting factor may therefore be defined as that quality of a thing by virtue of which it is placed in a given class of things. In these purposeful sortings that we call classifications, the major divisions are called categories and the minor divisions are called subdivisions or subcategories. A classification is like the harness of a mule team in that it is an artificial device for getting order out of chaos so that work may be done.

In concluding the definition of classification, we must point out the tricky ambiguity of the term *sorting factor* as here defined. If we think of sorting factors with reference to our hierarchical diagrams, we may speak of the genus factor as the *vertical* factor, defining it as a quality in which data are similar, and the species factor as the *horizontal* factor, defining it as the respect in which the species differ. Suppose we take a very simple classification, the sorting of flowers as they approach the three primary colors. We may say that we are sorting the flowers according to color and that our horizontal sorting factor is color. But in the performance we sort a given flower because it approaches blue rather than red or yellow into the blue category—thus its vertical sorting factor is blueness, not color. In discussing classification with others it is frequently necessary to make clear whether we are using the term *sorting factor* at the genus or the species level and whether we mean the respect in which they are similar or the respect in which they differ.

Corresponding to the process of selecting a relevant sorting factor and keeping accurate check on our levels of classification, when we deal with experience as structure we must decide on the nature of the principal parts and maintain a consistent type of structure analysis; for structures have different sorts of principal parts when viewed from the point of view of different purposes. The principal parts of the body, for example, from a mechanical point of view are its so-called members, from a physiological point of view its so-called organs, and from a dietetic point of view its so-called tissues. The physicist, physiologist, and chemist have different ways of taking things apart. Indeed, the structure analyses of the chemist turn out to be, like those of the thoretical physicist, hypothetical constructs or *gedanken* experiments.

In operation analysis critical procedure achieves its most complex development, for here the mind adds to the continuing processes of classification and structure analysis a regular method for dealing with occurrences as distinct from (but necessarily including) objects. In classification, we recognize likenesses and differences. In structure analysis, by the application of our power to classify we recognize parts and their interrelations within and to the wholes that they constitute. In operation analysis, by noting the changes in the relations of the different sorts of parts we translate raw occurrences into meaningful events and combine events into operations.

When classifying critically we must become clearly aware of our sorting factors; in structure analysis we must keep careful account of the changing sense of the basic terms *part, whole, structure,* etc.; in operation analysis we must extend our care to include the nomenclature of change. What do we mean in any given operation analysis by words like *time, occurrence, event, phenomenon,* etc.? We say, for example, that the basic act of this type of analysis is the division of an operation into its constituent stages. But what is a "stage"? Consider, for a moment, the interrogatory sentence you have just read, "But what is a 'stage'?" And above all, remember that we are discussing the events in your head when you read, not the structures of ink on the page. We may say that there are five stages, *But* being the first and *stage* the last; or we may say that *But* is the first, *But what* the second, *But what is* the third, etc.; or, finally, we may use *stage* to mean the instants of division that mark the ends (or beginnings) of the stages in either of the preceding senses. Thus, it would be accurate but confusing to say that we may divide stages into stages by means of stages. And if you are getting the real point of this stage business, and if you took note of the remark about goings on in the head, you are probably wondering why we didn't divide our sentence like this: "But what is a—stage?" The answer is that just as we classify the same things in different ways for different purposes, and just as we take the same structures apart in different ways for different purposes, so we divide the same operation into different stages for different purposes.

When we have carried the relevant analytical processes as far as circumstances and our capacities permit, our final step is to draw such conclusions as are relevant to the purpose for which the problem was approached. Such conclusions may range from simple inductions to the complex patterns of inductive and deductive reasoning exemplified by modern statistical procedures. These we will briefly consider in the following chapter on practical induction.

STUDY QUESTIONS

1. (**A**) Two synonyms have been given for the problem-solving function of language — *reason* and *reflection.* Look these two words up in your dictionary, consider their etymologies, and justify their use as synonyms for problem-solving.   (**B**) Again consider the author's statement in Chapter 2 that *reflection* is "a somewhat more emphatic term for reason or logic."

2. How are the communication and problem-solving processes *not* mutually exclusive?

3. How is the process of "making up our minds" more properly a process involving reflection, rather than sensation or emotion?

4. How can we more efficiently deal with the problems we now solve, and solve problems now beyond our skill?

5. The author has suggested that "the necessary first step in the reflective process is definition." How is this what the engineer calls "setting up the problem"?

6. (**A**) "A problem — the thing, not the word — is a state of mind characterized by the momentary awareness of a need to know something that is not then in the consciousness." Why does the author distinguish between the word and the thing?   (**B**) What is the difference between the definition of the word *problem* and the thing *problem*?

7. Describe and differentiate between the two sorts of problems described on page 144.

8. In Chapters 11 and 12 the author answered the question "What sorts of definitions are there?" in two different ways. What were these?

9. In this chapter the author is sorting words according to the work they do. Grammarians have traditionally come up with eight sorts, sorted according to the way they are used in the sentence.   (**A**) What are these eight sorts?   (**B**) Why have they "contributed very little to the clarity of

our thought"?   (C) How does the author's *horizontal* sorting factor differ from the grammarian's? Illustrate your answer by showing how the
grammarian might sort *gold standard,* and how the author sorts it.   (D)
Why, from the author's point of view, wouldn't *gold* be one of "the eternal verities"?

10. How is *demonstrable contact with "external reality"* a synonym
for the process of corroboration? Why is *external reality* in quotes?

11. Is the naming of the rock "Pete" simply incidental, or is there a
reasonable connection between the name "Pete" and the rock? Refer to
your dictionary.

12. (A) How is it possible that *Pete* (or any proper name) is a generalization? In answering this question, consider again these remarks,
made on page 100: "Suppose your name is Hamilcar. By saying that
Hamilcar is necessarily a genus term, we do not mean that you are of the
same sort as the conqueror or the cat (Anatole France's cat, that is), but
that Hamilcar is the name of the class of all experiences identified with
or as you. Whenever anybody, including you, is consciously aware of
you as you, Hamilcar or some other symbolic instrument of recognition
must be on hand to unite the present Hamilcarian experience to the series
that goes to make up your individuality in time and space. It is not only
by means of genus terms that we designate our pigeonholes, but it is by
genus terms that we create the pigeons that go in them. Of course, in
some areas of our conscious life those terms are not definite symbols like
words, but are rather like the indescribable private symbols in which a
blind musician thinks about music."   (B) Considering a proper name
operationally, how is it the name of an *undefined* operation?

13. (A) The concepts of *egg-shaped, smooth, hard, 16 ounces,* and
boulder were necessary for the author's reification of the symbol *Pete.*
As he introduces you to Pete, how will your reification differ from his?
(B) How, then, does a public proper name differ from a private one?
(C) In the quotation from page 100 the author said, "Of course, in some
areas of our conscious life those terms are not definite symbols like words,
but are rather like the indescribable private symbols in which a blind
musician thinks about music." Are *private* and *public* symbols being
used in the same sense as established in this chapter?

14. How would the *National Theatre of Mexico* differ for the engineer who built it and the author? How could this difference have caused
trouble to the author?

15. The author states that *proper name* is not used "in the loose sense
of 'capitalized noun' but in the sense for which most of us would use the
expression 'given name.'" Illustrate this distinction.

16. Which would have more "demonstrable contact with reality"—a public or a private proper name?

17. Our second type of symbol is the *recognized generalization*. Is *generalization* as used here different from *generalization* when we say "proper names are generalizations"? If so, how?

18. How would you differentiate between the two sorts of generalizations?

19. How are real generalizations *inductions*?

20. Which would have more "demonstrable contact with reality"—a proper name or a generalization?

21. If *induce* and *generalize* are synonyms, what is a synonym for *deduce*?

22. If the species must have all the characteristics of the genus, why isn't the term *species* a synonym for the term *genus*?

23. (**A**) What is a *syllogism*? What are its three stages? (**B**) What is a premise? How do a "major" and a "minor" premise relate to *Aristotle's Dictum*? (**c**) *Deduction* may mean the act of reasoning from the general to the particular or the conclusion so reached. How does the author use the term? (**D**) Explain the statement "Formal logic, so-called, is simply a set of exercises that leads the mind to an understanding of such concepts as *all, some,* and *none.*"

(**E**) "A little thought will convince you that in order to be sure that a given species belongs in a given genus, you must know *all* the qualities of the genus and must have examined the species for all qualities of the genus." Analyze the following syllogisms with the preceding statement in mind: (1) All mammals are warm-blooded; whales are mammals; therefore, whales are warm-blooded. (2) Some redheaded people are hot-tempered; Eric had red hair; therefore, Eric was hot-tempered. (3) All redheaded people are hot-tempered; Eric the Red was a Scandinavian; therefore, Eric the Red had a hot temper.

24. (**A**) Look up *implication* in your dictionary. How does a deduction symbolize an implication? (**B**) Of the two deductions *the moon is round* and *Socrates is a man,* which is more probably based upon premises that have been privately corroborated? Which is more probably based upon borrowed premises?

25. How would a *valid* syllogism differ from a *true* one?

26. (**A**) What sort of words are *symbolics*? (**B**) Do they have referents? (**c**) Is *ownership* a symbolic?

27. (**A**) How are the "notions" *Chiron, Alexander,* and *Bucephalus* different? (**B**) How do these "notions" differ from the concept *half-man–half-horse*?

28. How does an assumption differ from a deduction?

29. (A) Explain the statement "When we make an assumption we use a symbol that has a reference—that is to say, a corresponding thought—but no referent, no percept to which the thought refers." (B) How does a *concept* differ from a *percept*? (C) Why wouldn't assumptions have *percepts*? (D) Why would we use assumptions, since they are so "unverifiable"?

30. (A) What are the three sorts of assumption? (B) Of what sort is a corporation? (C) How is the word *God* different from the word *Mohammed*? (D) What does belief have to do with assumptions? (E) Why is it necessary to recognize assumptions for what they are?

31. How do hypotheses differ from other assumptions?

32. (A) What is a *datum*? (B) Is a datum a *specimen* or a *species*? (C) How do you know if a datum is relevant?

33. (A) What is the function of hypotheses in problem-solving? (B) Explain this statement: "The hypothesis (the reference of the symbol hypothesis) is like a light by means of which we search for truth; but it is a colored light that may render invisible the very object we seek."

34. How does a hypothesis grow into a theory?

35. What is a law? How can it be dangerous?

36. (A) Paraphrase the definition of *truth* as it is given on page 154. (B) How can truth "exist"? (C) If assumptions have no referents, how can they lead to "truth"? (D) Do you consider the formula $f = ma$ (force = mass × acceleration) as "true"? Why do you think it is "true"?

37. What happens when one of the parts in a system is not known?

38. What does *ultimate cause* as used by Sir William Dampier have to do with laws?

39. How does metaphor function in creating hypotheses?

40. (A) The author has used the term "demonstrable contact with reality" as applying to the concept of immediate sensory response. Thus, the proper name would come closest to "reality" in this sense, because it is as close as one can bring a name to a thing. However, the "reality" of the scientist with which he associates natural law and on the basis of which he predicts "results" is a different sense of reality from that in quotations in the expression "demonstrable contact with reality." In "I christen this stone here Pete," "this stone here Pete" stands for what we have called "reality" where the term in quotes stands for an immediate intuitive percept. The kinds of realities that scientists talk about are at the other end of our semantic spectrum as a result of inductive and deductive procedures. Thus, a scientist examines all redheaded men and finds they possess the quality of hot tempers. He then says that all red-headed men are hot-tempered; that a man, Eric, has red hair, and that therefore Eric is hot-tempered. Have both induction and deduction figured in this conclusion? (B) Is corroboration a deductive or inductive process? (C) Considering the definition of *corroboration* on page 131, would "reality" to the scientist be more dependent on contacts through sensory mechanisms or through logical abstractions? (D) Considering the definitions and etymologies of "*reality* and *actuality*," "*percept* and *concept*," "*subjective* and *objective*," look again at the statement, on page 131, "With the scientist, we who are studying semantics reach the paradoxical position of attaining objectivity by being more and more subjective." (E) Relate the terms *corroboration, concept, reality, subjective, induction, deduction.* (F) Relate the terms *actuality, percept, objectivity* (in the sense of meaninglessness).

41. How was the author's classification of linguistic functions designed to help us in the first step of problem-solving?

42. Would the selection of a working hypothesis be necessary in solving both kinds of problems? If not, why not?

43. Why is determining a purpose so necessary in classifying?

44. List and illustrate three good reasons for classifying the data of complex problems.

45. (A) What meaning in the universe of language does the difference between the English-style rider and the American mule skinner have for us? (B) In the process of achieving control over our language "mules," how do we make a few reins do the work of many? (C) How do *sorting factors* figure in the process? (D) How do horizontal and vertical sorting factors differ? (E) Is there any relationship between these two terms and ordinal and cardinal ambiguity? (F) If the horizontal factor in sorting flowers is *color*, how is it that the horizontal factor is the "respect in which the species differ"?

46. (A) What is the difference between the relation of a part to a whole and a species to a genus? (B) How would a change in purpose change the sorts of principal parts of a structure?

47. (A) How in operation analysis does "critical procedure achieve its most *complex* development"? (B) Define a *stage* as used on page 158. How does *purpose* enter into your definition?

48. The author states that after applying the relevant analytical processes, our final step is to draw conclusions. Explain how the conclusions drawn through modern statistical procedures are a result of *both* inductive and deductive reasoning.

Think upon what hath chanced.

MACBETH

14 CHANCE

ONE SWALLOW DOESN'T make a summer, says the proverb. "How many swallows does it take?" is the practical question we must now ask. How many data are required for a given induction, and how do we tell?

There are several ways of answering the question. A very practical one is that we learn to tell by experience. This is an Irish bull; it is equivalent to saying that we learn how to induce by inducing. But it may mean something deeper; there is a sort of inarticulate sagacity acquired through familiarity, which is not to be lightly ignored.

Another answer is that where exhaustive investigation is impracticable we should collect as many data as we can. The more data we know the less probability there is of a disturbing factor being present.

But the best answer, in an age increasingly dominated by the standards of scientific procedure, is that we should acquire at least an elementary knowledge of the science of statistics. It is neither within the scope of this book nor in the capacity of its writer to present an adequate statistical primer; but a brief introduction to the subject may provoke the reader to further study, or at least indicate to him its vital importance. For the citizen of the modern world stands in constant need not only of sales resistance but of some modicum of self-protection against figures that lie and liars that figure.

We have already suggested the likeness of the symbol to the tool. Just as the compound microscope vastly increased the seeing power of the eye, so the logical definition improved the capacity of the mind to organize experience. The compound microscope has now been superseded by the unbelievably powerful electron microscope. Simple induction has been similarly replaced by the new science of statistics. The one derives from the theory of the atom, the other from the theory of the sample. Both are based upon the doctrine of probability.

There is also an instructive parallel between the relation of these two ultramodern instruments and the man in the street. Popular ignorance of the fact that electronic pictures are not photographs of objects is paralleled by failure to recognize the deceptive ambiguity of the term *average*.

Let us begin, then, by doing our orthological duty. Here are some uses and definitions of *average*:

(1) *The average wage in this plant comes to exactly $7.87 per working day.* In this statement *average* has the strict mathematical sense. It is the quotient obtained by dividing the sum of all wages for a given period by the product of the number of workers and the number of days in the period. It doesn't imply that any particular worker receives $7.87 per day.

(2) *The average worker in this plant gets over $16 a day.* Here *average* is synonymous with *majority*. More workers get above $16 than below.

(3) *The average worker in this plant gets $265 per month.* This statement has the sense of "I've seen more pay checks for $265 per month than for any other amount."

(4) *Many writers call the various measures of central tendency* "*averages.*" An explanation of this statement will go far toward giving us our Pisgah sight of statistical induction. Of course, there are several other relevant senses of *average*.

Whenever objects or events are amenable to the sort of logical qualification which we call quantification (that is, whenever we can count them or measure them by some standard unit), the resulting data or "values" may be placed in various sorts of scalar order. Arithmetical qualifications thus arranged are said to be "distributed" and the order is called a "distribution." We distribute values in order to facilitate induction. Distributions, of course, are quantitative classifications.

Now when the data relevant to a given problem are either too numerous or otherwise too inconvenient to gather or report, we make or report our inductions by means of representative groups of individual items. The representative character of a group of data is determined in the light of two statistical principles—the doctrine of probability (law of averages) and the demonstration of central tendency.

Probability is a curiously unstable concept. Semantically speaking, it is an assumption, a pure artifice, a concept that may or may not be true, but nevertheless facilitates a logical process. It is not a hypothesis because, as you shall see, by its very nature it cannot be proved. Suppose we flip a coin that has a distinguishable head and tail. We must assume at the start that nothing about our coin influences its fall in favor of either side (or that all influences are counterbalanced by equal and opposite influences), so that we are completely ignorant of the coming result. In this state of ignorance we say that the coin has one chance in two of falling heads up, or that the probability of a head is one to two (one over two). Here it must be emphatically understood that the one-to-two is not "true" but is merely a species of the genus probability. In this particular universe, it is the sort of datum that probability refers to.

Next, suppose we flip the coin five times and it falls tails-up each time. What is the probability then that it will fall a tail on the sixth toss? When we began our series of six, we had 64 possible sequences of heads and/or tails. That is, the probability of throwing six tails was one in sixty-four. Does this in any way influence the one-to-two probability of that last toss? Isn't it reasonable to assume that, as we approach the last toss, one more successful tail toss becomes less and less likely? Not at all!

We have a fifty-fifty chance of a tail at the end of the fifth toss, just as we had at the beginning of the first toss. Let us diagram the possibilities. Suppose we flip the coin and it falls a head, and we place an h on our graph; the second flip may fall either heads or tails, so we put down both h and t; if h, then h and t again; if t, then h and t again; and so on to the sixth flip. A similar pattern may then be worked out for a first fall of tails. On the sixth line of each diagram will be found sixteen heads and sixteen tails; each throw may be traced back by the connecting lines to the original flip. Thus, there are sixty-four possible sequences in a six-flip series.

Now if we count the number of tails in each series, and the times that a given number occurs, we may plot the graph in the accompanying illustration. The smooth curve through the coordinate points describes a symmetrical figure known variously as the bell-shaped curve, the normal-probability curve, and the normal frequency distribution. It is called normal because in any universe of investigation where there is no discoverable controlling influence, the frequencies of chance occurrence tend thus to drape themselves. The tendency of the data points to cluster about the mid-position is called the central tendency of the data.

There are several common "measures of central tendency" in statistical thought, all of which are called averages. These commonly used measures are:

(1) The *mean,* or arithmetical mean, which is obtained by adding the values and dividing by their number. Thus, for the number of tails: $0 + 1 + 2 + 3 + 4 + 5 + 6 = 21; 21 \div 7 = 3$. On the perfect normal curve the mean will be the position of maximum frequency, and the maximum number of points will cluster there. If a point falls precisely on the mean position it might also be called a mean, or mean value.

(2) The ambiguous term *median,* which may have these senses: (a) that point or value above and below which an equal number of points or values are distributed; or (b) that position which divides the values in equal groups. Thus, according to (a) the median is 3; but according to (b) it is 3.5, which may not make sense to you, but does to those statisticians who have no scruples about theoretical families with 1.63 parents and 2.15 children.

(3) The *mode,* which is the value in a distribution that occurs most frequently. Thus, in our statistics for six tosses, the mode is three tails, which is another way of saying that out of sixty-four possible sequence-patterns, the three-tail pattern is the largest probable group.

When a distribution is normal, the values for the mean, sense (a) of the median, and the mode coincide so that if we know one we gain

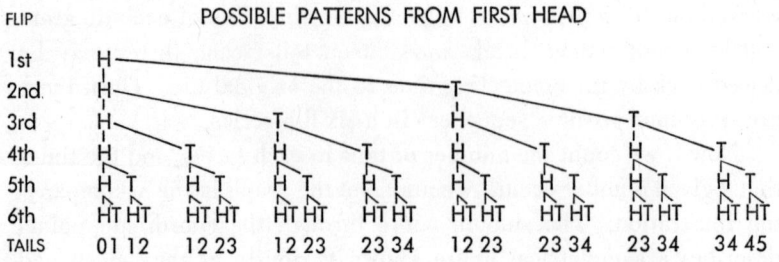

FLIP — POSSIBLE PATTERNS FROM FIRST HEAD

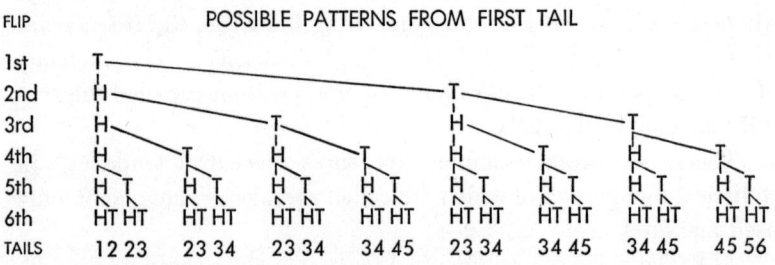

FLIP — POSSIBLE PATTERNS FROM FIRST TAIL

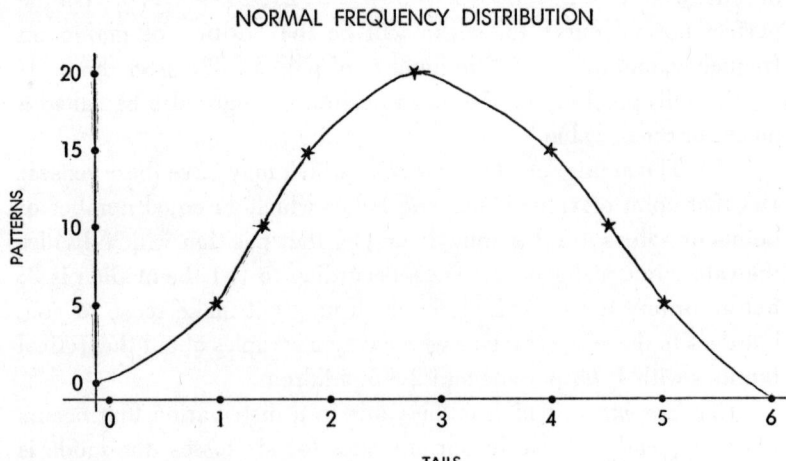

NORMAL FREQUENCY DISTRIBUTION

nothing by computing the others. But in distributions that deviate from the norm, comparison of the three measures may tell us much. Suppose we distribute the incomes of a family of five, composed of: an artisan; his wife, who takes in dressmaking; her sister, a stenographer; and two children, who have jobs in a factory. Let the separate incomes be $2,400, $1,800, $1,200, $900, and $900. The mean is $1,440, the median is $1,200, and the mode is $900.

The mean is at once the most useful and the most deceptive measure of central tendency. Because it takes account of the extreme range of the distribution, it is not always typical. If the father had the good fortune to double his income in a new job, the family mean would rise above the next highest income, but the median and the mode would remain undisturbed as indications of the nature of the distribution. Where the deviation from the mean is great, the median is therefore the better measure. The mode is frequently a useful indication of a significant bump in the curve.

Means, medians, and modes enable us to think with considerable accuracy about large groups of data that would otherwise baffle our meager capacities.

When the data in a given field of study are for any reason too numerous or inaccessible to consider in detail, we have recourse to the method of sampling. The assumption is that if a group of samples is taken at random, it will tend to display the same distribution as the whole body of data. Thus, if we telephone one number from every tenth page of a city directory, and inquire about the subscriber's favorite radio program, the tabulated result would be a random sampling of the telephone subscribers. If we seek greater precision, we can take the mean of several samplings. But note that such a mean would only *tend* to be more accurate, by the doctrine of probability. The first sample *might* actually be a more accurate representation of the field than the mean of many samplings.

The probable dependability of a random sampling is based upon the general dispersion of the data and the size of the sample. Telephone directories are tempting but treacherous sources of data about the entire population. Many who ride in Cadillacs and Lincolns have "silent phones," and many who go on foot have no "phones" at all.

In concluding these few words about statistical induction, we may point out that as systematic investigation develops in a particular field, the method of random sampling tends to be replaced by the so-called "scientific" cross section. To get such a cross section, the statistician attempts to apply his knowledge of those factors that are known to influence deviations from the normal frequency curve by giving some data more "weight" than others. He carefully selects his samples, not at random but in the light of known trends of the data.

As a final word, we must vigorously insist that a vast amount of the statistical information presented to the reading and listening public should be most warily accepted because of the failure to include clear definitions of the terms employed and some reasonably accurate account of the methods of acquiring and interpreting the data. A great national magazine, *The Literary Digest*, destroyed itself through unsound sampling in a presidential poll. And many a pollster dined on roast crow in the fall of 1948 because of faulty assumptions about human nature; these "scientific observers" had failed to allow for what Shakespeare would have called "a little touch of Harry in the night."

We shall now present a series of demonstrations designed to illustrate the principles we have all too briefly set forth. They will be oversimplified and in many respects inadequate, but we may perhaps alert you to the importance of these techniques by reminding you that it was by their means, and theirs alone, that untold millions of itemized men and munitions were for the most part put down at the right place and at the right time upon the roads and beaches of northern France, and that the successful application of these techniques would appear to be essential to national and individual survival in the modern world. Indeed, we might describe the adequate citizen as a vital engineer and the applied science of systematic analysis as vital engineering. We should add that the ultimate survival of civilization will depend upon our capacity to apply these techniques not in Pentagons but in Departments of State. The logistics of military supply is a stupendous manifestation of applied analysis. Dare the calculus of peace be any less so?

STUDY QUESTIONS

1. How many swallows make a summer? Discuss the three ways of answering this question.

2. What is an "Irish bull"?

3. Is it always true that the more data we collect, the less the probability of reaching a wrong conclusion?

4. (**A**) How is it possible for figures to lie?   (**B**) What is the sense of *lie* in the above sentence?   (**C**) Is this opposite to *truth* as defined in the last chapter?

5. (**A**) How is the new microscope derived from the theory of the atom, and the science of statistics derived from the theory of the sample?   (**B**) How are both based on the doctrine of probability?   (**C**) How is probability related to hypothesis, theory, and law? To deduction?

6. How is it that "popular ignorance of the fact that electronic pictures are not photographs of the object is paralleled by the failure to recognize the deceptive ambiguity of the term *average*"?

7. With the aid of your dictionary, give five senses of the word *average*.

8. The president of the Nadir Company receives a salary of $1,500 a month. The other employees, listed below, receive the following monthly salaries:

Mr. A: $300	Mr. G: $250
Mr. B: 200	Mr. H: 300
Mr. C: 250	Mr. I: 250
Mr. D: 500	Mr. J: 250
Mr. E: 250	Mr. K: 600
Mr. F: 200	

Define the words *average, worker,* and *salary* as used or implied in each of the statements below: (**A**) The average salary in the Nadir Company is $304.55. (**B**) The average salary is $370. (**C**) The average worker receives $250 a month. (**D**) The average salary is $300 a month. (**E**) The average salary is $558.33.

9. (**A**) If the public relations department of the Nadir Company were to claim that the average salary in their company is fifty per cent higher than that received by the average worker of its nearest competitor, would you be impressed?   (**B**) What information would you need in order to relate such a claim to the facts?

10. What is a *Pisgah* sight of statistical induction?

11. (**A**) What is *quantification?*   (**B**) Distributions involve what sort of analysis?   (**C**) Why are values distributed in statistical problems?

12. (**A**) When do we "report our inductions by means of representative groups of individual items"?   (**B**) How is the representative group of data determined?

13. How is probability an *assumption*? A pure *artifice*? What does *artifice* mean here?

14. Why is an assumption of probability not a hypothesis?

15. What is the relationship between ignorance and chance?

16. (**A**) If we know that one of two possible events is more likely to occur, is the probability of its occurring one over two? (**B**) Under what circumstances does each of a number of possible events have the same probability of occurring?

17. (**A**) Assuming that a coin is "unbiased" according to weight and other factors, what is the probability of flipping two heads in a row? (**B**) Three heads? Five heads? Ten heads?

18. If ten heads have been flipped in a row, what is the probability of flipping an eleventh?

19. (**A**) What is a frequency distribution? (**B**) What is a *normal* frequency distribution?

20. (**A**) What is central tendency? (**B**) What are three measures of central tendency?

21. Find the mean, the median, and the mode of these figures: 7, 8, 8, 9, 9, 9, 10, 11, 12, 14, 15, 16.

22. What happens to the measures of central tendency when a distribution deviates from the norm?

23. Consider the following salaries:

$225	$ 375
310	385
350	390
350	400
375	1,800
375	

(**A**) If the salary of $1,800 were tripled, how would the mean be affected? (**B**) The mode? (**C**) The median?

24. If a distribution deviates from the norm and we are interested in a "typical" value, what measure of central tendency should probably not be used?

25. When do we use the method of sampling?

26. (**A**) What assumption is made when a distribution is made from a random sampling? (**B**) What does such a distribution "represent"?

27. What factor makes a random sampling random?

28. What precautions may be taken in order to ensure that a sample will tend to correspond to actuality?

29. Assuming that adequate sampling methods are followed, what is the relationship between the size of the sample and its probable dependability?

30. How does a "scientific" cross section differ from a random sample?

31. What are the relationships between *sampling, ignorance, chance, probability, induction,* and *truth?*

32. Why must we accept statistical information warily?

That's a question. How shall we try it?

15 PROBLEM-SOLVING

PROBLEM-SOLVING is an operation. The changing structure involved is made up of the problem-solver, his apparatus, and his environment. Our objective is to identify and describe the principal stages. Like many another operation, problem-solving is best studied in the act, but performance does not necessarily lead to understanding. Understanding requires that the performer realize what he is doing and how he does it.

Our demonstrations must proceed with three unfortunate handicaps: artificiality, oversimplification, and incompleteness. They are really "samplers" or make-believe problems in which we shall consider a logical series of steps that in actual practice is neither as clearly defined nor as systematically sequential as our discussion would imply. Nor will we be able to illustrate the random process of exploratory digression that may profitably accompany the line of direct progression. And finally, we shall not complete our assigned tasks and thus enjoy the satisfaction of accomplishment.

The choice of problems has itself been something of a problem. We have sought to confront the reader with subjects that were not strange to him but were not likely to have been studied in a systematic way. The first was selected for three reasons: it presents an instructive exercise in definition; the working classification is elaborate without being difficult; and finally, it is a particularly fitting point of departure for discussing the difference between solving a problem and writing a paper. The second was chosen because it is a complex puzzle-problem that involves the use of a working hypothesis.

Let us assume that we have been assigned the task of writing the entry to appear under the word "hunting" in a forthcoming encyclopedia. As a matter of course, we ask the editor what he means by "hunting," but he parries by saying that he means whatever a good encyclopedia should include in the hunting entry. This is our first step, a tentative statement of the problem.

Our semantic inclinations prompt us to begin with a multiple definition of the word "hunt," but we forgo this because of a comfortable conviction that we know what hunting is not. We do not go hunting, in our present sense, for bargains, houses, or gold.

Two questions now pop up together. We were about to ask ourselves, "What is hunting a sort of?" But the thought "not for bargains" ushered in the question "For what, then?" The word "game" is sailing around in our heads, eager to be the answer to the second question, but we wave it off and judiciously consider the first. We get three answers. Hunting is a sort of sport; hunting is a sort of livelihood; and hunting is a human institution.

This operation disposes of *game*. Game, we conclude, is an animal pursued for sport and is a species of the more inclusive genus prey. We decide that prey is any living thing that we seek with the intent to kill or capture it. But this would include microbes, rats, and criminals. For various reasons, conventional, aesthetic, and moral, we now arbitrarily eliminate insects, common pests, and human beings. This means that, for us, beetle, butterfly, and other bug collectors are not hunters.

But what about fishing? Our impulse is to draw the line at fishing. We say either you go hunting or you go fishing. Well, what about harpooning? That's hunting, for you must chase your prey. In fishing, the fish has to chase you, or at least attack your bait. Does this make trapping and snaring hunting? Does bringing your prey back alive make you a hunter? This leads to a reconsideration of fishing. Our logical minds have taken up the eternal struggle with tradition. We begin to see how arbitrary the distinction between hunting and fishing may sometimes be. We finally compromise the problem by asking our editor to let us treat our subject under the dual title of "Hunting and Fishing." The absence of an inclusive term in English had, for the moment, tricked us.

We now revive our concern about the butterfly chaser and soon add to him the camera hunter. But they are ultimately ruled out. This ends our second step, the multiple definition—in this case a rather hasty consideration of the possible senses of key terms. We now set up our working definition: "The pursuit, with intent to kill or capture, of such animals as are generally regarded as capable of making that pursuit a source of amusement for its own sake and/or profitable because of the animals themselves." It is the clause "as are generally regarded" which rules out rat- and dogcatchers. This is our third step.

Although somewhat awed by the increasing scope of our task, we are in no sense puzzled by it. It is not a puzzle-problem. We have merely to give an account in the allotted space (say, five thousand words) of the nature and history of hunting and fishing throughout the world.

In terms of analysis our problem is a double one. Hunting and fishing are operations, and so far as our account is complete it will include a stage-by-stage operation analysis; but since we have many different types of hunting to consider, our next concern is a practicable working classification. We must sort hunting and fishing data according to some relevant quality that will probably be classifiable as primarily sensory, affective, or logical. This is our fourth step.

Shall we sort according to the type of sensory response involved? Probably not, at least not primarily. What about affective responses? The emotions of hunting as we have defined it may be its very reason for being, but they do not provide a practicable basis for a classification. A hunt that thrills one hunter may bore another. Thus, we are committed to the logical qualifications, the numbers, changes, sizes, forms, materials, times, or places of huntings.

The recommended procedure at this point may seem ridiculous, but we hope that you will try it nevertheless. It is simply a verbal method of reminding ourselves of the many ways in which the data have been or may be sorted. We record such practicable classifications as occur to us when we ask the following questions: What sorts of hunting and fishing are there? What kinds? What ways? What manners? Methods? Means? Classes? Types? Styles? Forms? Makes? Models? Grades? Brands? Species? Stages? Aspects? Phases? Ages? Fields? Degrees? Parts? Functions? Purposes? Causes? Statistics (how many huntings)? Patterns?

You may quite justifiably inquire about the reason for asking yourself the kinds or types when you have just answered the question "What are the sorts?" The reason is this: these terms are not necessarily synonyms; their senses vary either with the things sorted or the occasion of the sorting. ("What sort of potatoes do you have today?" "I have some good new potatoes." "What kind of potatoes are they?" "Burbanks." "What brand of clothes?" "What make of car?") The result is that different terms get established with different classifications. Running over the whole list (and even adding to it) increases the likelihood of mobilizing all your relevant knowledge. It may also suggest acquiring some that you do not now possess.

As we work our way along the list, we dismiss the word "model" as inappropriate until the term *conceptual model* comes to mind. Then we attend immediately to the fact that our subject is a dynamic human institution, and we reflect upon the desirability of an operation analysis and a conceptual model or models. (If we had passed the word "model," however, the words "part" or "stage" probably would have suggested the same point.) The basic model of the hunt seems to be composed of the hunter, an implement, and the quarry maneuvering in a field. We might, then, deal with our subject according to its parts. That is, we might sort our data under the headings: hunter, implement, quarry, maneuver, and field. We are inclined to guess, however (and this we confess to be a mild form of hypothesis), that the implement and the quarry tend to determine the pattern of the hunt and, therefore, will provide the more profitable sorting factors. But this much we know: any datum relevant to hunting will also be relevant to one or more of the parts, and the name of any one of the parts will yield us a horizontal sorting factor for sorting data on any one of the others. This suggests the possibility of using each one at a specific level. Say, then, that we sort the category level according to implement, implement according to quarry,

quarry according to field, field according to hunter. Graphically our classification takes the form of the hierarchical diagram shown in Diagram A. The hunter, it will be noted, is the concept by which we introduce the aspect of time. He is conceived as one living either in the remote or immediate past. His race or nationality as indicative of geographical location will also tend to be relevant (see p. 180).

There are at least four comments in order at this point: (1) The diagram is not our working classification; it is simply a device that enables us to use our eyes in the process of making up our minds. (2) It causes us to think carefully as to whether organizing our thoughts around the implement will give us a clearer, more meaningful grasp of our subject than organization based on the quarry. And in this regard we must always keep foremost in mind that our controlling purpose is the writing of a popular reference article, not a sociological or psychological treatise. (3) It suggests immediately the need for several subdivisions that will be inserted at various levels, such as sorts of firearms, sorts of fowls, sorts of animals, etc. (4) Consideration of our controlling purpose confirms the desirability of keeping the factors *historical* and *contemporary* at the lowest level because that will keep all the data conveniently sorted, even though we are not thinking of our problem as a double one—hunting and the history of hunting. We are generally motivated by the desire to know as much as we can about hunting, but we suspect that our conventional editor will want the customary historical sketch of the subject.

So far as procedure is concerned, we are now back where we started. We have the word *implement* to define and a classification of implements to work out. Our definition of implement may be derived from our conceptual model. An implement is the part of the hunt that is not hunter, field, or prey. Thus a dog, a falcon, a gun-boy, a beater, or a mount would be an implement. But, relatively speaking, a gun, rod, or falcon is a primary implement; gun-boys, beaters, horses, decoys, chum are auxiliary implements. Dogs are sometimes primary, sometimes auxiliary. Let us, therefore, seek a classification of principal or primary implements.

We first list various implements as they occur to us: guns, fishing gear, arrows, spears, boomerangs, riatas, bolas, traps, snares, pitfalls, falcons, cheetahs, dogs, cormorants, etc. Now we put the question: what sorts have we? After careful consideration, we narrow the primary categories down to five: missile-implements, hooks, snares, traps, and animals.

The process is repeated as before. We now define missile-implement as any device which forcibly propels an inanimate object toward the prey to stun, maim, or kill it. Then, what sorts of missile-implements are there? (And we should, perhaps, remind you at this point that whenever the term *sort* is used it may well be regarded as an invitation to try the full list of sorting words.) We can think, offhand, of bullets, shot, stones, arrows, darts, bolts, spears, harpoons, boomerangs. Here consideration brings out the distinction between missiles that are hunter-propelled and those that are explosive-propelled. We hit upon the terms nonfiring and firing. Arrows and blowgun darts would be nonfired; crossbow bolts and air- and spring-gun ammunition would be arbitrarily classed as fired for practical reasons.

It now seems high time to get our growing classification down on paper, where we can see it again. Needless to say, we had better use a rather large sheet. Diagram B is our tentative beginning of a working classification for sorting data relevant to "Hunting and Fishing." This is the end of the fourth step, the general plan of our working classification.

A point to be emphasized is that this is *not* the beginning of an outline for the assigned article on hunting. It is a graphic representation of the order in which we propose to sort the data that we shall ultimately be jotting down on suitable cards or slips of paper. The names of the groups of related data we expect to get will also provide us continually with suggestions as to what to look for or what to do next. The systematic addition of each new datum to our collection is the process that produces what we call a "grasp of the subject."

We are not discouraged upon glancing over our classification. It will obviously direct us through a survey of the various sorts of hunting, past and present, hither and yon. Moreover, it has already served to point out numerous areas in which our present ignorance far exceeds our knowledge. It is not within the scope or intentions of this demonstration to acquire the indicated information and pursue the project to the bitter end, but we will take up a typical example

DIAGRAM A
hunting and fishing data

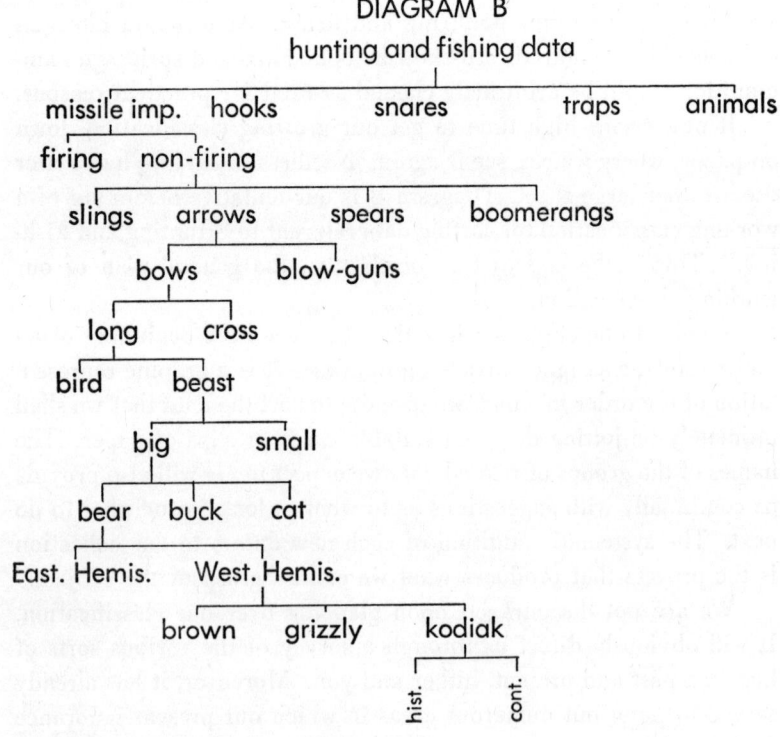

DIAGRAM B
hunting and fishing data

of a sort of problem that will frequently arise as we methodically plod through the headings saying, "What are the sorts of this?"

Our eyes have fallen on the word *spear*, and the word *harpoon* comes to mind. Since we define *harpoon* as a special sort of spear, we find that it may stand for either a fired or nonfired missile, the distinguishing characteristics of which are the barb and the attached line. We are, thus, moved quickly along to the definition of *hooks*. The final result is the discovery that, so far as hunting is concerned, harpoons have more in common with hooks than with missiles, and therefore we classify them as such—the dictionary to the contrary notwithstanding.

Perhaps it will be helpful to remind you at this stage that a two-ring circus is going on here; the writer is demonstrating a method of critical procedure, but you as a thoughtful reader are supposed to be absorbed in the subject of hunting and fishing. Now if you are keeping an eye on both rings, you may be troubled with this question: why do we attempt to plan a working classification before we have collected the data to be classified? The position is well taken and there are at least three relevant replies.

The first is that if you are working in a strange field your classification will necessarily be brief and subject to revision and amplification as your acquaintance with the incoming data develops. The second is that it is desirable to make a tentative working classification in advance, and to make it as detailed as possible because at this stage it is really an elaborate definition. In making it you are actually formulating a more precise and extensive idea of what you are trying to do. You will move in the field with a keener sense for what is relevant. The third answer combines a constructive suggestion and a word of caution. In working in an established field it is well to find out and use the standard, "tried and true" classifications. But you must not follow the sheep over the cliff. Sometimes the successful solution of an age-old problem calls for new methods of sorting the data if new insights are to be achieved.

We should also add that thus far we have been solely concerned with the sort of classification that aids the mind in grasping the meaning of the data. In extensive research where many data are being collected over a considerable period of time you will need classifications for ready reference. For example, you may give some appropriate name, number, or color to each datum so that it may be filed alphabetically, or in some other convenient order.

In returning to our encyclopedia assignment let us assume that, guided by our classification of implements, we have pretty well covered the subject of game. As we reflect upon such terms as *statistics, cause,* and *purpose,* we will broaden the focus of our thought to include other patterns of human behavior to which the institution of hunting is related or in which it is included. Considerations of ritual, costume, social, economic, and even political significance will be suggested by such terms as *aspect* or *phase.* And these may compete with the description of the hunt itself for a share of our five thousand words. Such ancient and traditional racial institutions as the fox hunt will test our capacity to select, generalize, and simplify.

Assignments such as ours have practical economic limits of time and funds, and as we bring our fifth step, the collection of data, to an end we find ourselves ready to take stock of an imposing assortment of notes, quotes, pictures, statistics, implements, trophies, etc. Now if we had the necessary space—say, a great hallway—we could chalk the diagram of our completed classification upon the wall. At the lower end of each vertical line not crossed by a horizontal one there would be a space laid out on the floor—a pigeonhole. Every datum would "belong" in one of these pigeonholes and we might put it there. This would be our sixth step. Thus we would have all our data assembled in such an order that there would be one or more meaningful relations between any one datum and any one or all of the others. We could then inspect the collection in any one pigeonhole, or set or branch of related pigeonholes, and so make some significant generalization concerning what we saw. This would be the seventh and concluding step of the problem-solving process—the set of inductions and consequent deductions derived from our systematic arrangement of the data. We would have solved the problem of getting ready to write our five-thousand word entry. The problem of the actual composition is another problem entirely, the discussion of which we shall postpone until we have analyzed a puzzle-problem.

Suppose that instead of asking the question "How have men

hunted?" we ask "Why do men hunt?" A quick glance suggests that we start our multiple definitions with *hunt*; let us assume the definition set up in the previous problem. *Men,* however, now takes on a new aspect. *Man* was simply a synonym for *hunter,* but now we become aware, as we ask ourselves all the things it might mean, that we have in mind a special sort of man—modern civilized men like Theodore Roosevelt, Ernest Hemingway, or Osa Johnson (Mrs. Johnson being just as much of a "man" in our sense of the word as her husband). We know why Eskimos hunt, but why do presidents, artists, and explorers do it?

Why brings up the whole complex problem of causality, and we may as well face it. Our basic sense of *cause* is any necessary link in a known chain of events: Tom might have become a hunter because he inherited a gun; Dick might have become a skin diver because he won an oxygen tank in a "giveaway show"; Harry might trace his archery to a job in a sporting-goods shop. We soon dismiss this concept of cause for the more psychological term *reason.* This line of thought reminds us that we rationalizing humans have two sorts of reasons for our acts—our own "good" reasons, and the "real" reasons that we are not always ready to admit. In the present instance our primary interest, at least, is in real reasons.

What sorts of real reasons do people have? The most general answer is that we all try to get pleasure and avoid pain, to get into good states and out of bad ones. Our problem, then, is the problem of motive, and two very thoughtful students of such problems have shown us very convincingly how to keep our thoughts ordered in this field. Kenneth Burke in his *Grammar of Motives* and Bronislaw Malinowski in his *Scientific Theory of Culture* have presented conceptual devices that must be used if our analysis is to be complete.

Mr. Burke makes his approach by means of what he calls the pentadic dramatism; and if you have ever taken a technical interest in journalism, you will be reminded of the "five *w*'s" of a good news story. Mr. Burke writes:

We shall use five terms as generating principles of our investigation. They are: Act, Scene, Agent, Agency, Purpose. In a rounded statement about motives, you must have some word that names the *act* (names what took place, in thought or deed), and another that names the *scene* (the background of the act, the situation in which it occurred); also, you must indicate what person or kind of person (*agent*) performed the act, what means or instruments he used (*agency*), and the *purpose.* Men violently disagree about the purposes behind a given act, or about the character of the person who did it, or how he did it, or in what kind of situation he acted; or they may even insist upon totally different words to name the act itself. But be that as it may, any complete statement about motives will offer *some kind* of answers to these five questions: what was done (act), when or where it was done (scene), who did it (agent), how he did it (agency), and why (purpose). . . .

.   .   .

A perfectionist might seek to evolve terms free of ambiguity and inconsistency (as with the terministic ideals of symbolic logic and logical positivism). But we have a different purpose in view, one that probably retains traces of its "comic" origin. We take it for granted that, insofar as men cannot themselves create the universe, there must remain something essentially enigmatic about the problem of motives, and that this underlying enigma will manifest itself in inevitable ambiguities and inconsistencies among the terms for motives. Accordingly, what we want is *not terms that avoid ambiguity,* but *terms that clearly reveal the strategic spots at which ambiguities necessarily arise.*[1]

When working from the point of view of individual psychology, the pentad is adequate. Malinowski, a cultural anthropologist, expands the focus to include an institution, or related group of individuals, and therefore introduces the terms *charter* and *norm,* thus providing a heptadic dramatism. The pentad would do very well for *Hamlet,* but we would need the heptad for Thomas Hardy's *The Dynasts.* As Malinowski wrote:

In order to make the foregoing analysis more definite and more serviceable in field-work and in theory, it will be best to represent it in a diagrammatic form, to give clear definitions of the various concepts we have derived from it, and to supplement it with as full and concrete a list of universally valid types as possible. The concept we have been elaborating is that of an organized system of purposeful activities. We have stated, first and foremost, that human beings are born or enter into already formed traditional groups. Or else, at times they organize or institute such groups. I shall define as the charter of an institution the system of values for the pursuit of which human beings organize, or enter organizations already existing. The personnel of an institution I shall define as the group organized on definite principles of authority, division of

---

[1] *Grammar of Motives,* pp. xv, xviii.

functions, and distribution of privileges and duties. The rules or norms of an institution are the technical acquired skills, habits, legal norms, and ethical commands which are accepted by the members or imposed upon them. It is clear already, perhaps, that both the organization of the personnel and the nature of the rules followed are definitely related to the charter. In a way both the personnel and the rules are derived from, and contingent upon, the charter.

. . . All organization is invariably based upon and intimately associated with the material environmental setting. No institution is suspended in the air or floating in a vague, indefinite manner through space. One and all have a material substratum, that is, a reserved portion of the environmental outfit in wealth, in instruments, and also a portion of the profits accruing from concerted activities. Organized on the charter, acting through their social and organized co-operation, following the rules of their specific occupation, using the material apparatus at their disposal, the group engages in the activities for which they have organized.

The distinction between *activities* and *rules* is clear and precise. The activities depend on the ability, power, honesty, and good-will of the members. They deviate invariably from the rules, which represent the ideal of performance, not necessarily its reality. The activities, moreover, are embodied in actual behavior; the rules very often in precepts, texts, and regulations. Finally, we have introduced the concept of function, that is, the integral result of organized activities, as distinguished from the charter, that is, the purpose, the traditional or new end to be obtained. The distinction is essential.

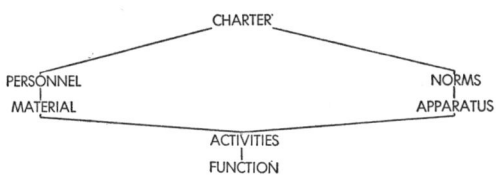

The diagram here presented gives a concrete, mnemonic illustration of this argument. It is not to be regarded as a mystical *eidos* or magical talisman. It is merely one way of relating, in a condensed manner, the results of the present analysis, and of impressing on mind and memory the relationship between the various points which we have set apart in the present analysis. It is also meant to show . . . that every type of effective activity has to be organized in one way and one way only. . . .

The diagram stands for the following propositions. Each institution, that is, organized type of activity, has a definite structure. In order to observe, understand, describe and discourse theoretically upon an institution, it is necessary to analyze it in the manner here indicated, and in this manner only. This applies to field-work and to any comparative studies as between different cultures, to problems of applied anthropology and sociology, and, indeed, to any scientific approach in matters where culture is the main subject matter. No element, "trait," custom, or idea is defined except by placing it within its relevant and real institutional setting. We are thus insisting that such institutional analysis is not only possible but indispensable. It is maintained here that the institution is the real isolate of cultural analysis. It is also maintained that any other type of discussion or demonstration in terms of isolated traits or trait complexes, other than those which would follow the institutional integration, must be incorrect.[2]

You will recall how in our encyclopedia assignment we conceived the simplest possible model of the hunt as composed of a hunter with an implement maneuvering in a field after a quarry. This was a dramatism. We did not, however, attempt exhaustive multiple definitions of our key terms because our problem was journalistic rather than scientific and we felt free to cut our Gordian knots with the swift blade of intuition. In our present task let us carefully approach our quarry to windward and in the process demonstrate the meaning of Burke's remark about how the terms of the pentad "clearly reveal the strategic spots at which ambiguities necessarily arise."

In our first problem our use of the undefined terms *pleasure* and *profit* allowed us to take the meaning of "purpose" for granted because our interest was focused upon the implement (agency), quarry (purpose in another sense), and field (scene). In our present enterprise we are primarily concerned with *purpose*, which we have already begun to discuss with the synonyms *why, motive, cause,* and *reason.* By consciously employing the pentad we may now explore the possible meaning of *purpose* in a systematically built-up collection of relevant respects in which hunter-agents achieve pleasure and avoid pain in the most inclusive senses of the words.

Let us begin with the agent term *hunter.* We put the question "What sorts of hunters are there?" on the assumption that different sorts of hunters have different purposes. Since people have been sorting people for a good many generations, we have at hand a goodly number of standard classifications—doctor, lawyer, merchant, chief; rich man, poor man, beggarman, thief; and so on. Economy requires a working hypothesis at this point; since we are already of the opinion

[2] *Scientific Theory of Culture,* pp. 52–54.

that our problem is basically psychological, we conclude that our best move is the selection of a standard psychological classification. If we are ignorant of the subject, we go to school, consult an expert, or get a book. If Dr. Samuel Johnson were doing the job, he would have studied the motives of sanguine, choleric, melancholic, and phlegmatic hunters; today we would peek into the minds of extroverts, ambiverts, and introverts, or into the brains of endomorphs, mesomorphs, and ectomorphs. If we were to find that most hunters are mesomorphs, we should have a partial solution to our problem; we could say that men are predisposed to hunt "because" of their psychophysical structure.

We next consider the act. What can we learn of hunters' motives by asking the questions "What sorts of huntings are there?" and "How do huntings differ in respect of the operations involved?" If we discover that some call primarily for courage, some for strength, some for skill, some for endurance, some for patience, etc., we get another insight into the possible satisfactions involved.

Approach from the angle of agency or apparatus reminds us that some may hunt because they enjoy using weapons, horses, dogs, falcons, boats, etc.

When we think of the scenes of huntings, the relevance to motive is obvious. The writer immediately recalls, for example, Ishmael's "good" reasons for hunting whales:

Chief among these motives was the overwhelming idea of the great whale himself. Such a portentous and mysterious monster roused all my curiosity. Then the wild and distant seas where he rolled his island bulk; the undeliverable, nameless perils of the whale; these, with all the attending marvels of a thousand Patagonian sights and sounds, helped to sway me to my wish. With other men, perhaps, such things would not have been inducements; but as for me, I am tormented with an everlasting itch for things remote. I love to sail forbidden seas, and land on barbarous coasts. Not ignoring what is good, I am quick to perceive a horror, and could still be social with it—would they let me—since it is but well to be on friendly terms with all the inmates of the place one lodges in.[3]

We are thus brought around to our starting point, the definition of *purpose,* but with an increased awareness of its many aspects. The

[3] *Moby-Dick,* Chapter 1, p. 6.

five terms turn out to be not only instruments of analytic discrimination but also demonstrations of the plasticity of thought and the protean character of its basic symbols. Purpose may not only be considered in relation to agent, agency, act, and scene, but may even be identified with them; and each may blend into one of the others with the shifting of our point of view. Suppose a man goes hunting to improve his health; since his health is an aspect of the man himself, purpose is identified with agent; if he takes to the hills in order to get vigorous exercise, then scene and agency are identified as well as act and purpose; a stream may be a part of the scene, but a part of the stream in the form of a drink may become a part of the agent, or an agency if he takes a bath in it. Thus the complexity of operation analysis is reflected in the subtle shifts of sense in the terms we use in thinking about it as they manifest their essential ambiguity.

Having surveyed the implications of our key term, we are now ready to commit ourselves to the precise sense in which we wish to use it. Do we propose a comprehensive study of the full range of human purpose—what the psychologists call "conation"—or shall we concentrate upon a particular set of purposes that we regard as more significantly related to hunting? Let us decide to identify those special pleasures and avoidances of pain that the hunter consciously seeks in the hunt. This is a momentous decision. It rules out, for example, the psychiatric analysis of a "hunting complex." Biologically, man is a predatory animal; hunting in some forms may be a vestige of his predacity; but by definition we exclude the primitive instinct to kill. We deliberately leave the latter-day troglodyte to the cultural anthropologist.

This selective definition does not, however, remove the need for Malinowski's social concepts of *personnel* (agents), *charter* (purpose), and *norms* (acts). For hunting as a "function" in civilized society has numerous motivational aspects. There is a hunter's "role" to be played and consequently a hunter's "status" to be achieved and maintained. The literature and lore of the chase constitute the charter and will be found to contain many a statement of the conscious purposes we have now set up as our objective. This amounts to a second working hypothesis, namely, that our data will consist mainly of the statements of hunters and that our procedure, if thorough, should probably include the use of interviews and question-naires as well as research in the relevant literature (manuals, mem-oirs, statutes, sports club constitutions, etc.).

And now let us make one more run at the target of *purpose* before summarizing our formulation of the problem. You will recall Mali-nowski's use of the phrase "system of values." What do we mean by "values"; are they the same as "purposes"? An unequivocal answer requires, of course, a pair of arbitrary definitions. We have already suggested (on page 17) the use of *purpose* for wholes and *function* for parts; and since anything toward which we have an attitude may be said to have value (positive or negative) it becomes profitable to speak of end-value and means-value, intrinsic and extrinsic value, purpose-value and function-value. The clear distinction of ends and means is the basic semantic difficulty in the analysis of any value problem. Is hunting an end in itself, or is it a means to an end? The facts that value assumes attitude and is therefore fundamentally af-fective and that the end-means relation is fundamentally logical sug-gest our final definitive step. Let us conceive of hunting as a system of private and social values and seek as our objective the general end-values realized by the three types of personality in the three areas of sensation, emotion, and reflection.

And now for clarity's sake let us review the steps we have fol-lowed. Step 1: We gave a simple statement of the problem by means of the expression "why men hunt." Step 2: We made a multiple defi-nition of key terms. Step 3: During the process of multiple definition two hypotheses turned up; we thought we had better consider the possibility of three types of hunters and that we should adopt both field and library procedures. Step 4: We restated our problem in the light of our multiple definitions and hypotheses. Here is the complete formulation of the problem: *In the three areas of consciousness, what are the general end-values realized by the three personality types among civilized men when engaged in the sport of pursuing with intent to kill or capture such animals as are generally regarded as suitable?* It should perhaps be emphasized that we have radically changed our original conception of the problem. We might go so far as to say that our interest has shifted from the question "Why?" to the question "How many?" We are stimulated by the conjecture that there may be three different value-patterns corresponding to three personality types, for the implications of this idea are profound and far-reaching. We may actually be taking a step in the direction of helping athletic Tom to realize why he does not always see eye-to-eye with slender Dick, or feel heart-to-heart with chubby Harry, in the choice of quarry, field, or implement.

On the other hand, as we have already remarked, our findings may show that hunters are mostly mesomorphic ambiverts (assuming that there is such a correlation between body-type and psychological behavior). This suggests one more working hypothesis and the main categories of our working classification. The inevitable trend toward specialization in civilized society produces imbalance in the life of the individual citizen. The "happy warrior," for example, finds himself trapped in an office swivel chair. It may be that hunting provides not so much a "change" or an "escape" as a rich combination of activities that satisfy the whole person. Its chief value may be an integration of several values.

As we begin to collect data relevant to end-values, let us therefore sort them either as primarily bearing upon the sensory, affective, or logical modes of consciousness, or as integrative or compound values. We frequently find use for such dichotomies, the usual terms for which are *simple* and *complex* or *special* and *general*.

Although our value problem is far more difficult than our encyclopedia assignment, our tentative classification diagram will be comparatively simple. The third level of subcategories might go something like this. For sensory, physiological, and psychological: enhanced body comforts following pronounced hunger, exertion, exposure, etc., would be physiological; sensations of rhythmic coordination in riding, paddling, rowing, portaging, etc., would be psychological. For affective, ethical, and moral: ethical will include such private values as we associate with terms like *courage, endurance, self-control, persistence,* etc.; they are subtly overlapping and their fourth-level differentiation will present nice problems of definition; moral will include such values as sportsmanship, comradeship, loyalty, responsibility, etc., and will present similar difficulties of definition. For logical: we get, at the present moment (the setting up of a working classification is tentative and exploratory), scientific (zoology), technical (woodcraft, marksmanship, etc.), and political; for many a hunter thinks of himself as a reservist in the act of maintaining his combat readiness.

Our main integrative or general category might well break down into partial and complete; partial might break down into aesthetic, philosophical, and scientific. Under *complete* we shall probably find ourselves trying to organize our thoughts and data on "great" hunters and the "good life."

With the conception of our problem as now set up, we proceed to collect and analyze as many data as circumstances permit and to draw such conclusions as the organized data imply. The conclusions are the "answers" to the problem; they are represented in our tentative classification, Diagram C, by the empty pigeonholes.

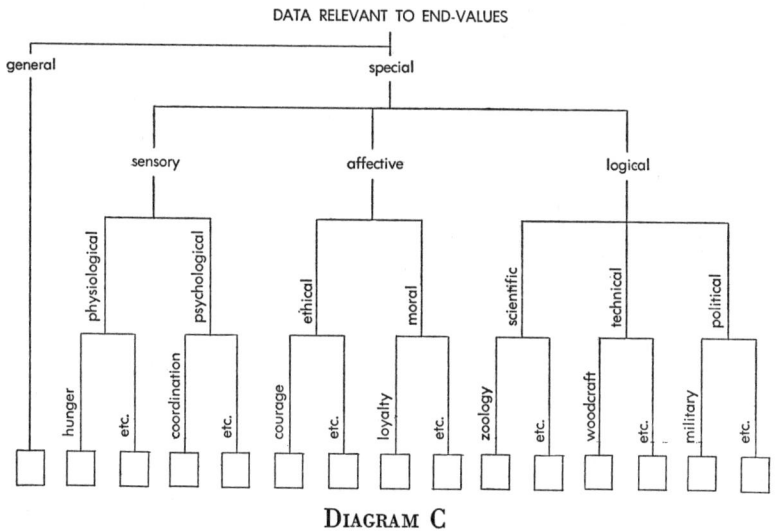

DATA RELEVANT TO END-VALUES

DIAGRAM C

The squares represent the pigeonholes in which the data are actually filed. "Etc." is not a sorting factor like "misc." but is placed in the diagram to represent the rest of an indeterminate set of factors at the same level.

STUDY QUESTIONS

1. Why is problem-solving called an operation?

2. What are some of the practical handicaps in any contrived demonstration?

3. The author has chosen two different sorts of problems for his problem-solving demonstration. Why did he choose each?

4. The author's first problem involves no working hypothesis. Why?

5. The first stage in operation problem-solving is the tentative statement of the problem. Let us say, for instance, that you have been assigned a project involving the novel *Moby-Dick*. Would you satisfy the first stage in problem-solving if you were to state, "The tentative statement of my problem is that I am taking a problem from *Moby-Dick*"? If not, what more would be needed? Could you make a tentative statement of your problem without having read the book?

6. (**A**) In discussing the second stage of problem-solving—multiple definition of terms—what methods discussed in the chapters on definition did the author employ? (**B**) Why was *game* discarded for *prey*? (**C**) Why were "bug collectors" eliminated? Was this an arbitrary decision?

7. Why does the author use the word *tricked* in the sentence "The absence of an inclusive term in English for hunting and fishing had, for the moment, tricked us"? In what way was he tricked?

8. (**A**) Why is the second step in problem-solving multiple definition rather than a single working definition? (**B**) How does the working definition differ from the multiple definition?

9. What is the meaning of *animals* in the working definition of the first problem?

10. Hypothesize a condition that would make the writing of an encyclopedia article a puzzle-problem.

11. If hunting and fishing are operations, why do we classify the data instead of performing an operation analysis?

12. (**A**) In his working classification the author rejected the sensory and affective components for the logical. Why? (**B**) Name a problem that would involve a classification of data according to sensory qualities; according to affective qualities.

13. Why does it help to go over the list of questions listed on page 177—the kinds, ways, manners, etc.?

14. How did the term *conceptual model* help the author in his working classification of hunting and fishing?

15. How did the author's "mild hypothesis" determine the pattern of the hunt? Why was it only a *mild* hypothesis?

16. (**A**) How does keeping the factors *historical* and *contemporary* at the lowest level on the diagram insure keeping all the data conveniently sorted, even though the problem is not hunting and the history of hunting? (**B**) How did the author's purpose make these factors pertinent?

17. (**A**) Why is it vital to define carefully the factors on each level?

(B) In considering *implements*, the author first defines it. Then he asks the question "What sorts have we?" After listing all implements that fall within his definition, he then asks, "How are these similar? How are these different?" Through this process he narrows his list to five primary categories—missile-implements, hooks, snares, traps, and animals. What did he sort according to, i.e., what was his horizontal sorting factor?   (C) How did his controlling purpose determine this factor? (D) Consider a problem in which it would have been more relevant to sort implements in a different manner.

18. (A) When considering *harpoon* the author placed it under the category of hooks, rather than missiles. Why?   (B) How was this placement contrary to the dictionary?

19. We have called stage 4 a "working classification"; however, this is the end result of the stage. The stage begins as a tentative working classification. It grows through a defining and redefining process with a constant reminder of purpose.   (A) Why do we attempt this working classification before we have collected our data?   (B) How will it change as we begin our data collection?   (C) How is it "really an elaborate definition"?

20. Problem-solving as an operation involves seven principal stages. What are these?

21. Our seventh step solves our problem. How is "the problem of actual composition another problem entirely"?

22. If you were getting ready to pack several thousand articles for an expedition, would you sort them according to value, perishability, availability, utility, or size? Give a suitable reason for using each sorting factor for your main categories.

23. Why was the term *cause* discarded for the term *reason* in the puzzle-problem?

24. How is Burke's pentadic dramatism a *conceptual device*?

25. (A) What are the five terms involved in Burke's analysis of motive? Define them.   (B) When Burke says, "We take it for granted that, insofar as men cannot themselves create the universe, there must remain something enigmatic about the problem of motives," what do you see as the cause-effect relationship indicated?   (C) Why does Burke say that he does not want terms that avoid ambiguity?

26. What makes *The Dynasts* different from *Hamlet* in terms of the conceptual devices needed in analyzing them?

27. Does Malinowski's heptadic dramatism include Burke's pentadic elements? How? What has Malinowski added?

28. Relate Malinowski's statement to the law of matrix.

29. On page 186 the author begins an analysis of "Why do men hunt?" utilizing Burke's pentad. (**A**) List the information obtained under each category. (**B**) Ishmael's "good" reason for hunting comes under which of the five pentadic terms? Which particular phrases or sentences place the quotation in this category?

30. Explain this statement: "The five terms (Burke's pentad) turn out to be not only instruments of analytic discrimination but demonstrations of the plasticity of thought and the protean character of its basic symbols."

31. The author arbitrarily decided to define *purpose* as "those special pleasures and avoidances of pain that the hunter consciously seeks in the hunt." Why did he do this? What does this definition exclude?

32. How does the application of Malinowski's heptad change the author's working definition?

33. (**A**) Are "values" the same as purposes? (**B**) How is "value" fundamentally affective?

34. Discuss the elements in the why-do-men-hunt problem that make it a puzzle-problem.

35. Explain how each stage in the solving of the second problem gradually reduces the puzzle aspect and leads toward the evolution of a static problem.

36. Study the classification on page 191. (**A**) Why is the genus term "Data relevant to end-values" rather than "Why do men hunt?" (**B**) There are two sorts of "Data relevant to end-values"—general and specific. Give examples of both of these. (**c**) Define *sensory, affective,* and *logical* as used in the classification. (**D**) How would an *ethical* datum under "affective" differ from a *moral* datum?

N.B. We got our "customary tale of seven" for the steps in our first problem by counting classification twice (tentative and final). In our puzzle problem we counted classification once in order to make way for hypothesis and to keep the count of seven. The object was to demonstrate the arbitrary nature of working divisions.

To try thy eloquence, now 'tis time.

ANTONY AND CLEOPATRA

16 EXPOSITION

BEFORE A MAN CAN BE in any capacity to speak on any subject, said John Locke, " 'tis necessary he be acquainted with it; or else it is as foolish to set him to discourse of it as to set a blind man to talk of colors, or a deaf man of music." The great philosopher was discussing the educational practice of his day, but the shoe still fits.

There are two very serious charges that may justly be made against contemporary procedure in general education. First, we do not make, nor do we train the student to make, a clear distinction between solving a problem and reporting the results. Second, we encourage, in the name of research, a sort of irresponsible trafficking in the reports of others. Composition thus tends to be an exercise in the rhetorical arrangement of other people's phraseology without an appropriate understanding of their ideas.

"Outlining," which should be a rigorous discipline, thus becomes a superficial activity regarded by the student as something of a nuisance. We shall discuss the outline for what it should be—a preliminary analysis of a proposed operation in the communication of ideas.

Here, then, is where we stand at the moment. Having proceeded from the premise that one is not ready to analyze the problem of saying something until he has something to say, and having presented an all too scanty chapter on the method of making up one's mind so

as to have that something, we are ready to consider the problem—
and it is a different problem entirely—of presenting our conclusions
to others.

Since our expositions of hunting or the reasons for hunting are
themselves problems, they are subject to the whole analytic procedure. One must examine his own dominant purpose. Is it to inform, amuse, arouse, or convince? One might set up a carefully
worked out hypothesis about the nature of his audience; what are
their prejudices and state of preparation? But we shall proceed intuitively at this point. Let us assume that our controlling purpose
is to inform convincingly and that our interpreters are very much
like us.

What, then, is the immediate practical problem? Clearly, it is a
problem in operation analysis. We are planning an operation in
which the utterer moves from the beginning to the end of an utterance in the hope that the interpreter will make a similar journey from
the beginning to the end of an interpretation. The problem is therefore a problem of order, the conscious determination of stages and
substages.

The ultimate units with which we must deal are words, but we
shall take the sentence as the basic stage for the purposes of our
discussion. We shall first set up a working classification for thinking
about the order into which sentence-statements may fall. Our second
step will deal with the paragraph as a sequence of related sentences.
And, finally, we shall start an outline for our hypothetical encyclopedia article.

The order we propose to determine may be either serial or linear;
that is, it may be the order of a series of sentences uttered one after
another in time, or it may be the order of those sentences as they are
lined up on a page reading from left to right and down in space. The
outline, which is the plan or "flow sheet" of our expository operation,
will, of course, be linear. The problem of whether the order should
be serial or linear is the problem of deciding when or where to start
and what to do next.

Generally speaking, there are three sorts of consideration that
tend to determine an order: the psychology of the subject, the logic
of the subject, and the physical circumstances of composition and

presentation. These categories and their useful subcategories yield a practical working classification of seven types:

(1) PSYCHOLOGICAL ORDER. Let us define psychological order as an order primarily determined by the emotional attitudes and interests of the utterer or interpreter; getting unpleasant points over with, working up to a climax, creating suspense, etc., are the factors that determine such orders.

(2) STRUCTURAL ORDER. A logical order derived from the relation of physical objects in space: New York, Chicago, Los Angeles; head, trunk, limbs.

(3) GENETIC ORDER. A chronological and therefore logical order in which events occur when interpreted as being in a cause-effect relation to one another. A more appropriate term in some universes would be "historical order." History may be defined as the historian's theory of a causal sequence of actual events.

(4) NUMERICAL ORDER. This is a logical order in which a set of items has been arranged according to a regular series of numbers.

(5) SCALAR ORDER. Logical orders of rank, degree, intensity, value, etc., are scalar orders. The terms "light air," "breeze," "wind," "hurricane," as used by mariners, are here arranged in scalar order from weak to strong.

(6) CONVENTIONAL ORDER. This type comprises orders of arbitrary arrangement such as alphabetical order; red, white, and blue; or good, bad, and indifferent.

(7) CONVENIENT ORDER. Any order determined by circumstances of composition or presentation and not by the inherent logic of the subject matter or the psychology of the communicants. A speaker, for example, might locate certain stages with reference to the anticipated late arrival or early departure of part of his audience.

We have now suggested that the problem of exposition is the problem of arranging sentence-statements in an ordered series and that for practical purposes there are seven types of order. But we do not intend to imply that all the sentences of a given discourse should be arranged in a single type of order. In a complex exposition there will be several relevant types, for there will be several levels of order. This is best illustrated in an outline, which is a written plan or program for an expository operation.

The primary stages, which correspond to the major categories of a classification, are usually the same for all expositions; we call them introduction, discussion, and conclusion, and their order is fixed. In brief expositions where single paragraphs suffice for the introductory and concluding stages, only the discussion stage requires further analysis.

A discussion may be defined as a series of connected "points." But *point* is a relative term; we can put small ones together to make big ones or break big ones down into small ones. We may say "The point is that the experts disagree about the meaning of the term *primary colors.*" Or we can say "The point is that there are seven primary colors." Or we can say "The point is that brown is not one of the seven." Whether or not a given point is major or minor will depend upon the context.

If the point of the whole discussion is that there are seven primary colors, then there might well be seven major points to be made —one for each color. If, however, the seven were divided into four primaries and three intermediates, then we might have two major points broken down into four and three minor points respectively.

Now when we consider the choice of a type of order, we mean the order of points of equal value. Thus, if we took red, yellow, green, and blue as our first minor series, the order would be structural if we took it from the spectrum, and scalar if we got it from the wavelength. If we took up the intermediate group as chartreuse, orange, and turquoise, the order would be conventional (alphabetical) and might have occurred to us because we were checking the terms in a dictionary.

It is relevant to notice the practice of the *Encyclopædia Britannica* at this juncture. The entry under "paint" gives the order as white, yellow, blue, green, red, brown, black, and lake; the entry under "paints" gives the order as white, yellow, red, green, blue, and black. One is moved to comment that it is helpful to have a reason for the order and to acquaint the interpreter with the reason; it gives him a firmer grasp of the data.

The problem of order is, of course, the same problem whether we meet it at the level of the sentence or the complete assembly. We speak of his Red, White, and Blue to an American, but of his Blue,

White, and Red to a Frenchman, thus adopting a conventional order. The Bible we arrange genetically into the Old and the New Testaments.

Let us now attack the most strategic sector of the matter of exposition. It is in the composition of the paragraph that the composer's grasp of the inherent logic of his subject and his awareness of the psychology of his interpreter are tactically brought to bear upon the problem of communication. For the paragraph is at once a logical and a psychological unit. An important psychological consideration is its maximum length, which is determined by the mental "span" of its utterer or interpreter. When eating normally we bite according to our oral capacities; the more work for our molars, the smaller the bite; the greater the need for salivation, the smaller the mouthful. With watermelon or cheese cake we can mouth a sizable bolus with comfort and gusto; peanut-brittle or bear steak calls for restraint. Symbolization is like eating in that we must not bite off more than the mind can masticate and swallow. A paragraph may thus be metaphorically defined as a mental mouthful. Three hundred words is an extreme upper limit; with less than fifty it approaches the scope of a sentence. We should note in this regard, however, that there are two sorts of paragraph—paragraphs of direction and paragraphs of discussion.

Paragraphs of direction are composed of one or two sentences used to make brief statements of introduction, transition, or conclusion. They do not develop ideas. Complete paragraphs of discussion are unit operations that state, develop, and summarize or conclude ideas. The statement usually takes the form of a single topic sentence. The development, which we shall here call *support*, is our present concern.

There seem to be just seven ways in which we may explicitly support an assertion:

(1) REPETITION. Perhaps the most effective way of impressing the human mind with a given symbol is to repeat it over and over again. American industry spends billions repeating a few words until we all become familiar with or even concerned about such things as "L.S./M.F.T." or "What is seepage doing to your loved ones?" This is support by repetition.

(2) RESTATEMENT. Sometimes it helps to say the same thing over in a different way. This is support by restatement.

(3) GENERAL ILLUSTRATION. It is almost always desirable to support a general statement by statements that are less general; e.g., "The President is not well. He has shingles and high blood pressure." "He has shingles" and "He has high blood pressure" are general illustrations.

(4) SPECIFIC INSTANCE. The form of support that usually registers immediate impact is the statement of an actual historical occurrence. "The President winced when his shingles blisters were dressed this morning" is a specific instance when used to support the statement "The President is not well."

(5) HYPOTHETICAL EXAMPLE. Certain types of proposition may be most effectively supported by the statement of an ideal or imaginary case possessing the precise characteristics we desire to place before the mind of the interpreter, e.g., "Some people get into a state where they can't seem to make up their minds. Take Sir Lawrence Olivier's Hamlet, for example." Here the supporting statement is a hypothetical example because Sir Lawrence's Hamlet never actually existed as a living central nervous system.

(6) TESTIMONY. It sometimes helps support a proposition to have almost anybody make some statement in agreement with it. When we make use of such a statement, it is testimony.

(7) AUTHORITY. If the testimonial statement comes from someone speaking with authority, it has a special significance, and we call it support by authority. It should be noted, however, that support by authority is not necessarily more effective simply because it is authoritative.

Here is a paragraph in which all seven forms have been used, directly or indirectly, to support the topic sentence. It is not to be inferred, of course, that it is usually desirable to employ so many forms together.

Theodore Roosevelt was a great hunter (Topic Sentence). He was the mighty Nimrod of his generation (Restatement). He had the physical aptitude and adventurous spirit of the true frontiersman (General Illustration). "There is delight," he said, "in the hardy life of the open; in long rides, rifle in hand; in the thrill of the fight with dangerous game." [Specific Instance] But he was more than a marksman and tracker of beasts, for he brought to his sport the intellectual curiosity and patient observation of the natural scientist (General Illustration). He bags a pair of ostriches: "The hen weighed two hundred and forty pounds," he writes. "Her stomach and gizzard, in addition to small, white quartz pebbles, contained: a mass of vegetable substance; the bright-green leaves and twig tips of a shrub; a kind of rush with jointed stem and tuberous root; bean pods from different kinds of thorn trees; and the leaves and especially the seed vessels of a bush, the seed vessels being enclosed in cases or pods so thorny that they pricked our fingers, and made us wonder at the bird's palate." [Specific Instance] But he was not a wanton killer (General Illustration). "Kermit and I kept about a dozen trophies," he confessed in *African Game Trails*; "otherwise we shot nothing that was not used either as a museum specimen or meat— usually for both purposes." [Testimony] It is amusing to contemplate this terrific little statesman boldly confronting a charging rhino for the sake of a primitive thrill and then turning the next moment to the methodical inventory of the craw of a tickbird in the interest of science (Hypothetical Example). And it was not a pose. "He was a keen naturalist," says Hermann Hagedorn, "accepted by scientists in his field as a trustworthy observer." [Authority] Perhaps this is why Roosevelt *was* a great hunter (Repetition). The mere size of the bag," he said, "indicates little as to a man's prowess as a hunter, and almost nothing as to the interest or value of his achievement." (The final quote is an authoritative restatement which, by implication, practically amounts to a definition of *great hunter*.)

Like the identification of the types of semantic growth (Chapters 7 and 8), the attempt to identify the form or forms of support in supporting sentences is an extremely profitable exercise in the basic acts of reason. Their deliberate selection in the process of composition will almost certainly fertilize and refine the entire operation. Conscious employment of this seven-category classification will not only generate ideas but will improve the quality, the logical relevance, of one's thinking.

Having taken the position that the setting up and solving of a problem is one thing and its exposition another, let us add to our partial account of solving the hunting-article problem a similar demonstration of the making of an outline. The first step is to get clear about the difference between a classification and an outline. We might sort animals into aerial, terrestrial, and aquatic, and the aquatic into lung-breathing and gill-breathing. It makes no difference what order, reading from left to right, we place the categories in, but when we set up the outline as an operation analysis of our proposed discourse, we must decide upon an order and record it. It is true that the several divisions of a particular level of a classification may determine a series of points of a certain value in our outline, but we must still determine their serial order. A still greater difference between the classification and the outline is that what constitutes a major point in the outline may be related to a single item in a pigeonhole of a highly subdivided classification.

When we undertook our encyclopedia project, our objective was to learn as much as we could under the circumstances about hunting throughout the world so as to be in a position to write the best possible article. Our attitude was primarily scientific. We wanted most of all to *know*. Now, having collected far more material than our article can specifically cover, we must generalize or ignore, and above all our account must be readable and, if possible, interesting. And thus the selection of specific instances and, when practicable, the use of photographs are indicated. Note that we now tackle a new problem. It is a puzzle-problem, so let us therefore seize upon the suggestion of pictures as a working hypothesis. Our first step is to select from our collection the most interesting set of pictures. Without describing the various techniques for determining such a set, let us assume that the selection has been made and that it includes photographs of prehistoric weapons and cave paintings, ancient representations of hunting and fishing in the art of Egypt, Assyria, China, Crete, and Greece, candid camera shots of several famous hunters with their kills or catches, and some particularly fine shots from the standpoint of artistic composition of an Indian tiger hunt, an Australian sailfish hookup, a Michigan lake duck blind, and an African rhino charge. Our problem now is to give a comprehensive account of hunting while at the same time putting our selected pictures to good use.

We have already suggested the conventional practice of historical introduction. Let us build our introduction around the primitive artifacts and the ancient art. This will mean that it will contain two main points, which we might call prehistoric and ancient. As we think of prehistoric hunting, however, we are immediately reminded of the present-day hunting pursued by primitive peoples. Let us then call one of our categories primitive hunting and divide it into pre-historic-primitive and modern-primitive. Let us put our ancient hunting in the chronological order of our pictured subjects and assume that this yields Egyptian, Assyrian, Chinese, Minoan, and Greek. In glancing over our pictures, a boar reminds us of some famous medieval accounts of the boar, fox, and deer hunts in the medieval romance of *Gawain and the Green Knight*; this in turn reminds us that our article belongs to an English publication for English-speaking people and that it should probably be "slanted" in that direction. Accordingly, we now add a third point to our intro-duction—medieval European hunting. And so we are faced with a fundamental problem of editorial policy that must be solved before we proceed with the main body of our article, technically called the discussion.

The medieval chase as presented in *Gawain and the Green Knight* was, like horse racing, a sport of kings. And its consideration served to alert us to the historical fact that democratization of society in-evitably brings with it the democratization of hunting. Shall our dis-cussion follow the gentle tradition of the *Encyclopædia Britannica* with its characteristic emphasis upon the fox hunt, or shall we ignore the social aspect and simply take up various kinds of hunting in our geographical or alphabetical stride without reference to the social status of the hunters? Let us assume that our editor is a liberal Republican and astutely elects to straddle the fence. We therefore check back over our pictures to make sure that our historical repre-sentations of kings and princes are effectively balanced with popular commoners like Theodore Roosevelt, Ernest Hemingway, and the Johnsons.

The policy question suggests a revision of the closing paragraph of our introduction. We now use it to make the transition from hunt-ing as a medieval, royal sport to the tremendous development of hunting and fishing in contemporary North America. This step suggests the desirability of organizing our discussion by continents. Thus our major points, those indicated in the outline by Roman numerals, will be North America, South America, Africa, Europe, Asia, the Indies, Australia, and the islands of the Pacific. You may well imagine that our increasing knowledge of the subject has impressed us with the importance of hunting and fishing in human affairs. Impressed by the colossal industry that has grown up in connection with hunting, you might further imagine that we have recommended to our editor an additional entry on the economic aspects of the sport. Let us assume that he approves of this. We

Introduction
  I. Primitive
    A. Prehistoric
    B. Modern
  II. Medieval
  III. Modern Anglo-American
    A. The fox hunt
      1. English
      2. North American
    B. The democratization of hunting

Discussion
  I. North America
  II. South America
  III. Etc.

Conclusion
  I. Hunting and fishing for fun through the ages
  II. Distribution of wealth and transportation as factors in making hunting a major sport
    A. Clubs and associations
    B. Records
    C. Laws
  III. Economics
    A. Manufacture
    B. Distribution
    C. Service

are thus provided with an organizing principle for our conclusion. It will contain three major points—the perennial importance of hunting and fishing as sports, the democratization of sports, and the resulting development in the democracies of the sporting-goods industry.

What is shown in the box is the first draft or skeleton of an outline for our encyclopedia article; its sequences have been determined in part by the nature of our pictures, in part by the relationship of the continents, in part by the editorial policy of our publication. When we come to the scheduling of subordinate points within this outline, the order will tend to be determined by the groupings in our working classification, but it will be frequently modified by considerations of interest and psychological association. For our outline is not a classification of remarks but an operation analysis, and it is therefore fundamentally concerned with the stages in which, one after another, a selection from our stock of knowledge is to be presented so as to achieve the purpose of at once entertaining and informing the reader.

We may now conclude these brief remarks on exposition by assuring you that an utterer or interpreter who checks from time to time with reference to the seven phases of meaning, the seven types of order, and the seven forms of support can hardly fail to improve the quality of his expository composition.

STUDY QUESTIONS

1. What is meant by *exposition* in this text?

2. The author has carefully distinguished between solving a problem and reporting the results. In the light of the John Locke quotation, why is this distinction vital?

3. In Operation Exposition why is outlining a "rigorous discipline" and not a "nuisance"?

4. If the immediate practical problem in exposition is one of operation analysis, what might be the considerations involved in the exposition as a structure? As a problem in classification analysis?

5. How does the consideration of *purpose* differ in problem-solving and exposition?

6. Name some problems best solved by operation analysis; then compare them in terms of the initial and closing stages of each. What determines the beginning and end of an operation?

7. What is the difference between serial and linear order?

8. Give examples of orders that are determined primarily from the standpoint of emotional data, sensory data, logical data?

9. Could you discriminate between a strictly genetic order and chronological order?

10. How is conventional order arbitrary?

11. What sort of order would you be using in the following examples? (**A**) If you organized your paper in the order in which the data were collected. (**B**) If you presented your data according to size, weight, or value. (**C**) If you presented your material in alphabetical order. (**D**) If a cramped time schedule required you to arrange your data in a certain way. (**E**) If you organized your paper showing growth. (**F**) If you picked especially bizarre or strange data. (**G**) If no special order is suggested by the data and you present your data by the numbers you gave them on collection.

12. How are there "several levels of order" in an exposition?

13. What is the "fixed" order of the primary stages of an exposition?

14. (**A**) Define *discussion*. (**B**) How is *point* a relative term? Relative to what?

15. Why must the points be of *equal* value in considering the type of order to use? What will determine this equality?

16. How does acquainting the interpreter with the type of order used help in his interpretation?

17. (**A**) How is the paragraph "at once a logical and a psychological unit"? (**B**) Explain the author's statement "A paragraph may thus be metaphorically defined as a mental mouthful."

18. (**A**) What are the two sorts of paragraphs? How do they differ? (**B**) To which type do the seven sorts of support apply?

19. (**A**) Give several illustrations of support by testimony for advertisements that you think were intended to carry the weight of authority. (**B**) Explain why Theodore Roosevelt's testimony is not authoritative. (**C**) Would it be a good idea for all discussion paragraphs to contain all of the forms of support? (**D**) How does conscious application of the seven forms of support aid the expositor? The interpreter?

20. What is meant by the "basic acts of reason" in the sentence "The attempt to identify the form or forms of support in supporting sentences is an extremely profitable exercise in the basic acts of reason"?

21. What is the difference between a classification and an outline? Illustrate your answer.

22. What circumstances determined the author's exposition of hunting?

23. What is the difference between ancient art and primitive art?

24. Is there an affective consideration in the problem of editorial policy? What factors must determine whether or not a writer will conform to the policy of a person in authority?

25. In what practical way will a check from time to time with reference to the seven phases of meaning, the seven types of order, and the seven forms of support prove profitable in exposition?

That old and antique song we heard last night:
Methought it did relieve my passion much.

TWELFTH NIGHT

My tongue will tell the anger of my heart,
Or else my heart concealing it will break.

THE TAMING OF THE SHREW

17 LANGUAGE AND ADJUSTMENT

BY WAY OF INTRODUCING the third primary function of language we were about to say that we now pass from the practical bread-and-butter business of communication and reason to the more idealistic aspect of linguistic behavior—to the angel food considerations, as it were. But we thought of the wise man of the East who said, "If I had but two loaves, I would sell the one and buy a hyacinth to feed my soul." Is there not something perilously impractical about an individual, a nation, or a culture that finds food for the belly a more vital concern than the diet of the soul?

"And what," you should insist, "do you mean by soul?" We must answer with a metaphor. We mean by soul a developed mind in a state of "collection." *Collection* signifies a sort of equestrian beatitude—Nirvana on horseback (if you don't mind a paradox). A good mount is spirited but well-trained. A good rider is spirited but well-disciplined. It takes a good man to make a good mount of a horse, and it takes a good horse to make a good rider of a man. The mount is swifter than the man; the man is smarter than the mount. The combination is superb. The horse is governed by hand and knee, which in turn are governed by the brain. When the mount and its rider are at their best, each knows himself and his fellow, and each trusts himself and his fellow. There is no ignorance, no weakness, no fear. The vibrant power of the beast is free and yet restrained, dynamically poised between the urgent knee and the curbing human hand. The knee and hands are likewise urged and curbed and likewise answer to the inclination of the brain. Thus the ensemble, mount and man and mind, make up a moving system in dynamic balance. This is a state of collection.

If we liken the mount to emotion, the hands and knees to senses, and the guiding brain to reason, then we may say that collection is that happy state psychologists used to call "successful adjustment." In the present phase of our semantic survey we are particularly concerned with the behavior of the horse. We seek to discover and describe the part played by language in affective expression and control. We begin with the spontaneous expression of primitive emotion.

An emotion is a state of nervous tension that seeks expression in some sort of physical activity. Indeed, a frustrated emotion may be as dangerously disruptive as a stifled cough or sneeze. Some of the pent-up nervous energy of such basic states as fear, anger, awe, contempt, yearning, pity, joy, and sorrow is normally drawn off by the more or less rhythmic repetition of conventional syllables or common names like *oh, ah, wow, oops, pooh, hurrah,* or *oh boy, man, rats, fiddlesticks.* Upon occasion a little salutary profanity may ease an otherwise destructive mood; in Hamlet's phrase, we may "unpack our hearts with words and fall a-cursing."

There is a rather subtle type of adjustment in which language assists in controlling the emotion of embarrassment we feel upon first meeting someone or during an awkward lull in conversation. We then "pass the time of day" or "discuss the weather." One may regard with justifiable suspicion the haughty soul who scorns such meaningless chatter and perhaps envy the happy extrovert who finds it unnecessary.

When an emotion is shared by a group its verbal expression may take a highly conventional form, particularly among children or uneducated adults. The communal expression of certain moods seems to give the individual a comforting sense of relationship with his fellow sufferers, or to enrich the feeling of camaraderie with his fellow celebrants. In some parts of the country a school ground fist fight is (or was, before the advent of "supervised play") accompanied by an ear-splitting chorus that goes *ay-yi-yi, ay, yi-yi-yi.* In Ireland choral "keening" relieves the pangs of bereavement; and in the Holy Land "the mourning women" are called that they may "come and take up a wailing." In America organized cheering is a curiously persistent vestige of primitive language behavior. Like the Highland pibroch, word patterns are also used by the group to incite and reinforce desired emotions in time of war or peril—men shout "Long live the Emperor!" or "Down with Caesar!" as they charge. We have already suggested the rhythmic tendency of emotional language. When developed, this tendency produces such highly utilitarian verbal structures as the chanty, barcarole, and marching song, in which the function of muscular coordination may even exceed that of emotional uniformity. Such communal compositions are the parents of poetry.

In the analysis of rhythmic patterns of emotional language we come to the consideration of man's most complex and elaborate achievement. Keeping in mind the threefold nature of mental behavior, let us observe the triple action of the c.n.s. as it operates to make human existence in the cosmic conflict bearable or even joyous. As we have already indicated, emotional states are states of tension which must be relieved by some form of action. If unduly prolonged or intensified they lead to "nervous breakdown." Language provides a definite, meaningful channel of expression. It not only enables us to "give voice" to our pent-up feelings, but where the expression is deliberate, complex, and sustained, the act of composition or interpretation becomes a form of occupational therapy. Like finger painting, the writing and recitation of poetry are sovereign remedies for the heartsick soul.

The theory that the subconscious is simply the unsymbolized suggests the desirability of adequate verbalization at the earliest possible stage of emotional development. It is the nameless fears and frustrations that defy analysis. Those that have names may be exorcised and dehorned. (Conversely, the fears and hopes whose only substance is a name must be exposed for the vacant ghosts they are.)

Our faithful categories, sensory, affective, and logical, again provide a fertile classification for the survey of poetic language behavior. The most obvious and immediate respect in which language serves emotion by stimulating the senses is the delight we take in conscious patterns of emphasis and sound. Rhythm, rhyme, and alliteration are the names for what we have in mind.

> One little, two little, three little Indians,
> Four little, five little, six little Indians,
> Seven little, eight little, nine little Indians,
> Ten little Indian boys

is an example of pure rhythm pattern. For rhyme we'll not take time. And Markham's immortal measure "To make a man to meet the mortal need" will do to demonstrate the repetition of initial sounds called alliteration (if not discernment in the identification of deathless dissyllables!).

This delight in what might well be called the ballet of language is a direct result of the sounds themselves. We also employ them as conditioned stimuli to call forth other imagery. Indeed, not Pavlov's pooches—no, nor all the other slavering slavs could him outsalivate whom Keats' enchanting bell hath taken in thrall:

> And still she slept an azure-lidded sleep,
> In blanched linen, smooth, and lavender'd,
> While he from forth the closet brought a heap
> Of candied apple, quince, and plum, and gourd,
> With jellies soother than the creamy curd,
> And lucent syrops, tinct with cinnamon,
> Manna and dates, in argosy transferred
> From Fez, and spiced dainties, every one,
> From silken Samarcand to cedar'd Lebanon,
>
> These delicates he heaped with glowing hand
> On golden dishes and in baskets bright
> Of wreathed silver; sumptuous they stand
> In the retired quiet of the night,
> Filling the chilly room with perfume.
> "And now, my love, my seraph fair, awake!
> Thou art my heaven, and I thine eremite.
> Open thine eyes, for meek St. Agnes' sake,
> Or I shall drowse beside thee, so my soul doth ache."
>
> *—The Eve of St. Agnes*

So captivating is the sensory delight we sometimes take in concrete imagery that a famous English critic could say to the reluctant reader of Spenser's *Faerie Queene*: "Just let the allegory alone and it won't bite you." This is tantamount to saying "Never mind what the man is trying to tell you; just see how much fun you can get out of the way he does it."

Even as we take pleasure in the composition and interpretation of musical and imaginative discourse, we also delight in the play of emotion for its own sake. By means of words alone, a skillful performer can sound any chord he pleases upon the verbal keyboard of human feeling. In fact, some of the responses of most of us are as easily manipulated as a toy piano; the mere words go right to work even without invoking the images to which they usually refer. Here are two songs designed to stimulate the love-for-mother system of responses (the whole system of which might be called a sentiment):

> If I were hanged on the highest hill,
>   Mother o' Mine, O Mother o' Mine,
> I know whose love would follow me still,
>   Mother o' Mine, O Mother o' Mine!

> If I were drowned in the deepest sea,
>   Mother o' Mine, O Mother o' Mine,
> I know whose love would come down to me,
>   Mother o' Mine, O Mother o' Mine!

> If I were damned of body and soul,
>   Mother o' Mine, O Mother o' Mine,
> I know whose prayers would make me whole,
>   Mother o' Mine, O Mother o' Mine!

MOTHER

> M is for the *million* things she gave me;
> O means only that she's *growing old*;
> T stands for the *tears she shed to save me*;
> H is for her *heart of purest gold*;
> E is for her *eyes with love-light shining*;
> R means right and *right she'll always be*.
> Put them all together, they spell Mother,
> A word that *means the world to me*.

It is not to our purpose to demonstrate the artistic superiority of the first (by Rudyard Kipling), or to cavil at the jejune banality of the second. The point is that as a sentimental composition, the second is the more efficient and therefore inevitably the more popular, because it arouses the desired emotion without requiring the use of thoughtful consideration. The italicized symbols set off the necessary stock responses immediately. Second thoughts would be disruptive, not to say downright fatal. Thus we have what may be described comparatively as a purely emotive verbal pattern.

But the feeling-content even of this effusion is not limited exclusively to the mother sentiment. Reinforcing it, and reinforced by it, is another affective activity dependent entirely upon the language— the delight we take in pattern for pattern's sake. Even the modicum of ingenuity required to find something nice to say about mother beginning with each letter of her name contributes its tiny quota to what is called the aesthetic emotion. (We take it that PA's initial appearance at the grand finale was purely coincidental!)

Consciously patterned language enables the intellect to participate in and organize the delight of the senses and feelings. By verbal objectification a method is provided of preserving in some degree the first fine careless rapture while at the same time enhancing its value by relating it significantly to the history of the individual. After the rich experience of "thumping his wet clay" the sculptor may step back and enjoy a higher delight (a "topgallant delight") as he surveys the outcome in perspective. Language offers a similar means of contemplating and evaluating moments that are not amenable to expression in the plastic arts. It is a source of profound satisfaction to verbalize a memorable experience, or, for that matter, to appropriate the verbalizations of others. And the greater the accompanying pleasure in the verbal design itself, the deeper and more lasting the satisfaction is likely to be.

The composition of musical pattern and the organization of imagery are not the only methods by which the rational intellect ministers to the emotions by the elaborate manipulation of language. There are two others, which we shall call compensatory composition and rationalization.

There is a certain type of mind that manages to compensate for its inability to take fortune's buffets and rewards with equal thanks by building a dream world remolded nearer to the heart's desire. In such a world a Dante may provide appropriate quarters for his heavenly Beatrice and condemn his political enemies to infernal torment. A Swift may speak his tortured mind upon the antic customs of his fellow men. A Shelley may escape to the Paradise of a *Prometheus Unbound*. Or a conscience-stricken Goethe may create a scapegoat Faust to perform the expiation of his sin. Perhaps a too frequently bankrupt civilization has overvalued these sublime insolvents who pay their score with the inflated currency of imagination. But it is a gorgeous coin they squander, and it does gloriously in the museum if not in the market place.

Then, there is the so-called philosopher whose nominal love of knowing is not sufficiently potent to cope with his love of perfection. He skillfully employs his rational wits to prove that "partial evil is universal good" in this best of all possible worlds. He picks out the assumptions he likes and so deduces the conclusions he wants. Old Omar unmasked the process in a *rubāʿi*:

> Myself when young did eagerly frequent
> Doctor and Saint and heard great argument
> About it and about; but evermore
> Came out by the same door as in I went.

These learned and sometimes holy gentlemen may be themselves not uncharitably described as exemplifying a lofty sort of arrested adolescence. Their world is an oyster in which the mote of their frustration becomes the pearl of philosophy. But for the child of modernity there is perhaps a deeper lesson in the oyster that manages to "contain" the mote that troubles it than in the mote that grows into a pearl. An intelligent oyster would probably eliminate the mote if it could, and might even regard the pearl as we do a gallstone.

We may acclaim the moving power and the exquisite beauty of the literary flowers of maladjustment or admire the intricate structure of a philosophic system without underwriting the questionable divinity of discontent.

Akin to the romantic poet and the philosopher whose reason panders his will is the astrologer, with his ancient and curious verbal fabric of preposterous assumptions and fantastic myths. His is a strikingly elaborate and intricate pseudo-science by which two objects are achieved: the individual is comfortably absolved of personal responsibility for the consequences of his behavior; and he can proudly take upon himself the mystery of things, as if he were God's spy.

It might be instructive to know why the wise Shakespeare commissioned his villains to speak for him upon this ancient but still thriving folly. "It is not in our stars, dear Brutus," the crafty Cassius said, "but in ourselves that we are underlings." From the otherwise lying lips of Edmund the Bastard we hear:

This is the excellent foppery of the world, that, when we are sick in fortune,—often the surfeit of our own behavior,—we make guilty of our disasters the sun, the moon, and the stars; as if we were villains by necessity, fools by heavenly compulsion, knaves, thieves, and treachers by spherical predominance, drunkards, liars, and adulterers by an enforced obedience of planetary influence; and all that we are evil in, by a divine thrusting on: an admirable evasion of whoremaster man, to lay his goatish disposition to the charge of a star! My father compounded with my mother under the dragon's tail, and my nativity was under URSA MAJOR; so that it follows I am rough and lecherous. Sfoot! I should have been that I am had the maidenliest star in the firmament twinkled on my bastardizing.

But, after all, in the hurricane and bitter cold of Shakespearean tragedy it is the heroes that are passion's slaves; they are the sick at heart. The villains are a healthy crew of enviably well-adjusted rascals. Or are they?

STUDY QUESTIONS

1. Why must the answer to the question "And what do you mean by soul?" be answered with a metaphor?

2. Define *collection* in the sentence "I mean by soul a developed mind in a state of collection."

3. Why is "Nirvana on horseback" a paradox?

4. Justify or correct the likening of the mount to emotion, the hands and knees to senses, and the guiding brain to reason.

5. Explain the logic of the word *conventional* in the statement "When an emotion is shared by a group, its verbal expression may take a highly conventional form, particularly among children or uneducated adults."

6. Give examples of the following: (A) Nameless fears and frustrations that defy analysis.   (B) Named fears and frustrations.   (C) Fears and hopes whose only substance is a name.

7. Given the definition of emotion on page 209, discuss the stages in the operation "where the expression of language is deliberate, complex, and sustained." Why does such composition or interpretation become a form of occupational therapy?

8. What sorting factors does the author use in classifying poetic language behavior?

9. Rhyme, rhythm, and alliteration are the three patterns employed to evoke a sensory response. Define and illustrate these.

10. What is a dissyllable?

11. (A) What sounds are repeated and what rhythm is apparent in the sentence "Indeed, not Pavlov's pooches—no, nor all the other slavering slavs could him outsalivate whom Keats' enchanting bell hath taken in thrall"?   (B) What does this sentence mean?   (C) What do you imagine to be the emotional state of the writer when he wrote this sentence?

12. *The Eve of St. Agnes* was used to illustrate which sort of poetic behavior? Why do you think it was a good choice?

13. Diagram the metaphor in the sentence "By means of words alone, a skilled performer can sound any chord he pleases upon the verbal keyboard of human feeling."

14. (A) Is it true that the arousal of an emotive feeling in listening to poetry necessarily involves an image to which the words refer?   (B) What is a *sentiment*?   (C) What second thoughts might destroy the sentiment in the popular "Mother" song?

15. Discuss the ways in which the unpoetic person may increase the pleasure he takes in the "verbal design" of his own accounting of a memorable experience.

16. What sort of poetic behavior is illustrated by compensatory composition?

17. (A) In what ways is a civilization "bankrupt" when it overvalues the dream worlds of famous artists?   (B) Under what circumstances does the "currency of imagination" become inflated?

18. What kind of person is implied as having "the mote that grows into a pearl"?

19. (**A**) How does the compensator differ from the rationalist? The astrologer? (**B**) Is Melville exemplifying one of these men in the following quotation? If so, what words determine this?

> To have known him, to have loved him
> After loneness long
> And then to be estranged in life
> And neither in the wrong
> Ease me, a little ease, my song!

20. According to the text, the astrologer achieves two objectives by following his pseudo-science. What are these?

21. Discuss the reasoning in Shakespeare's making his heroes "passion's slaves" and his villains well-adjusted rascals.

How mightily sometimes we make us comforts of our losses.

ALL'S WELL THAT ENDS WELL

18 THE NOBLEST
FUNCTION OF LANGUAGE

WE BEGAN OUR DISCUSSION of the affective function of language with
a definition of the dynamic control or balance that we called collection. After a brief glance at the basic types of the affective function,
we took up the subject of language as the medium of art, putting the
emphasis, however, upon such factors as escape, compensation, and
wishful thinking, which we usually associate, in their more extreme
manifestations at least, with the neurotic personality. But romantic
literature, whether it be in the heavy accents that arouse compassion
or in the brave measures of unconquerable hope, is not the ultimate
achievement that we mentioned at the start, nor does it represent
what seems to us the highest type of collection.

Psychiatrist and layman agree that the best sort of adjustment
is founded upon an acceptance of reality, rather than an escape from
it. It is not by fatuous attempts "to grasp the sorry scheme of things
entire" but rather by achieving order in the kingdom within that man
most honors himself. "There is one thing of even greater worth than
Faith," writes John Herman Randall, Jr. (*The Making of the Modern
Mind*, page 680), "and that is Thought"; he continues, quoting Ber-
trand Russell:

"Men fear thought as they fear nothing else on earth—more than ruin, more even than death. Thought is subversive and revolutionary, destructive and terrible; thought is merciless to privilege, established institutions, and comfortable habits; thought is anarchic and lawless, indifferent to authority, careless of the well-tried wisdom of the ages. Thought looks into the pit of hell and is not afraid. It sees man, a feeble speck, surrounded by unfathomable depths of silence; yet it bears itself proudly, as unmoved as if it were lord of the universe. Thought is great and swift and free, the light of the world, and the chief glory of man."

It is for thought in this sublime sense that language performs its noblest function. For thousands of years the thoughtful few, at least, have understood the miracle of high tragedy in which all man's knowledge, wisdom, joy, sorrow, triumph, and despair—and even the awareness of death's inevitable hour—may come together in a pattern of rhythm, imagery, reason, and emotion, in the weaving or beholding of which the mind may experience a moment of fear-free ecstasy. Philosophically speaking, tragedy, in the sense illustrated by *King Lear* or *Moby-Dick*, is a *realistic* solution of the problem of evil. The mystic solves the problem of death by endowing his protagonist with immortality. Thus the Passion of Jesus, which provides all the materials for sublime tragedy, is compromised by the epilogue of the Resurrection. The rationalist solves the problem by verbal sleight of hand. With a series of logical deductions he equates "partial evil" with "universal good." The realist accomplishes a dispersion (the figure is chemical) of the problem rather than its solution. He does not ask what "brought death into the world, and all our woe," but resolves the stress that death occasions by making it the essential factor in a comprehensive synthesis—the most all-inclusive pattern of his conscious life. Thus the very causes of his discomfiture (his passions and the destruction to which they lead him) become the instruments of the imaginative act in which he achieves his greatest poise.

In this view the creation and appreciation of tragedy would seem to be a sort of psychological prophylaxis. By taking occasional doses of the bitter fact of death sugar-coated with the beauty of rhythm, imagery, and rational pattern, the system of personality builds up immunity to the poison of its most toxic fear. This, in very truth, is an admirable evasion of deathmaster man to allay his craven disposition with the magic of a metaphor. "As flies to wanton boys, are we to the gods, they kill us for their sport" or "He hates him who would upon the rack of this tough world stretch him out longer" are bitter thoughts, indeed, but by the subtle alchemy of art they become delicious beyond description.

Or take the unforgettable speech of Richard the Second as he dismisses a halfhearted gesture of encouragement:

> . . . of comfort no man speak:
> Let's talk of graves, of worms and epitaphs;
> Make dust our paper and with rainy eyes
> Write sorrow on the bosom of the earth.
> Let's choose executors and talk of wills;
> And yet not so, for what can we bequeath
> Save our deposed bodies to the ground?
> Our lands, our lives and all are Bolingbroke's,
> And nothing can we call our own but death
> And that small model of the barren earth
> Which serves as paste and cover to our bones.
> For God's sake, let us sit upon the ground
> And tell sad stories of the death of kings:
> How some have been depos'd; some slain in war;
> Some haunted by the ghosts they have depos'd;
> Some poison'd by their wives; some sleeping kill'd;
> All murder'd; for within the hollow crown
> That rounds the mortal temples of a king
> Keeps Death his court and there the antic sits,
> Scoffing his state and grinning at his pomp,
> Allowing him a breath, a little scene,
> To monarchize, be fear'd and kill with looks,
> Infusing him with self and vain conceit,
> As if this flesh which walls about our life
> Were brass impregnable, and humour'd thus
> Comes at the last and with a little pin
> Bores through his castle wall, and farewell king!
> Cover your heads and mock not flesh and blood
> With solemn reverence: throw away respect,
> Tradition, form and ceremonious duty,
> For you have but mistook me all this while;
> I live with bread like you, feel want,
> Taste grief, need friends: subjected thus,
> How can you say to me, I am a king?

Childlike confidence in the saving power of a mother's prayer is a lovelier thing to contemplate than the bitter moment of a king's defeat. But unflinching recognition of the "antic" death as embodied in the Shakespearean metaphor is a higher—that is to say, a more stable—form of adjustment than the sentimental reaffirmation of an infant trust.

In the perception and appropriate symbolization of irony the rational intellect makes its supreme contribution to the psychiatric process we have been trying to describe. And what could be more fitting than the lavish employment of that fundamental irony of language, ambiguity? In the grave-digging scene of *Hamlet*, Shakespeare sears with jovial flashes the hyperserious fool who finds a pun the lowest form of wit. Here is part of that scene (as found in Wilson's Cambridge edition):

HAMLET (*clad in sailor's garb*) *and* HORATIO *are seen entering the graveyard.* FIRST CLOWN *digs and sings:*

> In youth when I did love, did love,
> Methought it was very sweet,
> To contract o' the time for a my behove,
> O, methought there a was nothing a meet.

HAMLET: Has this fellow no feeling of his business that a' sings in grave-making?

HORATIO: Custom hath made it in him a property of easiness.

HAMLET: 'Tis e'en so, the hand of little employment hath the daintier sense.

I CLOWN (*sings*):

> But age with his stealing steps
> Hath clawed me in his clutch,
> And hath shipped me intil the land,
> As I had ever been such.
>
> (*He throws up a skull.*)

HAMLET: That skull had a tongue in it, and could sing once! how the knave jowls it to the ground, as if 'twere Cain's jaw-bone, that did the first murder! This might be the pate of a politician, which this ass now o'erreaches; one that would circumvent God, might it not?

HORATIO: It might, my lord.

HAMLET: Or of a courtier, which could say 'Good morrow, sweet lord! how dost thou, good lord?' This might be my lord such-a-one, that praised my lord such-a-one's horse, when a' meant to beg it, might it not?

HORATIO: Ay, my lord.

HAMLET: Why, e'en so, and now my Lady Worm's, chopless and knocked about the mazzard with a sexton's spade; here's fine revolution an we had the trick to see't! did these bones cost no more the breeding, but to play at loggats with them? mine ache to think on't.

I CLOWN (*sings*):

> A pick-axe, and a spade, a spade,
> For and a shrouding sheet,
> O, a pit of clay for to be made
> For such a guest is meet.

> (*He throws up a second skull.*)

HAMLET: There's another; why may not that be the skull of a lawyer? Where be his quiddities now, his quillities, his cases, his tenures, and his tricks? why does he suffer this rude knave now to knock him about the sconce with a dirty shovel, and will not tell him of his action of battery? (*He takes up the skull.*) Hum! This fellow might be in's time a great buyer of land, with his statutes, his recognizances, his fines, his double vouchers, his recoveries: is this the fine of his fines, and the recovery of his recoveries, to have his fine pate full of fine dirt? will his vouchers vouch him no more of his purchases, and double ones too, than the length and breadth of a pair of indentures? The very conveyance of his lands will hardly lie in this box (*he taps the skull*), and must the inheritor himself have no more, ha?

HORATIO: Not a jot more, my lord.

HAMLET: Is not parchment made of sheep-skins?

HORATIO: Ay, my lord, and of calf-skins, too.

HAMLET: They are sheep and calves which seek out assurance in that. (*Drops skull.*) I will speak to this fellow. Whose grave's this, sirrah?

I CLOWN: Mine, sir, (*sings*)

> O, a pit of clay for to be made
> For such a guest is meet.

HAMLET: I think it be thine, indeed; for thou liest in't.

I CLOWN: You lie out on't, sir, and therefore 'tis not yours; for my part, I do not lie in't, and yet it is mine.

HAMLET: Thou dost lie in't, to be in't and say it is thine. 'Tis for the dead, not the quick—therefore thou liest.

I CLOWN: 'Tis a quick lie, sir, 'twill away again, from me to you.

HAMLET: What man dost thou dig it for?

I CLOWN: For no man, sir.

HAMLET: What woman, then?

I CLOWN: For none, neither.

HAMLET: Who is to be buried in't?

I CLOWN: One that was a woman, sir, but rest her soul, she's dead.

HAMLET: How absolute the knave is! We must speak by the card or equivocation will undo us. By the Lord, Horatio, these three years I have took note of it, the age is grown so picked, that the toe of the peasant comes so near the heel of the courtier he galls his kibe. How long hast thou been a grave-maker?

I CLOWN: Of all the days i' the year, I came to't that day that our last king Hamlet overcame Fortinbras.

HAMLET: How long is that since?

I CLOWN: Cannot you tell that? every fool can tell that. It was the very day that young Hamlet was born: he that is mad and sent into England.

HAMLET: Ay, marry, why was he sent into England?

I CLOWN: Why, because a' was mad: a' shall recover his wits there, or if a' do not, 'tis no great matter there.

HAMLET: Why?

I CLOWN: 'Twill not be seen in him there, there the men are as mad as he.

HAMLET: How came he mad?

I CLOWN: Very strangely, they say.

HAMLET: How strangely?

I CLOWN: Faith, e'en with losing his wits.

HAMLET: Upon what ground?

I CLOWN: Why, here in Denmark: I have been sexton here man and boy thirty years.

HAMLET: How long will a man lie i' th' earth ere he rot?

I CLOWN: Faith, if a' be not rotten before a' die, as we have many pocky corses now-a-days that will scarce hold the laying in, a' will last you some eight year, or nine year. A tanner will last you nine year.

HAMLET: Why he more than another?

I CLOWN: Why sir, his hide is so tanned with his trade, that a' will keep out water a great while, and your water is a sore decayer of your whoreson dead body. Here's a skull now: this skull hath lain you i' th' earth three-and-twenty years.

HAMLET: Whose was it?

I CLOWN: A whoreson mad fellow's it was, whose do you think it was?

HAMLET: Nay, I know not.

I CLOWN: A pestilence on him for a mad rogue! a' poured a flagon of Rhenish on my head once. This same skull, sir, was Yorick's skull, the king's jester.

HAMLET: This!

I CLOWN: E'en that.

HAMLET: Let me see. (*He takes the skull.*) Alas! poor Yorick! I knew

him, Horatio—a fellow of infinite jest, of most excellent fancy. He
hath borne me on his back a thousand times, and now how abhorred
in my imagination it is! my gorge rises at it. Here hung those lips
that I have kissed I know not how oft. Where be your gibes now?
your gambols, your songs, your flashes of merriment, that were wont
to set the table on a roar? Not one now to mock your own grinning?
quite chopfallen? Now get you to my lady's chamber, and tell her,
let her paint an inch thick, to this favour she must come. Make her
laugh at that. Prithee, Horatio, tell me one thing.

HORATIO: What's that, my lord?

HAMLET: Dost thou think Alexander looked o' this fashion i' th' earth?

HORATIO: E'en so.

HAMLET: And smelt so? pah! (*He sets down the skull.*)

HORATIO: E'en so, my lord.

HAMLET: To what base uses we may return, Horatio! Why may not
imagination trace the noble dust of Alexander, till a' find it stopping
a bung-hole?

HORATIO: 'Twere to consider too curiously, to consider so.

HAMLET: No, faith, not a jot, but to follow him thither with modesty
enough, and likelihood to lead it; as thus—Alexander died, Alexander
was buried, Alexander returneth to dust, the dust is earth, of earth we
make loam, and why of that loam whereto he was converted might
they not stop a beer-barrel?

> Imperious Caesar, dead and turned to clay,
> Might stop a hole to keep the wind away.
> O, that that earth, which kept the world in awe,
> Should patch a wall t' expel the winter's flaw!

In such ripe discourse as this the polysemous syllables literally
crawl with maggots of meaning for the epicure with a stomach for
poetic Gorgonzola. Note the semantic complexity of the superb play
on "fine" and the inspired similitude suggested by the physical resemblance between the parchment-like surface of the parietal bones
(with their suture) and a pair of indentures. Could it not be that
myriad-minded Shakespeare was even mindful that the "fine dirt"
was, in part at least, the dusty vestige of the mind itself? And catch
the gentle pun on "chopfallen." It is only in the world of symbols
that such stabilizing harmonies of grim humor and haunting melan-
choly can be struck, for the process is essentially reflective. "Here's
fine revolution, an we had the trick to see't."

With this brief suggestion of the function of language as an instrument of emotional adjustment, we reach the very frontier of lin-

guistic psychology. The student who would go farther must abandon the academic highway and pack into the wilderness of psychoanalysis. We shall be content to summarize the lessons of our journey thus far as they bear upon metaphor, the most vital and versatile of symbolic operations.

The great mistake the human intellect has made about language is to assume that language may exist independently of that intellect. Because our eyes can behold the print upon a page, the grooves upon a disc, or the staggered sound track upon a film, as something separate from and outside the mind, we quite understandably confuse the objective record with the mental operation to which it corresponds. This point must be emphatically made and firmly grasped if we are to be clear about the subtle subject of metaphor. For metaphors live within the minds of men, but they die upon forgetful lips and then lie figured as pious effigies in the vast catacombs of lexicography. The immortality of great literature derives, for the most part, from our imaginative capacity to breathe life into these once-vital symbols.

The act of re-creation is complex. We have not only to link the symbol to its proper literal sense, but also to see that same literal sense itself as symbolic of its figurative implications.

The primary functions of metaphor are the primary functions of symbolism. We may use a metaphor for simple communication, as in the lexicographer's statement (Merriam-Webster) "a metaphor may be regarded as a *compressed* simile." We may embody an emotion as in "O, that this too too sullied flesh would melt," or seek to arouse one as in "Nothing, but to show you how a king may go a progress through the guts of a beggar." Or we may define, classify, and organize the aspects of an abstract concept by means of such a metaphor as this:

> That monster custom, who all sense doth eat;
> Of habits devil, is angel yet in this,
> That to the use of actions fair and good
> He likewise gives a frock or livery,
> That aptly is put on.
> (*Hamlet*, III, iv, 161)

And metaphor may upon occasion perform all these functions in one synthetic operation.

There is a series of Rubáiyát toward the close of FitzGerald's famous adaptation that doubly illustrates our point. The allegorical device of the Potter's house and the Shapes of Clay not only serves to present in a concrete and meaningful way succinct definitions of several divergent philosophies, but is a figure introduced by FitzGerald himself to give order and pattern to various Rubáiyát that are "star-scattered" here and there among Omar's hundreds. This extremely logical operation, however, has actually accentuated the affective and sensory components of the total meaning experience. Here are the Rubáiyát:

LXXXII

As under cover of departing Day
Slunk hunger-stricken Ramazán away,
    Once more within the Potter's house alone
I stood, surrounded by the Shapes of Clay.

LXXXIII

Shapes of all Sorts and Sizes, great and small,
That stood along the floor and by the wall;
    And some loquacious Vessels were; and some
Listen'd perhaps, but never talk'd at all.

LXXXIV

Said one among them—"Surely not in vain
My substance of the common Earth was ta'en
    And to this Figure moulded, to be broke
Or trampled back to shapeless Earth again."

LXXXV

Then said a Second—"Ne'er a peevish Boy
Would break the Bowl from which he drank in joy;
    And He that with his hand the Vessel made
Will surely not in after Wrath destroy."

LXXXVI

After a momentary silence spake
Some Vessel of a more ungainly Make;
    "They sneer at me for leaning all awry:
What! did the Hand then of the Potter shake?"

LXXXVII

Whereat some one of the loquacious Lot—
I think a Súfi pipkin—waxing hot—
    "All this of Pot and Potter—Tell me then,
Who is the Potter, pray, and who the Pot?"

LXXXVIII

"Why," said another, "some there are who tell
Of one who threatens he will toss to Hell
    The luckless Pots he marr'd in making—Pish!
He's a Good Fellow, and 'twill all be well."

LXXXIX

"Well," murmur'd one, "let whoso make or buy,
My Clay with long Oblivion is gone dry:
    But fill me with the old familiar Juice,
Methinks I might recover by and by."

XC

So while the Vessels one by one were speaking,
The little Moon look'd in that all were seeking:
    And then they jogg'd each other, "Brother! Brother!
Now for the Porter's shoulder-knot a-creaking!"

Taking our cue from FitzGerald we may, in like fashion, express
the burden of the entire composition by the selection of a single *rubā'i*
or two. For example:

The Moving Finger writes; and having writ,
Moves on: nor all thy Piety nor Wit
    May lure it back to cancel half a Line
Nor all thy Tears wash out a Word of it.

Ah, Love! could you and I with Him conspire
To grasp this sorry Scheme of Things Entire,
    Would not we shatter it to bits—and then
Re-mould it nearer to the Heart's Desire!

This little book, however, was not developed as a plan for Omar's
cosmic conspiracy. We know something of man's cerebral capacity,
and in our very attempt to increase his reach we have discovered the
limitations of his grasp. Nor would we shatter Things to bits. On
the contrary, we have pursued our academic task in the religious faith
that the ability of the human intellect to generalize may be led to control its irresponsible appetite for "specialism" before it manages to
vaporize the organ that gives it life. We believe that the races and
the nations, the castes and the classes, the sects and the societies can
be brought to resolve their ethnic, social, and economic differences
through an enlightened realization of their human similarities.

Nor do we propose a new mould. We have no blueprint for perfection. Ours has been strictly a remodeling job—a modest attempt to contribute to a periodic overhaul. The title *Design for Thinking* was intended to refer, first of all, to the tripartite pattern of the organ of consciousness; next, to the implications of that pattern for a method of improving conscious behavior; and finally, to the practical kit of organizing concepts which our set of triads and heptads provides.[1]

We have formulated three basic assumptions: (1) that the human brain is the ultimate achievement of the evolutionary process as we know it; (2) that language behavior is, in turn, the crowning achievement of that brain; and (3) that individual freedom is the greatest value which that behavior can produce.

Two fundamental principles have determined our procedure at every step. The first of these we have called the law of matrix; we might well have called it the law of signs. The other we have called the doctrine of essential ambiguity, for which the law of symbols might have been a better name; it is an expression of the idea that if language is to function as the servo-mechanism of a community of free minds, some of its symbols must be conveniently polysemantic and most of them must be free to become so.

In concluding our discussion we spoke once more of metaphor, that subtlest of all creative instruments, which serves so well the triune heliotropism of the mind as it turns—in the sensory perception of the Beautiful, the affective intuition of the Good, and the logical formulation of the True—forever toward the Light.

STUDY QUESTIONS

1. If language can be considered the medium of art, how can it also be the medium of sensation and logic?

2. Why is the attempt to "grasp the sorry scheme of things entire" called "fatuous"?

3. What is the "noblest function of language"?

4. What is the difference between the fatuous attempt to "grasp the sorry scheme of things entire" and the understanding of "the miracle of high tragedy in which all man's knowledge, wisdom, joy, sorrow, tri-

---

[1] The ancient cult of the heptad is cleverly discussed by George A. Miller in *Psychological Review*, March 1956.

umph, and despair—and even the awareness of death's inevitable hour—may come together in a pattern of rhythm, imagery, reason, and emotion in the weaving or beholding of which the mind may experience a moment of fear-free ecstasy"?

5. (**A**) Define *mystic, rationalist,* and *realist* within the context of this chapter. (**B**) What sort of person tries to solve the problem of death by discovering who or what brought it into the world?

6. (**A**) Diagram the metaphor "By taking occasional doses of the bitter fact of death sugar-coated with the beauty of rhythm, imagery, and rational pattern, the system of personality builds up immunity to the poison of its most toxic fears." (**B**) What does the Richard the Second speech have to do with this metaphor? (**C**) What is the irony involved in the process of adjusting to death?

7. How is ambiguity the fundamental irony of language?

8. What is the tone of the speeches in the grave-digging scene?

9. (**A**) What is a polysemous syllable? (**B**) Diagram the metaphor "In such ripe discourse as this the polysemous syllables literally crawl with maggots of meaning for the epicure with a stomach for poetic Gorgonzola."

10. (**A**) Determine the various meanings of *fine* in Shakespeare's superb play on the word. (**B**) Why is the comparison of the skull to indentures a similitude and not a metaphor? (**C**) Why does the "relevant relation" of metaphor do away with the sensory resemblance that a similitude needs? How does this give room for more imagination? (**D**) What is the pun on *chopfallen*? (**E**) How does the use of pun and metaphor contribute to the adjustment of emotions? Is their composition primarily sensory, affective, or logical?

11. What does the "great mistake the human intellect has made about language" have to do with the statement "The immortality of great literature derives, for the most part, from our imaginative capacity to breathe life into these once vital symbols"?

12. (**A**) What are the primary functions of metaphor? (**B**) What is the abstract concept the aspects of which are defined, classified, and organized by means of this metaphor?

> That monster custom, who all sense doth eat;
> Of habits devil, is angel yet in this,
> That to the use of actions fair and good
> He likewise gives a frock or livery,
> That aptly is put on.

13. (A) Diagram the metaphor in the Omar passage:

> As under cover of departing Day
> *Slunk hunger-stricken Ramazán away,*
> Once more within the Potter's house alone
> I stood, surrounded by the Shapes of Clay.

(B) Restate the philosophies of the various pots.   (C) Who do you think the "Pot" and "Potter" are in the quotation?

14. What does the Omar quotation:

> The Moving Finger writes; and having writ,
> Moves on: nor all thy Piety nor Wit
> May lure it back to cancel half a Line
> Nor all thy Tears wash out a Word of it.

have to do with Hamlet's speech:

> There's a divinity that shapes our ends
> Rough hew them how we will.

15. Consider the four concluding paragraphs as a combination of realism and Realism, Aristotle and Plato.

16. Compare the passage with Arnold's *Dover Beach*.

17. Do you see any connection between the passage and I. A. Richards' Foreword?

INDEX

INDEX

Those entries which refer specifically to the basic triads, pentads, and heptads employed as working classifications in the text are starred.